WHAT THE WAR LEFT BEHIND

WHAT THE WAR LEFT BEHIND

WOMEN'S STORIES OF RESISTANCE AND STRUGGLE IN LEBANON

MALEK ABISAAB AND MICHELLE HARTMAN

TRANSLATED BY MICHELLE HARTMAN AND CALINE NASRALLAH

Syracuse University Press

Copyright © 2024 by Syracuse University Press
Syracuse, New York 13244-5290

All Rights Reserved

First Edition 2024

24 25 26 27 28 29   6 5 4 3 2 1

∞ The paper used in this publication meets the minimum requirements
of the American National Standard for Information Sciences—Permanence
of Paper for Printed Library Materials, ANSI Z39.48-1992.

For a listing of books published and distributed by Syracuse University Press,
visit https://press.syr.edu.

ISBN: 9780815638377 (hardcover)
9780815638384 (paperback)
9780815657095 (e-book)

Library of Congress Cataloging-in-Publication Data

Names: Abisaab, Malek, author. | Hartman, Michelle, author, translator. | Nasrallah, Caline, translator.
Title: What the war left behind : women's stories of resistance and struggle in lebanon /
Malek Abisaab and Michelle Hartman ; translated by Michelle Hartman and Caline Nasrallah.
Other titles: Women's stories of resistance and struggle in lebanon
Description: First edition. | Syracuse, New York : Syracuse University Press, 2024. |
Includes bibliographical references and index.
Identifiers: LCCN 2023048132 (print) | LCCN 2023048133 (ebook) | ISBN 9780815638384 (paperback) |
ISBN 9780815638377 (hardcover) | ISBN 9780815657095 (ebook)
Subjects: LCSH: Women in war—Lebanon. | Women—Lebanon—Social conditions—20th century. |
Women—Lebanon—Biography. | Women—Lebanon—Interviews. | Lebanon—History—
Civil War, 1975–1990—Participation, Female. | LCGFT: Biographies. | Interviews.
Classification: LCC DS87.5 .A263 2024 (print) | LCC DS87.5 (ebook) |
DDC 956.9204/409252—dc23/eng/20240108
LC record available at https://lccn.loc.gov/2023048132
LC ebook record available at https://lccn.loc.gov/2023048133

Manufactured in the United States of America

For Rula

Contents

9.
Sanaa Ali Ahmad
"You do what you have to do"   *178*

WHAT THE WAR LEFT BEHIND

1

"What the War Left Behind"

When talking about her life and experiences in the Lebanese Civil War, Wadad H. states bluntly, "War is the worst thing." She recounts a story, in fact many stories, that reveal some of the complexities of why and how this is true. As she insightfully points out, the issue is not only how the material and psychic impacts of war change everything about your life and that of the people around you but also how it changes people so profoundly— how they act, how they think, and even who they are. We draw the title of this book from the way in which Wadad characterizes these changes; the impact on the very essence of who people are and how they express themselves is, in her words, "what the war left behind."

We have chosen to frame this book with Wadad's words because we believe that her notion of the war leaving behind traces of itself within people and of people being inherently changed is crucial to trying to understand the experience of war. If wars are the "worst thing," then what does it mean to people when parts of it are left behind inside of you and become a part of you? What does a war leave behind inside people? How does it change us? How do people cope with and live through war? What do we do, what actions do we take? These questions and others are posed within the pages of this book through the stories of eight women. This volume is an oral history built from the stories that women told us about their lives and experiences in the Lebanese Civil War (1975–90). They all were active in wartime in many ways, including as community workers, organizers, activists, and militants. By putting their stories together here in the form of an oral history, we hope to offer some ways of thinking about and understanding the impact of the Lebanese Civil War, specifically on

1

women, with a focus on how people react to, struggle within, and survive war as well as how war changes them.

Like Wadad's, the other stories presented here also affirm how terrible war is. It is notable, though, that even as every single story recounts the horror of war, telling of truly dreadful experiences people live through, they all also discuss the ways in which wartime helped them grow as people, build solidarity with other women, and find alliances across class, geographical, sectarian, political, and ideological lines. These tensions and contradictions unfold throughout the narratives collected here. War clarified for many women in this book the importance of being active in life—more than one person related to us how when faced with unthinkable adversity, you have no choice but to react and take action. You cannot be afraid, Umm Ziad counsels us, or you won't be able to do anything. A common theme running throughout their lives is that when they met awful, unthinkable circumstances in life, they couldn't simply stay home, close out the world, sit still, or do nothing. As yet another person, Sanaa A., puts it in the chapter that closes this volume, "You do what you have to do."

Women's War Stories: This Book's Backstory

The bulk of the book you are reading is focused on eight stories of women's resistance and struggle in the Lebanese Civil War. Each chapter consists of a full story told by one of eight women, but each is also representative of so many more stories told by so many more women. To put together this oral history, in fact, we had conversations and conducted interviews with forty-five women. We collected so many stories that we couldn't include all of them here; we chose these eight stories to be exemplary of the larger group in order to present a history of the Lebanese Civil War through their narrations. The stories of struggle and resistance told by these eight women also tell us a great deal about the lives of many other individuals, women and men, as well as about communities and about a collective experience of war.

The oral histories consist of the eight women's own narrations of their lived experiences, told in their own words, and translated from Arabic to

English. Based on our interviews, the stories we present here were those chosen by the women themselves to tell. We asked them to talk about their lives in the war—to say whatever they wanted in whatever way they wanted. What came out of the process is that women spoke about and analyzed a huge variety of different aspects of their lives during the war: experiences, challenges, achievements, and reassessments. They talked about their activism, militancy, paid and volunteer work, families, partners, children, and so much more. One major focus that emerged from this process of talking, discussing, and collecting stories as well as in translating and reworking them for publication is women's deep and broad implication in politics, activism, organizing, and resistance work broadly conceived. In these women's war stories, we can read how they survived the war, worked and struggled to make things better in their world, and participated in life around them, whatever circumstances they found themselves in.

To present our project at the outset, we would like to underline and emphasize that this book and our oral history project are feminist; they were conceived and created in the tradition of feminist oral histories and oral histories of women, though they diverge from many of these projects in significant ways as well. In this vein, we believe it is important to assert that this is a project of recovery and documentation of women's narrations about the fifteen-year-long war. There is little documentation of the lives of ordinary people during the war and even less of women. While some of the women included in this history held prominent positions in their local communities and played extraordinary roles in their lives as militants, activists, and organizers, they also are "ordinary women." We see this in how they talk about the balance between being active and publicly engaged but also ordinary people—mothers, sisters, daughters, wives, and so on.

This oral history built from a collection of women's narrations is therefore a corrective to the kinds of limiting stories and histories often written about women and war, especially those from the region. All too often, women's lives and experiences are slotted into narrow boxes and reductive categories. This is why stories like those found within these pages are so helpful in offering fuller and more authentic views not only of how such women experienced the war but also how they think about and talk about their experiences. For example, some women may have worked with a particular political party, but not all of their political work was necessarily done merely in function of that party. Women's own actions, activities, and political engagements are much more complex, and even though some of them struggled with patriarchal structures and their limitations, they were never merely appendages of men.

A benefit of this kind of feminist oral history project that presents an open-ended collection of narrations with many different points of connection and analysis is that it works against clichés and stereotypes of women's lives and activities in wartime not only in its content but also in its very premises and structure. We do not sort or categorize the women or their stories, and we work against labels that would dichotomize them—as either fighters or peace organizers, for example. In challenging stereotypes of women in war, moreover, we make clear that we are not claiming a singular experience for "women," nor are we seeking to define who is or who counts as "a woman." We have chosen the category of women for analysis because it is a social category meaningful in the context and meaningful to our participants. The concept of "woman" is laden with meaning, and we are using it in a way that we hope is not limited or limiting. We are well aware that strict definitions of "woman" and "man" are increasingly contested, with people challenging binary understandings of gender. By focusing on "women," we do not intend to negate or undermine this reality but rather to reflect a category of experience relevant to the people whose lives make up the core of the book.

The Development and Evolution of the Project

The making of this book dates back to 2016, when we, as two colleagues, made a plan to research and write about women and the Lebanese Civil War. The idea initially came from Malek, a historian, whose work has focused on women's labor struggles and other elements of women's history in Lebanon. He proposed this idea to Michelle, who works as a literary scholar and translator focused largely on Lebanese women's fiction, literary language(s), and transnational solidarity. We discussed our plan to structure this study, and over the years we have worked together on it every step of the way. Based at McGill University, our project titled "Women's War Stories: Building an Archive of Women and the Lebanese Civil War" received funding from the Social Sciences and Humanities Research Council of Canada. Over the past five-plus years, we have been documenting, collecting, and archiving stories of women's lives in the war.

We shaped and changed the project over time, keeping our focus all along on women's lives—in particular their political involvements, struggles, and resistance. We began by collecting women's testimonies, stories, and histories through formal and less formal means, which included interviews, upon which much of this book is based, and a variety of other less formal conversations. We collected and then indexed and archived these interviews, discussions, and many other documents. To make as much of our work as accessible as possible, we created a website, Women's War Stories: An Archive of Women and the Lebanese Civil War, where our publications and activities are recorded (https://womenswarstories. wordpress.com/). On this website, you can find more information about other parts of the project as well as about the events we have convened in Montreal, including film screenings, book conversations, lectures, and a major multiday symposium commemorating the Sabra and Shatila massacre. We have mentored students at our university who created 'zines (also found on the website) and are currently working on recording a podcast, *How to Tell a War Story*, drawn from material in our larger archive.

We have also already published works from other parts of the project. Two books—one in Arabic and one in English—consist of the memoirs of Nawal Baidoun: *Mudhakkirat al-munadila fi mu'taqal al-Khiyam* (Baidoun 2020) and *Memoirs of a Militant: My Years in the Khiam Women's Prison* (Baidoun 2021). Nawal Baidoun is a militant, activist, and educator from Bint Jbeil in South Lebanon. She was imprisoned in the women's section of the Khiam prison for her role in planning the assassination of the notorious Israeli collaborator Husayn Abdel-Nabi. When we interviewed her as part of this project, she not only told her story but also revealed that she had already written her memoirs. At the time, she was not sure where they were because she had given them to a publisher, but she feared they had been lost or forgotten because she had not heard from the publisher since that time. After some research, we managed to locate the manuscript and return it to her so she could read and remember it once again. With her permission, we then transcribed the handwritten pages, which she penned after her release from prison and before personal computers were commonplace. In collaboration with her, we then edited the manuscript. Michelle and Caline Nasrallah translated the book into English, and it was published. Her story appears in much more detail in these books, so we did not include a version of it here as a chapter. It is notable that the final story in this collection, told by Sanaa A., mentions Nawal Baidoun; their perspectives on the war and their shared time in the Khiam prison as cellmates are fascinating and instructive to read together.

Another book-length publication that developed out of our project is our coedited collection of essays on labor and the creative arts produced by women in the Lebanese Civil War, *Women's War Stories: The Lebanese Civil War, Women's Labor, and the Creative Arts* (Hartman and Abisaab 2022). It contains essays on visual arts, performance art, fiction, poetry, cinema, art therapy, and women's labor movements. Containing essays by six scholars, this book asks the question of how we might tell a "better story" (Georgis 2013) of women's labor and creative production in war. In the collection, we propose some ways that we might think of work and labor as a story and investigate what kinds of stories women tell about war through their creative labor.

What the War Left Behind is not only a centerpiece and anchor of a larger project but also another written portion representing one more selection of what we have collected, learned, and shared in the archiving project. We dwell here on the diverse parts of the project to emphasize our focus on building a larger picture and understanding of women's lives in the Lebanese Civil War, which cannot be captured or summarized in one publication. *What the War Left Behind* underlines how the organizers, activists, and militants who lived through extraordinary things during the Lebanese Civil War were also ordinary, everyday, real women. Their stories highlight women's achievements and the many roles they played during the war, both as individuals and as people deeply connected to communities, families, friendship circles, and political networks.

Writing on Women and the Lebanese Civil War:
The Broader Context

There are few histories of the Lebanese Civil War. When we began this project and explored readings to situate it, we found ourselves returning to many of the same few works (*Irth Lubnan* 2013; Nasr 2013; Petran 1987; Traboulsi 2007; *Yawmiyyat* 1977). Several studies deal with specific moments, places, or events, such as the massacre at Sabra and Shatila (Mundus 1974, 1977; Nofel 2006; Nuwayhed al-Hout 2004; Safa 2021). Even fewer works deal specifically with Lebanese women in the Civil War (Eggert 2022; Maksoud 1996; Schulze, Stokes, and Campbell 1988; Shehadeh 1999), and there is no dedicated history of women's lives, experiences, or activities in the war, though two Arabic-language oral histories—both also translated into English—do focus on experiences of Palestinian women in Lebanon (al-Hilou 2009, 2022; Abdul Hadi 2015a, 2015b).

Two collections devoted to women in the war are multidisciplinary edited collections with a focus on arts and literature as well as other areas: *Women and War in Lebanon* (Shehadeh 1999) and our recent collection, *Women's War Stories* (Hartman and Abisaab 2022). Other studies of creative work and politics in the Lebanese Civil War also add to making thought about the war more complex (e.g., Maasri 2008). Further exceptions to this sparsity of writing on the war include older literary studies of women and the war that focus on literature—one that contrasts women writing about peace with men writing about war and fighting (Accad 1990), another that focuses on women writing about daily life and struggles (cooke 1996). These two works were written when the war was still being fought—and perhaps reflect their times. Another important exception is related to the work done in our study. Jennifer Eggert's studies of women fighters in the Lebanese Civil War uses a political science approach and interviews with participants to build a picture of women in militias. Although adjacent to our work, her book *Women and the Lebanese Civil War: Female Fighters in Lebanese and Palestinian Militias* (2022) is different in how it defines its parameters—studying fighters only—and in its methods.

All these studies provide insights that support the work our oral history project is doing in *What the War Left Behind* because there is so little available written work on women and the war. Our study does challenge this existing scholarship in several ways, most evidently in that it works to break down in its very premise and structure the dichotomy that asserts people, in particular women, as fighters *or* resisters, as engaged in war *or* in peace. The thin line between these dichotomies in a civil war situation is evident in many women's stories collected here. The meditation of Rima Z. in chapter 3 shows this when she half-jokes that her children would find her a hypocrite for saying that she always has rejected violence, knowing that at moments in the war she did take up arms. Moreover, our study also shows that women were active in a wide range of political formations and actions, resisting war while participating in those political forums, and that their resistance to occupation and oppression did not always mean that they could be opposed to violence or military action. One of the important scholarly contributions that we make in this book is to show how complex and nuanced the lives of politically engaged women were by detailing the many roles they played, their actions and activities, and their own analyses of what all these things meant to them and can mean now.

Although there are relatively few studies of women and the Lebanese Civil War, histories or oral histories that cover women's experiences in it, a number of women have used the genre of life writing or autobiography to talk about their experiences. Because our project seeks to center women's life stories, a brief discussion of the genre of life writing adjacent to the kind of history we are producing here and of a selection of these works offers useful insight into our own project as well as into the larger context of women and the Lebanese Civil War.

In 1988, the Palestinian political activist and poet May Sayegh published a full-length autobiographical account of her life and work in the war, especially the siege of Beirut, *Al-Hisar* (The Siege) (1988). Written in Arabic, this text reflects Sayegh's feminist and revolutionary sensibilities and highlights gendered tensions and conflicts within Fatah, the political organization she belonged to, especially with respect to the experiences of war and displacement.

Sayegh's perspective is echoed in the memoir by Eva Stahl (Samira) Hammad, *An International Who Didn't Leave the Tal* (2000), a Swedish nurse who lived through the siege and massacre at Tal al-Zaatar. In the same year that Sayegh published *Al-Hisar*, 1988, Jocelyne Saab made the documentary film *La tueuse* (The Killer) about another woman activist in the right-wing Phalange Party, Jocelyn Khweiri (Saab 1988). A first-person account by Khweiri was also included in the edited volume *Women and War in Lebanon* (Shehadeh 1999). Unlike Sayegh's autobiography, Khweiri's memoirs received great attention in France and Lebanon and became somewhat sensationalized by the media, reflecting mixed fascination and confusion about a young "attractive militant woman" who put down her arms to join the Maronite church, then went back to Lebanon a few years later to preach for a militant defense of Christian Lebanon in the right-wing Christian party the Lebanese Forces (Khweiri 1999, 210). In 2005, Nathalie Duplan and Valérie Raulin wrote *Le cèdre et la croix: Jocelyne Khoueiry, une femme de combats* (2005), shedding light on new features of Khweiri's life.

The memoirs of another activist affiliated with the Lebanese Forces, Antoinette Chahine, appeared in French in 2007 under the title *Crime d'innocence* (Crime of Innocence), which received scant attention outside of Lebanon, where it was translated into Arabic by Marie al-Touq as *Jurm al-bara'ah* (Chahine 2007b). Chahine discusses her perseverance and strategies of survival during episodes of psychological and physical torture in Lebanese state prisons after being falsely accused of assisting her brother, Jean Chahine, in assassinating Father Sam'an Boutros Khoury in 1992. Regina Sneifer, another political activist in the Lebanese Forces, narrated various aspects of her militancy in defense of Libanist Christian ideals and highlighted her disillusionment with her party in her book *Guerres maronites, 1975–1990* (1995). In 2006, she then published her memoirs, *J'ai déposé les armes*, which gained the attention of diverse French and Lebanese audiences (see also the Arabic translation Sneifer 2008).

In contrast to these right-wing women, Souha Bechara was a militant Communist who fought against the Israeli occupation and details her exploits as a militia member in her widely circulated memoir, *Résistante* (2000), translated into English as *Resistance: My Life for Lebanon* (2003). Written with Gilles Paris, a journalist for *Le Monde*, this memoir discusses her mission to assassinate Antoine Lahad, the right-wing, Israel-backed leader of the South Lebanon Army, in 1988 and depicts her day-to-day experiences with imprisonment and torture in the Khiam prison for ten years. When the memoirs were translated into Arabic as *Muqawama* (Bechara 2002) and into English as *Resistance*, they reached broad audiences throughout the Arab world and beyond. In 2011, she produced a second autobiographical work, *Ahlamu bi-zinzanah min karaz* (I Dream of a Prison Made of Cherries), written with Cosette Ibrahim, another woman activist detained in the Khiam prison, which was also translated into French (Bechara and Ibrahim 2014). Bechara has become the most famous of the women imprisoned in Khiam and something of an icon of resistance, with her struggles documented not only in these well-known books but also in film. It is notable that Nawal Baidoun, whose memoir we edited and translated, as well as Sanaa A., whose story is the final chapter of *What the War Left Behind*, were imprisoned with Bechara at Khiam. Reading their narratives and stories together can help us gain more context and detail for the situation and experiences of women held by Israel and the South Lebanon Army in this prison.

We have dwelled only briefly on such written autobiographical accounts; there are others that offer compelling stories. More works in English, French, and Arabic detail life and struggle during this war, from the memoir of the intellectual and professor Jean Said Makdisi, *Beirut Fragments* (2007), to the now famous *My People Shall Live: Autobiography of a Revolutionary* (1975) by the Palestinian revolutionary Leila Khaled (see also Bizri 2017; Ghoussoub 1998; and Mikdadi Tabbara 1979). But even this short account demonstrates how they can provide points of comparison and contrast with the recorded and spoken life stories we provide here. For instance, in just this brief overview of women's published narrations of the Lebanese Civil War, the disproportionate representation of Christian women or women of Christian backgrounds is notable. We also note that several of these women are of right-wing political orientations, whom, as we discuss later, we had less access to in our interviews than left-leaning political women. In reviewing written works dealing with women and the Lebanese Civil War, we noted that many involve life writing, first-person accounts, and direct narrations of lives. The book you are reading adds to this material but in a significantly different way as an oral history.

Women's War Stories: Why Oral History?

Researching, understanding, and writing about women and the Lebanese Civil War present myriad challenges, all of them linked to how any attempt to reconstruct the past is fraught with obstacles. Oral history allows us to produce one such reconstruction of the past that pushes us not only to think in different ways and new directions from the perspectives of people who lived the historical moments and events in question but also to query the methods and processes by which we produce history. In the case of the Lebanese Civil War, especially women and the war, there is a marked absence of documentary materials, statistical records, or quantitative data of any kind on specific events, historical moments and developments, and other aspects of the war. This absence can be compared to efforts to collect data on other major conflicts in the region—for example, the important oral history work done by the Palestinian Revolution website hosted at Oxford University (Nabulsi and Takriti 2016). This related oral history project shows how the method allows us to gain unique perspectives on historical moments and proposes particularly useful ways to understand them.

More specifically, oral history is a method of inquiry that lends itself well to a feminist perspective and framework. Some of the common goals of feminist oral history—that we share—include analyzing women's subordination within patriarchal structures and producing alternative histories rooted in women's experiences and truths (Srigley, Zembryzcki, and Iacovetta 2018). Moreover, while oral history builds on stories told by individual voices and often makes use of specific life stories, it also is possible to use these voices and stories to decenter individuals and individualism and to think more about collective experiences. Like other feminist oral historians, we are attuned to a focus on marginalized and excluded stories but also to accounting for the power dynamics inherent in producing this project. We have formed and built relationships over time in working with our participants and shared many hours of conversation (Patai 2018, 54).

Oral history is of course not without its own challenges, and we detail in some depth in the next section how we took up the methodological issues in producing a work of this kind. But even beyond the specific steps we took to produce this book, we also must highlight at the outset some of the larger issues that affect oral history projects. For example, the ever-changing social environment of the subjects of the study inevitably affects human memory, just as the passing of time changes people's perceptions, perspectives, attitudes, and even values. Not only the way memory changes but also the way people choose to present their memories can be signifi-cantly altered because of various circumstances. We are keenly aware of this variability in how we have produced our study. This is one reason why we use this chapter to offer a contextualization of ourselves and our project as well as a transparent, detailed description of our process so that you as a reader can think critically about what we have produced, even as we are asking you to learn from it. Particularly when we think and write about the past through the prism of the future, possible change in memory is one of the crucial questions we must pose about any historical account, especially one based on oral history. Within these parameters, we offer this oral history that we have crafted judiciously in full recognition of its limitations as well as of its strengths.

Oral history is a method and form that we believe also suits the study of women and the Lebanese Civil War in relation to our work together in a research partnership. As a historian and a literary scholar, we find common ground in working on producing an oral history. Oral history is a particularly appropriate method for us to work together. Unlike other kinds of documentation and writing, for example, oral history allows us to combine our historical and literary approaches into a feminist method of rethinking and retelling the past. It also helps us to balance between a larger focus on the war and women's experiences in the war in general, on the one hand, and individual specific stories, on the other. Other forms of historical writing, such as the life history method, have a different tra-jectory and focus, with more attention paid to the individual and their understanding and analysis of their own stories. While we build out from specific, individual stories, we are also narrating a history that is not only of individuals but also of collectives and communities.

Methodologically, therefore, this book is not simply a series of related individual stories. As the steps we outline in the next section indicate, we have deliberately constructed a history through these stories and through our more comprehensive reading and research in the area. The way we chose our participants, listened to, read, wrote, and rewrote their stories, selected sections for inclusion, and, importantly, worked with and framed them all is what makes this book history. Further, crafting an oral history has much in common with storytelling. All good historians think deeply and critically about the stories they are telling as they formulate the histories they write. Literary approaches and analysis can offer a great deal to understanding the production of historical writing because they are concerned with how stories are told and the tools and methods used to do so. Feminist oral history is a method that lends itself well to this kind of intervention in that it explicitly privileges the empowering of the participants and makes the intersubjectivity of the project transparent (Srigley, Zembryzcki, and Iacovetta 2018).

Such a project underlines poignantly some of the stakes of historical writing in working with the stories of others and conveying them in both words and meaning. Retelling someone else's story in your own words, after they have told it to you and entrusted you with it, also has a great deal in common with the work of translation—in this case both figuratively and literally. The ethics and practice of translation and storytelling therefore have provided us with crucial theoretical insights to consider as we crafted this book and the history told within it. We are working with a location and period about which so little has been written in English, and we are writing about women whose lives and stories often go unnoticed or misunderstood but who lived through life-altering and devastating events.

We take very seriously the trust given to us in telling these stories and crafting a larger history out of them, and we are deeply aware of the ethics of accurately and sensitively representing the information and experiences so generously shared with us. Because the context in which we are producing this history is one that is often hostile and unwelcoming to the women whose stories we are sharing, we took special pains to remember this as we put together the book. In the next section, we detail at some length the steps, procedures, and processes we followed in the production of *What the War Left Behind* so as to give a clear and transparent insight into how the book you are now reading came to be.

Methods and Process

Eight stories of struggle and resistance, each told by one woman, follow this opening chapter. The following eight chapters are subtitled with quotations taken from the stories. We borrowed these phrases not so much as summaries of the stories—which are indeed much too rich and complex to be summed up this way—but rather to give a glimpse into both the content and the mood of each account. The chapter subtitles also speak to and echo each other as well as point to some of the themes this history covers when read as a whole. In addition, we have provided a short introduction for each chapter, summarizing some context and personal information from within each woman's narrative. We also link each chapter to the one that precedes it to help form a fuller and more complete narrative for the history, but without overinterpreting or distracting from the narratives told by the women themselves.

In building the oral history in this way, we were inspired by many oral histories that came before ours. One of the most influential is the classic of labor history *When the Mines Closed* (1998) by Thomas Dublin. Dublin captures so well the end of the useful, working life of a mining town in the United States through the stories of interconnected men and women, paying attention to labor, gender dynamics, and the rise and fall of middle American towns from a working-class perspective. Our oral history is different, however, in a number of ways, including the fact that it focuses solely on women's stories in a much different context—Lebanon and the Civil War. Rather than telling the story of a place that was shaped by an event through people, we here are telling the story of a long process and its impact on people who lived in roughly the same general area but in diverse specific locations and personal contexts.

Working within the feminist oral history tradition, we have also drawn inspiration and analysis from the classic collection *Women's Words: The Feminist Practice of Oral History* (Gluck and Patai 1991). Many of the chapters in *Women's Words* resonate with our project today and are fundamental to the way we conceptualized this project as one that highlights people whose work in and stories about the war have been forgotten or marginalized or both. We record these stories and give them value as history in ways outlined by early feminist oral historians. In line with these projects, we propose to use these everyday stories "from below" as integral to understanding the war and larger social and political processes; we focus not just on the lives of individual women but also on how they are powerfully connected to something bigger. Though we do not explicitly identify our work as advocacy oral history, as defined and advanced by Sherna Berger Gluck and Daphne Patai (1991), our book does have elements in common with this kind of work in that we understand our contribution to be political and to intervene in important questions about the lives of underrepresented people. We also share the belief that research can potentially have the purpose of empowering participants and transforming social realities in that our history of women's organizing, activism, and militancy is connected in multiple ways to the struggles and resistance of women in war and under occupation.

Our focus on struggles and resistance, especially in an anticolonial framework, very much resonates with the way feminist oral history is being rethought and reshaped today. The anthology *Beyond Women's Words: Feminisms and Practices of Oral History in the Twenty First Century* (Srigley, Zembryzcki, and Iacovetta 2018), an update of and in explicit conversation with the now classic *Women's Words*, in fact locates a focus on anticolonial thought and methods as one of its major contributions to the field (Iacovetta, Srigley, and Zembryzcki 2018, 13). The reflexivity advocated in this collection and its focus on rethinking the ways historians relate to their inquiry and the women they are in conversation with have influenced our methods and conceptualization of the project.

First Steps

To begin this project, we worked together to devise a plan for the study that would draw on our complementary but different knowledge and skills as researchers. We are colleagues who work together at the same university and have a shared interest in women's lives, the Lebanese Civil War, and feminist approaches to scholarship. Yet we are located very differently in this regard. Although both of us have lived and worked in Lebanon, Malek is Lebanese and grew up in and lived in Lebanon, including during this war, whereas Michelle came to Lebanon for the first time as a student a few years after the war ended. Malek is a man, and Michelle a woman. All of these details led to different kinds of connections and bonds with the women we spoke to in our research. Malek has extensive contacts within different Lebanese communities and political groups, whereas Michelle's connections in this project are more concentrated in the area of literature and the arts. We spoke to many women as part of the overall project, and those we began with led us to meet and speak to others. In the process of finding people to participate in the study, we drew on networks and communities we knew, which also then led us to others. We built our archive of interviews and stories from there.

Beyond the work of preparing and familiarizing ourselves with the context and process of oral histories, we began our project by locating a large sample of women who might be willing to talk to us and help us to build our study. At first, as in many studies, we were most concerned with finding enough people and a wide range of people of different backgrounds and experiences. Our challenge at this point was to determine where we could find women who had a story, were ready to tell it and have it recorded, and of course—importantly—would agree to make it available to a wider range of researchers and readers through translation into English. We expected to interview about fifty women and rapidly learned that we would have that many and more participants very quickly. We had to start limiting interviews even in the beginning of the project, though we never turned anyone away who contacted us and was willing to speak to us as the word spread between communities of women. We thus used a method of meeting people that is often referred to as "snowball sampling," with people referring us to other people.

Sometimes people told friends, relatives, people they worked with in community organizing or political parties, or fellow political prisoners. The vast majority of the interviews were conducted in Lebanon in Arabic, though some were in mixed languages, and one interview took place in Montreal. We did not use sectarian, religious, or community background as a determining factor of who we would or would not interview, though we kept track in an informal way to be sure that we were not unconsciously overprivileging members of one or another group and not ignoring particular groups. Having said this, we noted all through the process that we spoke to more women of some backgrounds than others and took this into careful consideration in our final decisions about inclusion.

We also kept an eye on our participants' political and ideological backgrounds and their regions of origin in Lebanon and Palestine—knowing that because of our own backgrounds we might inevitably include more people from leftist political orientations and from South Lebanon than North Lebanon. Throughout the project, until the very end, we spoke to all the women located through our networks who were willing to meet and share their stories about the Lebanese Civil War. We did not require any specific criteria for interviewing them, though because we found people through networks of women who were politically active in different ways, most of the people we spoke to were politically active as well.

By using these techniques, we were confident that we would find people willing to discuss different strategies they used to navigate life during the Civil War in Lebanon, with a focus on resistance of different kinds. We kept an ear out for stories of militancy, political engagement, incarceration, community organizing and activism, pedagogical engagement, and daily survival. Not every woman we spoke to initially was willing or able to participate. Some women whom we met refused in the end to narrate their stories, talk about their struggles, or share their suffering. It was clear to us that many wounds had not healed. These women's stories were not recorded or used in any way. We have drawn upon and worked with only the stories for which we had full, informed, written, and verbal consent to use. By the time we stopped actively meeting with people, which coincided with the beginning of the COVID-19 pandemic, we had collected forty-five full interviews.

Setting up and Conducting Interviews

The stories collected in this book are based on these individual interviews with participants. The interviews ranged in time from one hour to several hours, some even lasting five or six hours or more, depending on how much the women wanted to speak. We formulated each interview as an open-ended conversation, and although we did have some questions prepared ahead of time, we often did not use them. The questions were meant to help people remember the era we were speaking about, and we modified them on the spot depending on what women chose to speak about. We at times intervened to ask for more details or guide the participant back to issues related to the war if the conversation strayed very far off. We did not set a specific time limit or timeframe, and participants were invited to speak freely and as much as they wanted to speak. They spoke into a voice recorder placed on a table near them.

The interviews took place at a variety of locations that were convenient for the women being interviewed—some at home, others in cafés or offices. In the overall sample of forty-five interviews, only one was conducted in Montreal, the rest in locations around Lebanon, as noted earlier. All of the interviews were conducted in Arabic by us, Malek Abisaab and Michelle Hartman. The interviews that formed the basis of the stories in this book were conducted from 2016 to 2019. More than one person was present for some of the conversations if the people being interviewed wanted others to be there. Many of the women interviewed also met Malek or Michelle or both more than once in follow-up conversations and discussions in person and then remotely later on to check and approve the materials during the COVID-19 pandemic.

The basic structure of the interviews was informal. Before beginning, all of the women gave their verbal informed consent, and we explained the project to them in detail. They then also signed a written consent form, which was provided to them in Arabic and English and had been approved by our university's research office before we began the interviews (included in the appendix). This form detailed the project, and for anyone interested we also discussed the larger project in as much detail as they wanted. They therefore were aware that they were telling their own story or stories about the Lebanese Civil War in any way they wanted and focusing on what they wanted to. They knew that their stories might be later used as part of an oral history of the Civil War and translated into English. They were asked if they wanted to share their real name or choose a pseudonym. Of the eight women whose stories are included here, seven chose to go by their real names and one chose a pseudonym.

When we listened to the tapes after our meetings, we noted that most of the recordings sounded more like a long storytelling session or conversation than an interview, except when people stated their names and professions for the record. Some women desired prompting or to be asked questions—for instance, asking the interviewer(s), "What do you want me to talk about now?" In most cases, however, they began speaking and carried on from there with very little intervention. Many women told long stories and indeed spoke for much longer than the anticipated hour or two; some asked what we were interested in or what they should talk about, but this was less common.

In reviewing the recordings, we noticed that although the conversations share many common features, they also reveal a great deal about the personalities and experiences of the individual women—in their form as well as their content. For example, the conversations start at different moments of their lives, even though most began with us asking the exact same thing: "Tell us about yourself and your life in the war." Some start with a brief factual biography—name, place of birth, childhood. Others plunge right into what they were doing in the war or a notable feature of their wartime experience. As we listened to the interviews again, it became even clearer that their nature as "semistructured" led them all to move in different directions.

"Semistructured" means that as interviewers we did not stick to a list of questions or try to guide the conversation in particular directions. The kinds of follow-up questions that we asked were related to whatever the topic was at the time or to prompt the speaker to continue or follow an idea she had started. The participants were guided in the interviews from time to time to speak about the war, usually when they would pause and ask what they should speak about. Most speakers, however, needed no such prompting. As stated earlier, there were no set questions, and the follow-up questions greatly depended on what the women actually said. If they started speaking about their family, for example, then the follow-up question or comment might be one that would ensure they have finished their thought about this topic or to guide them back to a point they had begun and not finished.

The method of questioning used here is one developed out of feminist inquiry, particularly in combining the focus on storytelling and less intervention in the production of the story than in other more guided methods. Our goal here was to ensure that the women produced the stories that they wanted to tell about the war—their own "war stories." This approach does have some things in common with other methods—for example, the "life history" approach, which also favors people telling their own stories with few prompts. Here, however, the method was not used to prompt participants to reflect on or analyze their own stories—though many did—but rather to offer the space for them to shape and guide what they were talking about. Because most of the women we spoke to were and are politically active and implicated in activism and organizing, they have told some of these stories many times. However, they shared or told new details or offered new reflections in our conversations. We wanted our method to be able to contain all of this richness.

Transcription and Translation

After the interviews were finished, we set about transcribing them from the recordings. Because the interviews were conducted in spoken Lebanese or Palestinian Arabic or both, the transcription took somewhat more time and effort than it might have if the recordings were done in the formal language used for written Arabic. Moreover, the women not only spoke with different accents but also at times used words and expressions particular to their region or generation. The first round of transcriptions was done by student researchers, and all of them were corrected and read many times by at least the two of us, if not by others as well. In one case, Michelle worked closely on transcription with Caline Nasrallah, with whom she cotranslated seven of the eight stories recounted here.

The translation process was considerably more involved than the transcription process. The translations were completed mainly by Michelle and Caline. We relistened to the recorded interviews more than once and worked closely to move the texts into English. Of the eight histories that appear here, seven were translated by Caline and Michelle and checked by

Malek. One was translated by Michelle and checked by Caline and Malek. We translated using the audio recordings and written transcripts together and worked collectively with much discussion and back-and-forth in the process. More interviews were translated than the eight that appear here, and some of the others will be incorporated into different elements of our larger project.

The translation process was painstaking and time-consuming. Being entrusted with the words of someone's life story added layers of meaning to the translation process for us all—speakers and translators alike. Moreover, knowing that the texts would go through multiple drafts and be edited for length made our desire to produce good, effective translations even stronger. We faced many specific challenges as translators during this long process, which we draw attention to here.

One of our first goals was to be sure to produce a distinct narrative voice for each of the women in English, knowing that the translation can never fully capture the nuances and features of each woman's spoken language. As translators, we are aware that we inevitably put a mark on the texts, and as a team we worked to mitigate this impression by creating individual narrative voices for each woman. Further, many words and expressions that are evocative and meaningful in spoken Arabic simply do not have the same impact when translated into English. Funny or powerful expressions can simply become flat—and we were acutely aware of this problem. This was all the truer in the case of these stories because we were translating from a vibrant spoken Arabic idiom to a much drier written form of English. Translating between spoken Arabic and a written language (be it English or another language, even written Arabic) means that multiple levels of loss are involved. This was certainly true of these translations, and we had to make choices about how to render colorful language, spoken-language idioms, and words with localized meanings, among other things.

As Arabic–English translators, we are also aware that quirks of language, turns of phrase, or unusual speech patterns can read as "wrong" in translation. But we did not want to take the life out of the translations and flatten them into a dry and drab English, either. This issue comes through in many if not most of the stories in how many women moved from using the first to second person when speaking about difficult topics. This pronoun shift is widely acknowledged in psychology and literary criticism as a way to cope with life trauma. It therefore seemed important to render such shifts in translation as they appeared in the original. Thus, we have kept them as a part of the narratives rather than "cleaning them up" for the translated version, even though the stories are edited in other ways.

Editing and Rewriting

We transcribed and translated many more interviews, stories, and histories than we could use in this book—many more than eight. It was extremely difficult to make the decision about which stories would feature and even how many we could include in a book like this. We had to balance the need for readability and the length of the book with wanting to include the widest possible number of voices. We could have included more, shorter, less detailed stories or fewer longer and more detailed stories, for example. We landed on eight stories to balance this choice and to include what we hope are stories long enough to provide deep and rich portraits of women's experiences, lives, and analyses. We were keenly aware that to produce a book that was too long would limit its readership, and we decided that it was important to balance our own desire to be complete and tell more stories in more detail with the importance of attracting a wide readership.

To help us make the decision of what to include and what to exclude, we relistened to the interviews many times and discussed them. We often had prolonged engagement with the participants in the interview process, but we also needed to think rigorously about the interviews in and of themselves to help us choose which to include in the book. We listened to the recordings again and again, took notes on them, and compared them to each other. In some cases, we spoke to participants again—asking for more clarification on some things they said or about sections that might be obscure or contradictory. Sometimes we asked if they would be willing to expand on sections that had parts missing or topics that they had started speaking about but got distracted from in the course of the open conversation. Of course, we were aware that some ambiguities were perhaps deliberate—some people purposely elided memories or made vague statements. We let these gaps remain if the participants preferred to tell their stories this way. But follow-up questions and conversations also allowed us to ensure that the stories and information that we had from the women participating were as complete as possible and that participants felt their stories reflected what they wanted to say.

Perhaps the most difficult part of this process—in some ways even more difficult than witnessing and then relaying the extremely traumatic stories the women recounted to us—was how to choose which stories to include. Every story told to us was important, every woman's experience unique, extraordinary, and compelling in its own way. Thus, to create an oral history we had to exclude many stories that we genuinely wanted to include. This process took a great deal of back-and-forth between us and a great deal of reading and debating. We felt that it was important that the stories were different from each other and covered different things, but we also wanted them to have things in common and to speak to each other. If two narratives felt too similar, which few did, we considered possibly leaving out one or the other.

We did also value the need for the stories to achieve a sort of balance—but not necessarily in traditional ways. For example, the labels of women as Christian or Muslim, Sunni or Shi'i or Druze, left wing or right wing, were in our minds as we made the decisions, given the nature of this war as one dominated by sectarian and political ideologies. At the same time, this was not the primary way in which we engaged or thought about the narrations that we were listening to and reading. Some women strongly identified with these communities and labels, others did not, and still others powerfully rejected them. Moreover, we were also thinking about many other categories of belonging that might be brought into this balance. Some of the women we interviewed were well known, others less known, both in their own communities and in the region and world. Some are Palestinian, others Lebanese; they hail from different regions of the country; some are based in Beirut and others outside Beirut; some spent the majority of the war in the occupied South, others did not.

We paid attention to the participants' class and socioeconomic backgrounds and educational levels as well as to their generations—we spoke to women who were adults with children and families when the war broke out and others who were teens when the war began and were just coming of age during it. We did privilege the inclusion of women who spoke directly about particularly significant episodes of the war and who lived and worked in some of the most active war zones. We considered all of these factors in relation to the question of achieving "balance" in producing our oral history.

In the end, we chose the eight stories you will read here by weighing a combination of these factors, favoring stories less on the external features of women's backgrounds and more on the way they told their stories and what they chose to include. We looked to narrations of the war in which women were able to express a range of experiences and talk about themselves and what they did both in public and private spheres. Because politics—in one way or another—is important to all of the women we spoke to, we chose stories that think and talk about politics in diverse ways. As we narrowed down our group of stories to about twelve, we found that we had achieved a representation across many other lines as well.

Though most of the women in these twelve stories, like the final eight, were Muslims or from diverse Muslim backgrounds, in particular people from the South, and with left-leaning political orientations, they were broadly representative of society in other ways, including across class, socioeconomic background, generation, and political experience. We have included both secularists and Islamists. We did and do not distinguish and divide the stories as being by religious or secular, conservative or progressive women because we do not find these labels helpful in understanding how the women relate to their own militancy and activism or how the stories relate to each other in narrating a history of the Lebanese Civil War. Previous research by Malek Abisaab and Rula Jurdi Abisaab (2017) has complicated the notion of Islamist activism by the Shi'a community in South Lebanon.

One notable absence in this book is stories by right-wing Christian women. This was not our intention or goal at the outset of the project but evolved into a more concrete choice as we continued. At the beginning, we knew that we had a relatively small number of women from this group whom we were able to interview, though we did speak to several. However, as we worked more and more and our project became focused, it was clear that we did not want to include these stories simply to achieve some kind of token inclusion of "both sides" of this war—a concept we reject as inaccurate, in any case. Nor did we wish to pretend to cover "all sides." Through our discussions, we made the decision, therefore, to focus on producing a narrative history of this war told through the stories of women who were working for a better society along principles of anti-colonial struggle, broadly conceived. All of the women we spoke to, for example, were in one way or another involved in the liberation of Palestine and South Lebanon from Israeli colonialism. Our decision came naturally as the stories of activism, militancy, community work, and other involvements shone through in stories so many women told.

Beyond the very difficult choice about which stories to include and not include, the hardest part of the editing and rewriting process was to cut down the stories and shape them from the translated transcripts. Because these transcribed stories were reproductions of how they were told, once translated into English they felt like not quite exact reproductions of the conversations we had. We endeavored in our translation process to be accurate literally and to convey meaning, but as translators we also know that all translation is on some level interpretation. We were painfully aware that we were already changing and interpreting the stories once through translation, so the editing and rewriting process was a further difficult challenge to us that we took very seriously.

In our early conversations, we spoke at some length about how much shaping of stories we needed to do because many of the interviews felt so well articulated even as raw transcriptions. As oral historians, however, we were aware that rewriting the stories and crafting them from the words spoken make up a crucial and integral part of the method. At the same time that we wanted to preserve individual voices, we were also aware of the value in making the stories speak to our readership. Michelle's background in translation and translation studies and her close work with cotranslator Caline Nasrallah gave additional insight and skill to this process. We therefore discussed and debated, working hard on how we approached the translation, editing, and rewriting process. In choosing what would and would not be included in this oral history of women and the Lebanese Civil War, we tried to be sure that we respected and honored the narrations as they were articulated by the individual women narrators.

Shaping the Stories

To give the stories a shape and make them speak to the reader through translation, we embarked on the lengthy process of editing and rewriting. In this rewriting process, we attempted to intervene as little as possible in each text, especially because we were conscious of the interventions that we had made by translating these stories from spoken Arabic into written English. Several drafts of translation had already moved the words our participants spoke into a recorder in Arabic onto the page in English. To produce the words that you are reading within the covers of the book, we edited and reworked each story, chapter, and then all of them together. One concern we had was to make the chapters approximately the same length and to fit eight of them within an overall word count that was appropriate to a book of this kind. Because our conversations were often long and discursive, this meant that some of the stories had to be edited and some parts cut out to make them shorter.

Editing academic work often involves eliminating repetition, ideas that stray from the main point of an argument, or something that "goes off on a tangent." In storytelling, however, these moments are often what makes a narration work. Thus, we were faced with an extremely difficult process. At times, we did eliminate small asides and comments that made the stories richer and more interesting. These types of comments also point to the ways in which people chose to tell their stories, especially those that are about very difficult or moving topics. The same is true of repetition. Some women repeated details and parts of stories several times. This is an important part of storytelling—it is a way to indicate emphasis, a subconscious process many of us use to work through difficult ideas or experiences when speaking. If we were to eliminate all repetition in shaping the stories, we felt that we might not capture well the way a woman chose to speak her story. We balanced the desire to keep these moments in stories and the need at times to cut out some repetition for concision and to allow other elements to remain. Part of the editing and rewriting process involved painstaking work on how features such as detail and repetition that can seem "extraneous" may also be crucial to a person's technique or style in telling a story. We paid close attention to maintaining the integrity of each story, working with the written words and recorded conversations at the same time, moving between the Arabic and the English as we finalized the manuscript.

Another intervention we made during the rewriting process was to eliminate the voice of the researchers from the stories. Questions and comments made by the interviewer(s) do not appear here. Once again, an interviewer's insertions can be an interesting feature of a conversation to analyze. For the stories to flow as narrations and for them to fit together as a coherent history, however, we eliminated these insertions together. This choice was not very difficult because all eight narrations were completed with ease—there was very little prompting and few questions asked. Some traces of the interviewer in the narrations were maintained in editing, such as where the narrative voice of the story asks herself a rhetorical question. For example, in Rima Z.'s story about women's empowerment, she asks, "What can I tell you about the experience of war and women's empowerment and liberation? In my opinion, yes, for sure, the experience of the war was a path to women's liberation." Her rhetorical question was originally asked by an interviewer. Another example in Wadad H.'s narrative is when she asks, "Maybe I'm straying too far from the subject?" This is a question she asked in her conversation, and the interviewer then reassured her that was not the case and that she should carry on. To keep the flow but remove the interviewer's voice, we then edited this part of the conversation to be all in her voice: "No? OK, to continue on. . . ." These examples show the remnants of the interview process that we chose to preserve without spoiling the narrative drive and coherence of the stories.

In finalizing the stories for publication, we recontacted all of the women whose stories we had used and shaped this way. We also checked in with them to be sure they still wanted their names used. Seven of the eight women had originally chosen to allow their real names and details about their lives to be published, as was the case of most of the women in the overall study. In general, the people we spoke to were eager to tell their stories, share their experiences, and have their names and details about their lives attached to them. One of the eight, like a minority of the women interviewed overall, asked us to choose a pseudonym for her, which we did. One woman had passed away, and the remaining ones opted to keep their identifications as is. In this process, some small details in these stories were also changed in consultation with the women and according to their wishes. We did not change any major details, and no women asked us to omit any major parts of the stories they had originally told us.

We contacted all the women whose stories are included here, if still alive at the time, at least twice in the process of working with their stories to prepare them for publication. The first time was after the translation process to ensure that no mistakes or inaccuracies were made and to ensure they agreed with the way it was translated, and the second time was just before publication to ensure that they agreed with the editing and reducing of the stories as well as the publication going ahead. We were particularly concerned that though all the women had given informed written consent for their stories to be recorded, they should also feel good about what was being written and represented as their stories and their lives in an oral history of the war that we had crafted.

The Story of Women's Struggles
and Resistance in the Lebanese Civil War

After going through this long and involved process, in particular letting the subjects themselves guide the direction of the oral history, we then worked together to think more deeply about what we would write here in relation to the stories and to an overall story of the Lebanese Civil War. The way we think about which themes, issues, and topics stand out in this study is guided by our own readings, individually and inclusively, and by our conversations with each other and our cotranslator, Caline, but also with the women. Moreover, we had been engaged in a lengthy process of reading about and researching the Civil War and what preceded it before we embarked on the interviewing, and that engagement continues to this day.

As mentioned at the outset, we familiarized ourselves with other narratives by women about the war published in the form of autobiographies and memoirs. But we also consulted a wide variety of research and scholarship on the war in Arabic, English, and French. For example, we worked with newspaper reports, published party records, articles, and written works by politicians and other public figures active during the Civil War. Much of this material we drew from the archives of major Lebanese newspapers because records of the major Lebanese political parties from the time were inaccessible. Together with graduate researchers, we did much of this work by accessing the libraries of universities in Lebanon, including the American University of Beirut, the Lebanese American University, Université Saint-Joseph, and the Lebanese University. We consulted the archives of the Maronite Church at Bkerké to have more information about the period leading to the war, though we could not access official Civil War documents from 1975 to 1990 because they are not yet declassified by the church.

This research work connects deeply to the stories of the women presented here. The oral history that we have produced is focused on what the war left behind in individuals, but these individuals have lives that are deeply embedded within families and communities. It is a story of deep family support even in families that are not perfect and that one might not immediately identify as such on the surface. This is a history full of difficult relationships, close comradeship with partners and husbands, even if marriages sometimes ended in divorce, as well as the joys and challenges of motherhood in wartime. The stories and overall story produced often invoke bravery and strength of character, working toward not being afraid. *What the War Left Behind* shows how people display everyday bravery born out of necessity, which in its ordinariness often becomes extraordinary. Key elements running through this history include women's activism in informal political formations and more organized political parties, which shows how the structure these groups give to political work affects women and how fraught with difficulty such hierarchies are. Many stories dwell on challenges for young mothers and families who are working and organizing while taking care of children. Others focus on the specific struggles of women in prison.

How to Use This Book: A Guide to Reading

We have purposely limited the scope of this first chapter so as not to over-shadow and overanalyze the stories of the women as they tell them. We know that all our choices in collecting, transcribing, translating, editing, framing, and presenting the stories influence how they are read, but we would like the stories to be the main experience of the reader of this volume. This is why we are not offering extensive analysis and contextualization for them here or in the remaining chapters. Each chapter is titled with a quotation that is taken from within the story, which does not fully sum up the rich and powerful words but, we hope, offers a glimpse into each tale. Moreover, we have written one short paragraph for the beginning of each story to weave them together and provide the briefest of contextualization of each woman.

In this final section, we offer some of our own ideas about what themes thread through these eight stories and others we collected to offer some guides for reading them. In addition, we have included a reading guide at the end of the book, where we offer very short definitions of people, places, events, organizations, newspapers, and other key historical references in the stories, which we have indexed to the chapters where they occur. We opted to do this rather than explain things through extensive footnotes in order to make this volume more readable and accessible. This reading guide is meant to provide a brief orientation to events such as the assassination of Maarouf Saad, the port strike in Saida, the Israeli invasion and occupation of 1982, the Aoun "War of Liberation" in 1989, and other things the women refer to in telling about their experiences. Where possible, we have pointed to additional resources to make learning more about specific things related to this war possible.

Although the reading guide cannot address all of the issues and questions that will—and should!—inevitably arise in reading these eight stories, which are rich in historical, political, and personal detail, we hope it can show readers where and how to pursue some issues further. For the remainder of this chapter, we have identified three main themes around which other issues crystallize and that recur in all of the women's stories—in different ways and for different reasons. We offer a brief discussion of these three themes not to limit readings of these histories but, we hope, to expand them: family and community support, the Israeli invasion of 1982, and the importance of taking action.

Family and Community Support

In the context of narrations of the Lebanese Civil War and in the eight stories told here, the importance of family and community support emerges as a key theme. Especially for publicly active and engaged women, like those featured here, the role of the people surrounding them is emphasized again and again. It is so important to underline and highlight the role of other people because this communality often contrasts with narratives about extraordinary or "exceptional" women. The women whose stories appear here might be thought of as both extraordinary and exceptional, but in other ways they are not, and they say that they are not. The sole focus on exceptionality, however, is very much the way Arab and Muslim women are often depicted and discussed in English-language settings—for example, when their works are translated into English. Many scholars have shown how problematic it is when women who are deeply embedded and engaged in their families and communities are shown to be at odds with them, when conflicts are exaggerated, and when they are proposed to be exceptions to their culture or religion rather than a part of it (Amireh 2020; Hartman 2020; Kahf 2014).

With this in mind and taking seriously the methods and goals of a feminist oral history project as we have defined it, we read and draw out how these stories are not solely or even mainly those of individuals or individual achievements. In a project where people narrate stories and are asked to talk about themselves, of course the individual is immediately privileged and might be expected to be highlighted. We did speak to individual women, but when we were working with the stories, we immediately noted how the theme of family and community support was highlighted by the women themselves. This explicit focus reinforced our own ideas about the importance of families, community, support networks, and other ways of being connected. Some women might have difficulties with their families of birth or specific family members. But it is striking how again and again women narrated themselves in relation to others and communities, while always aware of their own roles and own lives.

We see, for example, that the women's stories talk about how they fit into their families and family structures. They speak about siblings, parents, partners, children, and other people in their lives as important to them and as a part of their stories. They all talk about their families and their family support for what they did during the war, particularly in relation to activism, organizing, militancy, and other work. We found it notable that even within families in which the women faced difficulties or in marriages that went wrong, the narrators of the stories found support and positive reinforcement. The realities of their family settings were by and large a source of strength for the women who tell their stories here. Where they were not, the women contextualized many reasons how and why this was true. Batul H., for example, talks quite extensively about challenges with her daughter, especially after her divorce. Umm Ziad describes taking her children with her to a military training camp, where she learned to use weapons; Hajjeh Zahra talks about dodging bombs and crossing checkpoints with her five children while participating in political organizing. Wadad talks about the extraordinary support she received from her parents-in-law after her husband—their son—was disappeared in the war. Their care for her was mirrored in her care for them throughout a period of immense pain and struggle.

Living in and engaging with family and community are related to the complexity of women's lives as told in these accounts. Women talk about how they are agents of their own lives and play many roles, often at the same time. They are at once activists, organizers, militants, fighters, members of communities and families and political parties, mothers, daughters, wives, and sisters. It is clear that these stories challenge any notion that politically active women in the war were somehow tools used by political parties, serving as mere extensions of their fathers, husbands, or brothers or somehow as pawns in a larger game. Where women faced challenges for these or other reasons within the family, marriage, or patriarchal society, they discussed them. Indeed, we find within these stories sharp political, social, and economic analyses of the war, Lebanon, and their own lives, including the way their home life and family life were affected by all these social factors.

Solidarity and the Invasion of 1982

These women's lives, deeply woven into the social fabric of their communities, were drastically torn apart in the war, which officially began in 1975, though it had shown signs of beginning even before then. For many women, the war did not simply end with the Ta'if Accords of 1990; its effects lingered for years and still linger in some cases. Many of the women begin their narration of this war before the official outbreak—narrating events from their life or political events that are connected to it. For example, the importance of the year 1948 and the Nakba in Palestine is usually mentioned. Highlighting different key dates and events underlines the different kinds of lives these women led and how certain moments were salient to their experiences. The reading guide at the end of the book offers some ways of thinking about dates, events, organizations, and places, helping to remind us of how diverse and vast the eight women's experiences were.

Taking this diversity into account, it was all the more striking to us that a shared traumatic event running through all the stories was the Israeli invasion of 1982 and the occupation of large sections of the country. In addition to the devastating impact that this event had on people and how massively destructive it was, it features in all eight of the stories here for other reasons. One is that most of the women we spoke to were based or have origins in South Lebanon. Several were from Mount Lebanon, and all of them spent time in Beirut, but the participants are much more representative of the southern region, which suffered for the longest under Israeli occupation both before and after the invasion of 1982. The descriptions of war as the "worst possible thing," as Wadad puts it, are often very much connected to events in this period. Some of the specific stories and details of the invasion detail brutality and horror as well as strategies of resistance and coping—as in Rima Z.'s confrontation with Israeli soldiers in Saida.

Another thread that emerges from the extensive discussions of the events of 1982 and their aftermath is the solidarity built in these terrible circumstances. Even in the most devastating stories also often come the most inspirational ways in which individuals and communities found support against a common enemy during this invasion. Arab L., for example, describes the 1982 invasion as the most violent part of the war. Yet she also talks about how such horrible moments of war brought all kinds of people out into public together to protest and how "the people on the streets were awe-inspiring, in full solidarity with each other despite the fact that they all were strangers." In these kinds of revolutionary moments, she reminds us, "people's minds are opened, and they are much more able to stand together in solidarity than they otherwise might be." Arab is not the only person to experience or observe this solidarity; the discussions of the invasion and occupation collected in this book show the remarkable relationships forged in these times.

"You Have to Act!"

The final theme we have chosen to focus on is one deeply connected to both community support and the terrible impact of war's violence on people. This is the idea that when someone is faced with drastic circumstances, the only response is to take action. As Elissar Z. describes living in wartime, "We had to run around and do things, we had to just act. But this made us stronger, in a way, to cope with these kinds of situations. Even now, I can't see someone in need and do nothing. I just can't." Using different ways and words to express this idea, most of the eight narrations here explicitly emphasize the need to act in a situation of crisis or need, faced by all the women highlighted here. Whether this need is framed as acting rather than doing nothing, being active instead of sitting still, or going out rather than staying in, the women whose stories we record here felt compelled to be engaged in the world around them.

Linked to the notion of action is also that you have to be brave and strong when you are faced with the situation of living through a war. Umm Ziad repeatedly points out the importance of not being afraid to act in wartime. What bravery and strength mean to each woman is conveyed dramatically differently, but in one way or another we see the women implicitly or explicitly telling stories of their own and others' bravery. One story that stands out in this regard is that of Sanaa A., whose narration closes out the book. She speaks of herself as being very brave and becoming even more so during her time as a political prisoner in the Khiam prison. She jokingly says about her time in the prison, "My bravery multiplied tenfold. I became stronger, and I'm still standing tall today despite all the suffering I've endured. What do you think? Am I strong or not? You say I am the model of strength? I'll tell you something, I'm not afraid. I'm bold and frank. I don't lie."

It perhaps comes as no surprise that a group of women who are identified as activists, militants, and organizers would choose to be particularly active—especially in a time of personal and societal adversity. This is one reason why we find it also crucial to link this notion of how women talk about feeling compelled to action to the notion that what they did was not of their own choosing. As becomes evident in reading their narrations, none of the women in this book wanted or sought out the roles they took on in the war. Living different lives and experiences in different places and in different communities, they all have this in common. One of the most frequent observations they offer is that war is terrible, but you learn from it, and it sharpens you. You gain experience; people come together and learn in the struggle together. The women tell stories of coming together, offering and experiencing solidarity, finding shared ways to combat sectarianism, and enjoying their roles in organizations and communities.

Despite these inspiring and compelling stories of what they did and learned during the war, the women here narrate that, given a choice, they would certainly have preferred to live a life with no war and never to have had the experiences they did have. Again and again, they reiterate that no one would ever choose to live in war. We may read their stories today as those of women who lived extraordinary lives in which they were and are still politically active participants in their communities and societies. But they think and speak of themselves as ordinary women who reacted accordingly when forced by circumstances into extraordinary situations. It is the stories of these ordinary extraordinary women that make up the next eight chapters of this book. We hope that in reading them you will gain some ideas and insights into what the war left behind.

2

Wadad Halwani

"War is the ugliest thing in the world"

Wadad H. is one of the few internationally recognizable names in this collection, known for her work with the group she founded, Committee of the Families of the Kidnapped and Disappeared in Lebanon. Her militating for this group began the night her husband was taken from their home "for just five minutes," never to return again. Her story highlights the challenges of becoming a single parent overnight, working to support her family on one salary, and simultaneously implicating herself in the struggle on behalf of her husband and the seventeen thousand people who were kidnapped and disappeared during the Lebanese Civil War. She discusses how her supportive family and in-laws gave her the strength to do this work but how at the same time she felt quite alone. Her emphasis on working across artificial divides of religious communities and geographical regions is echoed by many women in the book. While telling her own story, Wadad H. also offers an incisive political analysis of the years 1975–90 as "an Israeli era" and describes how after the war ended, those who fought were rewarded, while others who resisted—like her—were punished. Looking back on the war and everything she did at the time, she emphasizes how no one chooses war and how it is the "ugliest thing in the world."
[b. Beirut, 1951]

My name is Wadad Halwani. I am the wife of someone who disappeared during the war, in 1982. I have two sons who were still young during the war—around three and six years old. I'd like to mention another thing

36

about myself as well. In 1982, about a month and a half after my husband was disappeared, I brought together families—women who, like me, had had a loved one go missing: a husband, son, brother, and even in some cases a whole group of relatives. The majority of us—I mean myself and the families I brought together—were women, of course . . . considering that the men were generally either missing or taking part in the fighting. The war hadn't yet ended. And in November 1982, we formed a committee. We called our association the "Committee of the Families," and our name later became the "Committee of the Families of the Kidnapped and Disappeared in Lebanon."

My husband was disappeared in September 1982, and we formed our group in November that year. In a few months, he'll have been missing for thirty-four years. And yet we are still trying, to this day, to demand our right to know what happened to so many of our loved ones, all the people that the war stole from us.

Let me say first of all that war is ugly. It's the ugliest thing in the world. Nothing about it is comforting or joyful or reassuring. It's awful to return to those memories. Another thing is that none of us chose this path: not me, not any of those women or families of the missing. We didn't choose to be the families of the kidnapped and disappeared, nor did our children. That reality was imposed on us by the war, the terrible war, and it's been perpetuated by the Lebanese state and its governments, one after the other—from back then, during the war, to this day. It has done so by brushing this issue aside, marginalizing us and keeping us on the sidelines, completely ignoring our rights, and threatening us. It's used all the methods it has at its disposal to pressure us to drop the matter. The war impacted me badly. I lost a husband, a lover, a partner, a comrade, the father of my two young boys, who have now grown into men.

My husband was kidnapped in Beirut. We used to live in Ras al-Nabaa, a neighborhood right on what we used to call the "demarcation line"—the line separating the two parts of Beirut: East and West. We were living in Ras al-Nabaa on September 24, when the Israelis withdrew from West Beirut, the capital, and after—or because of—the withdrawal, the Jammoul operations by the National Resistance Front, began. . . .

The War: An "Israeli Era"

I don't want to go back to that time. If I had to sum it up, I'd just say it was an Israeli era. I don't really want to talk about politics, either. But there were no military actions being carried out against the Israeli occupation at the time. The militias all seemed to have allied themselves with the occupation somehow, and there weren't any individual operations against it, either. I don't really want to go into the details . . . it's enough to say that everybody knows that we didn't vote at the time. We didn't. And yet the president was elected during the Israeli war, meaning that a parliamentary majority had been secured to vote him in. I'm telling you all this just to try to explain what I meant by saying it was an "Israeli era."

To keep it short, what followed was a wave of punishment, kidnapping, and torture, mainly against people who were openly hostile to this policy of submitting freely to the Israelis. In the case of my husband, Adnan, specifically, he was kidnapped because he was a political activist; he wasn't in the military. He was a member of the leadership of the Communist Action Organization; his work at that time was humanitarian and social, 100 percent work on the ground. Obviously, I'm not saying this to try and absolve him of anything; I don't mean to imply that he was unique or different than anyone else. Not at all. There were dozens of people who were part of the struggle like Adnan was, and I could probably even say with confidence that they were against the war, too.

Now, what did this look like on the ground? Seeing as he was a secondary-school teacher, he would call on other teachers to open up the schools during cease-fires and truces. Students, high school students especially, fueled the war. They were at an impressionable age, and Adnan wanted to keep them in school so that they wouldn't take up arms and join militias. I mean, all the Kalashnikovs and guns and bombs and money were tempting, as were hashish and opium and whatever else. . . . All of these things were being used to lure kids in. Maybe I'm straying too far from the subject?

No? OK, to continue on, this is why I would say that my husband, Adnan, was one of those people working against the war without explicitly stating that he was against it. He was helping people to believe that they could endure the Israeli invasion. Or trying to, at least. There was a siege, you know, and all essential goods were being rationed so people could survive. He helped get flour to the bakeries, to secure diesel fuel and medical supplies for hospitals, so that they could continue to treat the sick and wounded. It was really the law of the jungle back then.

I can summarize this by saying that Adnan's work was outside the norm of what people were doing, which made him an enemy to the Israelis and their supporters. He thus had to be removed from the equation. This is how I'd sum up the war. Adnan and so many others paid the price. All Lebanese people paid a price, in one way or another. But having someone kidnapped is like paying an extra tax, and it's not really just a tax, you know . . . it's the worst possible tax that can be imposed on you.

When someone is disappeared, and you don't know anything about what happened, you can't defend them. You have no idea where they are; you don't even know if they're dead or alive. . . . You know nothing, nothing at all—you can't even call yourself a widow, you can't say you're divorced, sometimes you can't even tell if you're a woman or a man. You know what I mean?

When you live through something like this, you become someone different from who you were before. There is your character, how you are built, but also the impact of all the things that happened to you and all the changes imposed on you by the injustice you were forced to endure. And then there's how society treats you and how people's views of you change . . . not to mention the huge changes in daily life because of your different circumstances.

You could say that people in society implicitly view you a certain way when you lose your husband. You don't really have an identity anymore; people are confused about how to act around you. I mean, because women in my position kind of become widows but are not officially widows, it's like they just don't have any identity at all anymore. They really don't. I'm not sure if this kind of dynamic also exists in the West or if it's just here, in the Arab region. I don't know. But it's a real thing that happens. You have to become very strong and, you know, claw your way to get the things you want, with your bare hands if need be. You need to become strong, no matter what it takes, so that you can stand up for yourself. Otherwise, you'll be eaten alive.

On top of everything you had to live through, the situation also made you vulnerable to people who wanted to do you harm. Morally, psychologically, economically—on all levels. So, really, how could I even begin to tell you about the effect the war had on me? It's like you're always trapped between a rock and a hard place. When people pity you, it shows in the way they look at you, in the way they look at your kids, kids who are completely blameless. Why would anyone look at them like that? I really used to lose my mind over trying to protect my children. You know, I wanted to protect them from more than the shelling, guns, and snipers; I also had to protect them from the looks in people's eyes, from their behavior and words. Those things can sometimes hurt as much as gunfire and war.

Political Party Experience

Before the war, I joined a political party. I was a member of the Communist Action Organization—that's where I met Adnan. It wasn't the war that pushed me to leave the organization. I was political even before the war, but I left the party when my first child was born. Being a new mother, responsible for a child, I simply didn't have any time left for political or party work. Being a mother was a new experience, as was living through the war. War was something new, and with a firstborn on top of that. . . . When the baby was about five months old, I realized I was unable to take on any real work in the party. I didn't want to just be a guest of honor—I didn't want to belong to the party in name only. I really couldn't take on any responsibilities, so I left in 1976 or 1977.

The war was raging everywhere, and moving from place to place was impossible. Both me and my husband were committed to our political beliefs, but I stayed home to raise our children. Adnan and I discussed this, of course. We knew that one of us had to continue doing political work. Because he was in a leadership position, he was the one who continued on the political path. And I was the mother. At the end of the day, a mother always knows better how to take care of a baby, especially a newborn. Even if

I had Adnan helping me out at home, the fact is that there are things only a mother can do—I mean, Adnan wouldn't have been able to breastfeed, you know?

Thinking about the war and to what extent it affected my character . . . obviously, there were things that I learned more about, and you could say that in one way or another this developed my knowledge. For example, we didn't know anything about war: we used to see it in movies or read about it in books, but there are so many other things you learn about by living through it. Not just war things but issues that go with it. Perhaps you never thought that the war would pick you, that it would come into your house—or, rather, break into your house—and steal something essential to you, your partner. Where there used to be two pillars, suddenly there is only one. You become weaker because of this. And this weakness means you lose your equilibrium. And this, in turn, means that you are forced to learn new things that you maybe knew nothing about, out of no desire of your own. You have new responsibilities, and on top of that war has its own methods, its own culture, and its own logic. It's a logic that people adopt—the logic of militias, of political parties.

So in one way or another, we still to this day—I mean, knowing to what extent I was against the war and keeping in mind how long it's been since it "ended"—we still to this day use what I call "war expressions." When we speak, even if we are not talking about war, we've built this whole vocabulary of what the war left behind.

Really, we still see manifestations of a militia-like logic. For example, when people are in some sort of political disagreement with someone who lives in a building, they say they want to lace it with explosives. And then there's the things you overhear in the streets. Unfortunately, when people argue over trivial things, it can escalate into a mini reenactment of the war. There never was true reconciliation—no one in the country did the work. I mean, the war started and ended just like that, and no one was held accountable. Nobody told us why it ended or why it happened in the first place. It just did. You know? And this means that to this day, any political dispute between the leaders that have been imposed on us is immediately reflected in society. The memory of the war immediately rushes back. Checkpoints, asking for IDs—I look at yours, you look at mine—and the narrative of *my* area versus *yours* and the ever-present *what brings you here?* Unfortunately, the mood of the war still clouds everything we do, even though right now there is no war. Inshallah, the shooting won't resume.

The Israeli Invasion of 1982

Now at the time of the Israeli invasion—I mean, when Israel arrived right in the heart of Beirut—we weren't in Ras al-Nabaa. I'm not defending Israel, but it's not the reason behind Adnan's kidnapping; it's not directly responsible, in any case. Protection-wise, Adnan had a bodyguard, but he only escorted him when Adnan was going from place to place. But at home there were no special security measures.

They took him from our home. And they did so under false pretences. They lied. Adnan had just gotten into a car accident, and they told him they just needed to speak to him about it for five minutes. Things were so chaotic back then, and, like we said, our neighborhood was right on the demarcation line. It was a mixed area, with communities of different sects living there, and it was the only neighborhood that Israel did not directly invade.

He was being tracked at that time; no doubt they followed him back to our house. Definitely. I refer to that time as an Israeli era par excellence. Back then, I couldn't even read a thing. It felt like something had just dropped on me, like I'd received a really strong body blow, and I didn't have it in me to keep up with the news. But when you do start reading again later on, you realize that what happened to Adnan and people like him was meant to discipline and punish those who resisted against the situation, or at least tried to. I mean, Adnan was one of the people helping make sure that the population of Beirut could make it through the Israeli siege, so that Israel couldn't take the capital. His kidnapping was to discipline and punish him.

Unfortunately, we now know that the people who started the war have been rewarded, as have their leaders. First things first: no one was held accountable. And not just that—I don't want to stop there: the amnesty law was declared immediately, in 1991. Sure, no one was against the amnesty law, in general. But before we absolve the warlords, couldn't we at least hold them accountable for what they did? And before I even talk about accountability—couldn't they have been made somewhat liable, these people who still live among us, before being pardoned by a general amnesty?

I mean, could we have expected anything more from warlords? Here they are, still living among us, moving around freely among us. Actually, they don't even live among us; they have positioned themselves as our masters, our rulers. They are omnipresent in positions of power and administration. They occupy high-ranking positions in public administration and everywhere else. There has been no accountability. All that happened is that the criminals were pardoned, further entrenching the victims in their victimhood. How is it that you're a victim of war but also a victim of peace? A victim many times over! And meanwhile reality is unchanged. This is so much so that the wartime sanctification of the *za'im*, the all-powerful political leader, still holds today. Politics has been personalized.

In that sense, the dominant forces triumphed. They triumphed in favor of the powerful, whose hands are still dripping with blood today. And this means that they have erased or marginalized the victims and the value of their struggles as much as they could. It is always the case here in Lebanon that justice only means whatever the leader or ruler decides it does. Truth is reserved for the powerful.

And—let me say this, if you don't mind—this is what played out in Lebanon during the biggest crime of recent times, in 2005, when Prime Minister Hariri was assassinated. The things that politicians said back then! The very same politicians we were demanding justice and truth from. Listening to those politicians demand justice and the truth back then, you couldn't but feel like *they* were the families of the missing and disappeared, so insistently did they claim that they wanted to know who had been behind the assassination: its planning and execution and, and, and. . . .

We thought, great! At least half the people we're asking for justice are starting to get it, are starting to talk about concepts like "justice" and "truth." We thought we were close. We really did. But as it turned out, we weren't. Justice only matters when it comes to important public figures, to leaders and powerful people. I mean, of course we strongly denounce the assassinations. They impacted everyone, without exception. But why is it that truth and justice only count when it comes to political leaders, to public officials, while the same demands made for the nearly seventeen thousand missing and disappeared are framed as threatening to reignite the war? This is the response we were met with whenever we demanded the truth about what happened to missing and disappeared people—that we were putting civil peace at risk.

To briefly talk about the experience of establishing the committee. As I said, it all happened very spontaneously. I mean, I wasn't planning for it; I didn't plan to set up a committee and do that kind of work. I always say that when I was looking for my husband, I realized that I was actually looking for thousands of people. It wasn't really a conscious decision. Every time I would go see some official to try and find out where Adnan was, I would be shocked to hear that there were other people in the same situation. But they never gave me names—not out of a concern for people's privacy—to the officials, people were just numbers. They're no better than the ones who did the kidnapping.

Back then, I was continuously coming up against a wall. So I made an appeal on the radio. I thought that if there were a lot of other people in the same shoes as me, then two or three others would show up and work alongside me. That way, instead of going to see the president or prime minister or mufti or patriarch or whoever by myself, I could go with three or four others so that we could have a stronger impact and could apply more pressure. I hoped these people would be a little older than me and even a bit more physically imposing, so we could be taken more seriously. I was so young back then, I needed others to help apply pressure.

Anyway, I put out that call on the radio and showed up at the time and place I'd announced in the ad. I was truly surprised by the number of people who showed up! I hadn't expected so many. I'd been hoping for two or three, and instead I was shocked to see hundreds of women and children . . . mostly women and children. I really hadn't seen that coming; I didn't think that so many people could have gone through that kind of injustice in so little time. It wasn't just me. Remembering that scene still makes me emotional.

I mean, I could hardly believe that so many people had missing family members. And we all were experiencing this at the same time! I knew we had to do something about it. This was my train of thought at the time. When I was meeting with the people who showed up to my call, I used my loudest voice. As I'd been a high school teacher who taught classes of forty girls at a time, I'd learned to project my voice, and I didn't need a microphone or anything. Keep in mind I truly thought that I was going to be meeting with only three women at the most! I'd suggested that we meet somewhere close by, so we gathered in Corniche el-Mazraa by the Abdel Nasser Mosque.

The nearest place we could go to from there was the government serail in Sanayeh—where the Ministry of the Interior is now. I suggested that we try to meet with the minister of the interior, and we did. That was our first mobilization. A group of people crowded together to support our protest, but at the time there'd been a state of emergency declared, and all demonstrations were completely forbidden . . . so it was brave of us to do what we did. We didn't have anything left to lose.

We weren't afraid of anything anymore—What could we lose that we hadn't already? What more than we'd already lost? It's not like we'd lost a car or money. We'd lost human beings whom we loved, who meant something to us. We'd lost parts of ourselves. So we went full steam ahead; we weren't afraid of challenging the emergency laws, like the curfew, and we didn't back down from threats, guns, or repression. The authorities eventually had to negotiate with us. Eight of us went to meet with the prime minister, but the government's condition was that we had to stop our protests before we could actually see him. We stopped protesting and went to meet with the prime minister. It was Shafik al-Wazzan back then.

Obviously, he played up the emotional angle when he came down to talk to us; he asked us our names and who in our families was missing . . . that kind of thing. And that was it. We decided that we had to push harder. The first thing we did was to start keeping records of the names of the missing and disappeared because every official we spoke with would always tell us that there were lots of other people in the same situation. All of these missing people have families, they have names . . . so we started keeping records. We started in November 1982, and we're still working on this to this day.

Our wartime struggle has not ended. The struggle began during the actual war, with bullets and missiles and snipers and threats everywhere. We were shot at. We were subjected to all kinds of things. We were intimidated into paying bribes. Umm Nabil was even killed because of this. They kept extorting money from her, telling her they'd let her see her son if she brought them money—just bring the money, they said—and they kept taking more and more from her, and when they finally realized she could no longer get her hands on any more, they killed her.

In that sense, the war never really ended. We were subjected to all kinds of torture, abuse, threats, baiting us—you name it. And back then, baiting us meant, for example, that they'd come, and . . . militias or militia members would volunteer to kidnap people from another opposing sect to set up an exchange. They used us to fuel conflict. This phase was very difficult to live through, and, you know, we were out there risking our lives . . . we could have died at any moment, our kids were so young, and we spent all our time in the streets demanding the release of all the missing people.

At first, there weren't any people from East Beirut with us . . . because there was a whole story with the militias there. Some people had been trying to come, but the predominant militia there was the Lebanese Forces. They'd tried to get in touch, and they did eventually, to say that they also had people who'd been kidnapped and disappeared. We called the number that the state had set up for inquiries about the missing people, and it turned out to be the number of the Phalangist offices, Beit al-Kataeb, in Saifi. We met with them. Then the House of Representatives invited us, as the families of the missing and disappeared, to speak with them. And so we did. Back then, the House of Representatives was located at the Mansour Palace in the Mathaf neighborhood. We headed there from West Beirut, and a group also came from East Beirut.

We didn't have any issue meeting with the families of the missing and disappeared who were Christian. I mean, Umm Pierre was no less distressed over Pierre's disappearance than Umm Ali was over Ali's. When they came, we all met. We showed them that we weren't strangers, that we were no different from them. They told us that the Lebanese Forces kept tight control over their movements. But we started coordinating together nonetheless: some of them would figure out who was in charge in their areas, and they'd apply pressure on them, on behalf of us all, to release whatever people from West Beirut they were holding. And we'd do the same in our areas for the people from East Beirut who were being held.

All of the warlords were responsible for kidnapping and killing people based on their sectarian identities. The militias all did this back then. Of course, now the leaders blame it on the war, claiming that war always harms the innocent.

Then peace was declared in 1991. We thought that since the war had taken our family members away, we could expect peacetime to bring them back. Let me conclude my memories of the war with this: the war was a very difficult time—all we got from it were promises. I don't know how justifiable it would be to claim that they were all empty promises. I don't want to be unfair—but there were definitely some lies in there. Also, government officials claimed that the militias' power was stronger than their own—they always claimed their hands were tied, stuff like that.

The war ended, peace was declared, fine. But where were all the missing people? The officials changed their tune then and started saying that it was time to look forward, not back; we were beginning a process of reconstruction and development. But I couldn't, I couldn't just turn the page and move on. Before I could be expected to start thinking about the future, I had to at least be standing on solid ground. My present needed to feel stable first, and that couldn't happen until I figured out my past. But they kept insisting that we not look back. . . .

In response, we continued to say that it was our right to know what had happened to our missing loved ones. Of course, we were marginalized even further after this, at all levels, and even by the media. We knew that if whatever we did wasn't picked up by the media, the general public wouldn't hear about it, and therefore it wouldn't make any impact at all.

There was a lot of pressure put on us, including by the media because at some point even the different media outlets were pretty much divided by sect and political affiliation. So there really was a media blackout.

But in late 1999, we and a group of loyal supporters managed to launch a campaign. We kept gathering more and more supporters from every part of Lebanon, all echoing our message that finding the missing and disappeared was the responsibility of the entire country. I mean, sure, we'd lived through a war, and people were afraid. People were still picking themselves up and dusting off everything the war had left behind. But how were we supposed to rebuild? How could we rebuild a nation when we had no idea what the fate of so many of our people had been? Had we still been at war, I'd have told the families myself that the war was still going on and not to expect anything while it was still alive and kicking.

The Committee's Work and Government Indifference

But, I mean, the indifference of the authorities was just another legacy of the war. So we launched this campaign, and we were able to force the formation of an official committee to investigate the whereabouts of the missing and disappeared. This was during the mandate of Prime Minister [Selim] al-Hoss [in 1998–2000], and we considered it the first actual recognition of our campaign. Unfortunately, the committee that was formed only operated for six months before it published a report saying that it had not found any of the missing alive and that it had found mass graves all over Lebanon. The report actually named them the "East" and "West" graves, implying that everyone had gotten their hands dirty—and such is war. Government officials thought they'd be able to get away with telling us that all the disappeared had died, meaning that it was time for us to go back home and that they'd done their part.

It's not that they didn't know. They did know, but they probably just wanted to buy our silence and get it over with. They know that a mass grave is a crime scene and that people must be held accountable for it. This means that I am not able to say, for example, there is a grave in Mar Mitr or another in the Martyrs' Cemetery in Horsh Beirut or in the English Cemetery in Tahwita or that some corpses were thrown into the sea. Because the report that came out was an official report, the committee considered that it had done its part.

Of course, the report was never officially signed and stamped. When it was released, we were all still collecting ourselves and supporting each other—its release came very abruptly. And all of a sudden, our missing were starting to be referred to as "martyrs" or in similar ways. Can you imagine? We were still picking ourselves and each other up and trying to heal. Some of the women even were being admitted to hospital . . . and then this.

Some women were practically on the brink of death, they were so distressed by the disappearance of their family members. Our tears had not yet dried when fifty-four people were suddenly released from Syrian prisons. Some of the released prisoners had been, of course, among those reported dead when the Syrian and Lebanese security services announced that they'd found mass graves. You can guess what had happened. You killed them with the stroke of a pen, but soon enough they start popping up alive. What must their families have felt?

We collectively revolted. But as we all know, our great Lebanese authorities cannot make one useful decision. They formed yet another committee, this one in charge of receiving complaints from the families of the missing and disappeared. They asked these families if anyone had proof that their missing loved ones were still alive. These were the kinds of impossible questions they were asking. I mean, if I could know for sure where my disappeared husband was or if he was still alive, what would I need the government for?

I'd been shouting in the streets all those years, so how could they think that I knew whether the person I was looking for was alive or not? Anyway, this committee was even less useful than the one before it. It dragged itself through its tasks and didn't accomplish a single thing.

Accomplishments in the Face of Adversity

Now, what did we do, and what was done to us? Wartime and peacetime—like I told you, we were victims of both. All kinds of weapons were used against us. If I were to summarize what we went through looking for our loved ones, I'd have to emphasize one point: what we managed to accomplish as the Committee of the Families of the Kidnapped and Disappeared. Keep in mind we were not an actual committee or an NGO or anything. It's like there was an oppressed, marginalized group of people, and some of us stood up and started asking for our rights to be recognized. And we were silenced. The committee was just a group of people whose loved ones had gone missing—like I told you earlier, we came together to support each other.

Over the course of those years, we managed to accomplish *something*, even if we weren't able to locate the disappeared or free those who were kidnapped. Their fates remain unknown. But we still did important work. We do need to take into account how many obstacles, difficulties, and weapons were—and still are—used against us.

First of all, we were able to join our individual cases together and make the question of the kidnapped and disappeared a national issue. Second, we managed to keep our struggle outside the orbit of sectarianism, militias, and political parties. And third and finally, we created a truly democratic structure despite the turbulence of the war around us. We still use it today. All social groups were a part of our group; regardless of confession, sect, region, ideology, affiliation, or nationality, we include everyone living in Lebanon, including Syrians, Palestinians, and anyone else. Anyone who'd been kidnapped mattered. Back then, even Camille Chamoun—the president, you know who I mean—gave us the name of someone to search for. It was of a relative of his, an American.

None of the political parties, none of the militias, nobody was able to extract an official confession to war crimes, but we were. We, the families of the missing and disappeared, were the ones who extracted this confession. We enshrined the right to know the truth—a right that is recognized internationally in treaties and covenants—in Lebanese law. This was a decision issued by the highest administrative judicial body in Lebanon, the State Council, in 2014.

We stood our ground against the political powers that be, and the judiciary was on our side, agreeing that, yes, the families do have the right to know what happened to their missing relatives. What else can I tell you? I mean, I've barely scratched the surface telling you about just a few obstacles; they were much more complex and difficult than this. And they weighed heavily upon us over all those years. That's why when I talk to my fellow committee members, I always compare us to an army of ants, trying to move a giant rock.

But I mean, sure, we'd accomplish one small thing every couple of years. Most recently, we've got a new weapon on our side—a judicial decision in our favor. It's a really proud moment for the Lebanese judicial system. The decision compelled the political powers to release their report to us. They'd never shared a copy of it with us because they claimed it would ignite another war! We knew the report was about mass graves and claimed all the missing and disappeared were dead. We'd been challenging them to show us proof. So they hid the report, their excuse being that giving it to us would start a new civil war.

But when the State Council's decision was issued, it forced them to release the report to us. Unfortunately, it was nonexistent. It was nothing but the forms submitted by the families of the disappeared. We told them then that if they were recognizing the validity of those forms, it meant they were recognizing us. The council's decision was binding, and they didn't have the choice not to follow it. In the end, we told them that we weren't going to make this public and shame them; we wouldn't tell people that that they'd basically done nothing and that there was no report. But we needed them to officially recognize us by doing two things.

First, they had to take DNA samples from us. Like everyone else, we get sick, grow old, and eventually die. At some point, we'll all be dead. Our DNA is our identity. If you recognize our existence, you are going to need to know who we are and therefore collect our DNA. Without this, how could they identify the disappeared if they did come back, dead or alive? How could they do this if they didn't have our DNA? Keep in mind that Lebanon was teeming with construction sites, and we were hearing a new story every day about how they'd found bones while digging them up.

I mean, come on, when you map people's DNA, you can at least better distinguish whether the bones being dug up are the bones of an animal or a human. That actually happened—I'm not making it up. The authorities discovered bones that later they found out belonged to a mule. With the DNA samples, they'd be able to identify the disappeared whether or not their family members were still in the country or even alive. We decided that the authorities should collect DNA samples from all the families. The International Red Cross started doing just that, collecting biological samples from the families of the disappeared.

The second thing we demanded was to implement the draft law that we'd spent so much time and effort working on with experts, lawyers, specialists, and judges. . . . We'd woven it, as they say, one thread at a time—and there it was, lying in some drawer of a desk in the House of Representatives. We kept telling the House deputies every day that nothing was more important or urgent than this legislation. We'd laid out a comprehensive plan, which detailed each step that needed to be followed in order to close the case for good. It should now have already reached the administration and the Justice Committee and after that will be referred to the Parliament. At the end of 2016, the draft law still hadn't reached it. Tells you a lot about what we've been through and the obstacles we've faced.

I have something very important to say about costs and expenses. I can say with certainty that we are the only group in Lebanon that operates without any funding. We don't submit funding proposals to the European Union or any embassy. When we work on our campaigns, we pay out of our own pockets; friends and supporters help us out. For example, I consider you both new friends of ours now. Give me your contact information, and when we need some money, we'll reach out to you and our friends and all the people who support our cause.

We have a huge project on the backburner right now: we don't have a physical office space. We have no money for it. We've kept on at Lebanese Labor Watch about this, so they've given us access to this room we are in right now. I make use of being here and like to work in their conference room. We really don't have any money, and this project we're working on now definitely needs lots of it. . . .

We're still working as volunteers. We have a whole team of volunteers; no one is paid, even the specialists who helped us out, like those who gave us workshops on how to document, digitize, take photographs . . . all these things—they even taught us how to make storage boxes for our archives. That workshop was run by volunteers from the American University of

Beirut and the National Archives. In the end, our archive is part of a larger national archive. It's national heritage, and therefore it must be publicly funded. We're going to launch a campaign to recruit some more volunteers to help us out. Our team of fifteen is not enough. But this is a public national project, so it needs public funding.

Family, Motherhood, and Work

As a mother, I suffered a lot. It was very difficult. It's not just that I had to juggle my work in the committee and being a mother, but there was also a war going on. There was shelling everywhere. I remember once wishing I could swallow my children. Swallow them back inside my womb. I was afraid of being destitute, of dying. I don't know how I managed everything. I mean, I made mistakes, I felt so guilty toward them, so much was going on. You might see me talking about these things comfortably now, but that's because I've reconciled with my children, which means I've reconciled with myself.

There were certainly times when I fell short in my professional work and in my work in the committee, too, whether doing things I wanted to or those I was compelled to do. I certainly fell short during the war. I used to be a public-sector employee. And I was attacked accordingly. Because I was always following up on our legal case, I was often subtly condemned. I mean, for example, when I retired, I was told I wasn't eligible to receive a pension even though I was eligible—I'd completed and fulfilled all the academic and administrative conditions. But when I left that job, I was at the same level I'd been hired into. I never got a promotion. That was the indirect war they were waging against me on an official level at my job.

I never got any kind of pension. They forbade it. They said they couldn't give it to me because when you advance in your work, you move from a category 3 to a category 2 and then a category 1. When I started my job, I was a category 3, and when I retired a year ago, I was still a category 3. There are some things that administration offers to some employees, like committees that help you make extra money, but I didn't get offered any of that. None of it. It's like they were telling me that this was the price I had to pay for what I was doing.

But they couldn't fight me on everything, and they never said that I violated employee regulations, even though I used to grant authorization for statements without official permission from those in charge. I also at times would publish articles in my own name. I never asked for permission to do this, even though employee regulations stated that I had to request it from my superior. But I couldn't follow those rules. They didn't punish me for that, though—only because the punishment they had in store was much more painful. They kept me in the same employment category though they knew that my struggle to find out what had happened to the disappeared never came at the expense of my work. If there was ever even an hour of overlap between the two, I'd take the day off from work without pay. I'd take a whole day off without pay to do that one hour of work for the committee because I didn't want to let anyone say that I took advantage of my job or that I didn't fulfill my duties because I was at a protest or a press conference. So that's how things went at work.

But my family, my husband's family, never gave me any trouble about this, definitely not. They were worried about me, but they couldn't do anything about it. My family is from the North. And I did pay a lot of attention to my husband's family because Adnan is their eldest, and his father wasn't in great health. I had to look after him and his mother; she was also a great woman . . . may she rest in peace.

They gave me a lot of moral support. But at the same time, I had to support them, too, on all levels. They depended on me. Whenever they saw me, they'd ask what updates I had and if I had any good news. What good news could I ever have given them? But you have to put their minds at ease. . . .

I treated them just as I treated the other families of the disappeared. I indulged them. Maybe I even indulged them more than the others—it's a kind of selfishness, maybe, because I knew how sensitive they were, and the last thing I wanted to do was hurt them. So, yes, there was a lot of moral support. Now, when it comes to other kinds of support, like material support, none of us could offer much to the other. On the contrary, sometimes you had to . . . I mean, what can I say? Sometimes things are just . . . I don't know, never mind. I don't want to talk about it anymore.

And they helped me out with my kids. I mean, sometimes I had to leave the house, but the kids weren't in school or at daycare. Umm Adnan, my mother-in-law, who was the sweetest woman, would babysit them for me. I was the only one who was taking care of everything at home, from A to Z, because all of a sudden a person was just missing from our life. Our family life had disintegrated; it was a big change for us. Even when it came to work, we'd been a double-income household, and then my income alone had to cover everything. I had to look for additional work to be able to provide my children with their basic needs. School fees, medical care, you know? And it's not just that, but everything in my children's lives. . . .

We'd run the household with two incomes, and then there was only one. This was another challenge that forced you to, yes, go beg for another job, a job that didn't have a set schedule. Before noon, I had my teaching job. My second job couldn't have long hours because I had to manage to do some things around the house after. And I also wanted to be with my kids. Often you ended up doing work that was completely out of your field, work you weren't interested in at all, because you just needed money. You were forced to take up work you had nothing to do with just because it gave you a little something in return—a little, but it still helped. It did help, you know, so you took up that work. I had to take up work I knew nothing about, work I had no experience in. I did some translation, some seamstress work, some manual labor; I even worked in sweatshops. It was forced labor, isn't that what they call it? Nonetheless, I had to it. You had to get your hands dirty.

And these weren't stable jobs. You had to constantly keep your eyes peeled so you could find more work to make some more money. I filled out forms for institutions, stuff like that, you know? Nothing was—I mean, you'd get to a point where there was no shame in anything anymore. You'd do whatever you could get your hands on. And all this is happening at the expense of your children, your time, your rest. You didn't have a minute to yourself.

After the War

Finally, I'd like to say that the purpose of the work we did was to assert our right to know the truth of what happened to our family members.

Everything we've done over the years, everything we're still doing, has allowed us to lay some foundations for true citizenship and a real homeland. One of our goals was to declare the day the war began, April 13, a National Day of Commemoration. We also demanded that a monument be erected for all victims of the war and not just the missing and disappeared.

These demands do have meaning. Today, we do collectively commemorate the date of April 13, even if we haven't managed to make it an official holiday. People have their own holidays, religious and national; we wanted to have a day for every Lebanese person, a day that would bring the Lebanese people together, a day of remembrance—not just a tribute to the martyrs of the war. We want to be able to say, "Remembered but never repeated." People may have forgotten what war does, what it takes from you.

To this day, we believe that our group—the families of the missing and disappeared—is unique; I even say we are like our own unique sect. I believe that when the state decides to sit down and start operating like a state is supposed to, our cause just might be the right issue to begin with because it will be a kind of salvation for our country. This is why I keep repeating that our basic demand is so very important: we must learn the fate of our missing loved ones. If this is actually achieved, we'd be contributing to building a true nation with enough space for all of its citizens.

3

Rima Zaazaa

*"I can't just go home, shut
the door on the world, and forget"*

*Like Wadad H., Rima Z.'s activism and militancy during the war were
deeply connected to her upbringing and later to working with her husband
as well as to her long-standing commitment to acting on her deeply held
principles. She repeats in many different ways, as her chapter title highlights, how she always felt she had to stand up for what she believed in. Like
Wadad, she did not set out to be an activist or militant but found herself
compelled to act because of her circumstances and inability to "sit still." She
can't do nothing when she sees people in need around her, so she becomes
politically active. This feeling of being in constant motion is echoed by many
of the women in the stories that follow hers. Having met her husband in
the People's Democratic Party, Rima Z. credits their political and personal
partnership with propelling her ability to contribute so fully to political life.
She also analyzes the political implications of calling this war a "civil war."
And like Wadad, she emphasizes the missing and disappeared as a major
issue still affecting Lebanon today "after the war." Rima Z. speaks about
how war ironically empowers women while at the same time harming them.
Her recounting of the Israeli siege and occupation of her hometown Saida is
the centerpiece of her story.*

[b. Saida, 1960]

My name is Rima Zaazaa; I am Lebanese, born and raised in Saida. My
mother is Palestinian, from Haifa, and that's why I speak with a Palestinian accent in Arabic. I sound so Palestinian because my father always used

to speak to my mother in Palestinian Arabic. So, anyway, the topic we're discussing today is "women and the war in Lebanon". . . . Everyone says that the war in Lebanon was essentially a civil war. This is 100 percent true. The Civil War began at the very beginning of 1973 and expanded in 1975. But from the outset of this conversation, I must emphasize that the war wasn't just a civil war; it cannot be separated from the constant attacks by Israel against Lebanon.

In some phases, we're talking about something like a civil war, but we should never forget our confrontations with Israel and Israel's many attacks against us, especially those against South Lebanon, most of which was initially liberated in the year 2000. I'm from Saida, the capital of the South, and those of us here, we always lived the war with Israel first and foremost—we knew this was the basis of any war being fought even if it presented itself as a civil war.

What I would like to say is that my first experience of the war in Lebanon was in 1975. And when the Syrian army entered Saida just after this in 1976, it was a result of what had been building up at the time, during the Civil War. It had spread throughout the country by then but hadn't yet reached Saida.

Childhood and Family Life

I got married in 1980, and I have three children. Rashid is my eldest, then Jana in the middle, and Tariq is the youngest. I was pregnant with Rashid in 1982, during the huge Israeli invasion when they occupied most of Lebanon; Israel even reached Beirut in this period. I was in my sixth month at this time, and we lost our very best friends—Rashid Broum; his wife, Suad; their son, Ghassan, and daughter, Samia. This was the first major shock we'd ever had in our lives. Rashid and Suad weren't just friends, but they were really our brother and sister in struggle—those supportive people in your life who you feel are just like you in so many ways; you share opinions and have so much in common. Even the things that you didn't agree on completely, you always, always knew there was a lot of room for discussion, for give-and-take.

This loss was the first really big blow for me personally as a result of the war in Lebanon. I didn't hesitate at all to name my eldest son "Rashid" when he was born. He now carries this name that means so much to both me and my husband, Majid. Honestly, their passing was an enormous loss. You can feel today how much we need people like this, people who have ideas like Rashid Broum, God rest his soul. He was so dedicated, so committed to the cause—and at the same time had a critical view of things. He was able to create a space for all things to be put on the table and discussed openly. He would say there is no such thing as "we must do this" or "we must not do that." We lost him . . . and it was a huge loss.

My father was very supportive of my militancy and activism during the war, the opposite of what you might think. I was one of those people . . . we were six kids in my family, I was the only one not to leave Saida. I never left Lebanon. All my siblings went abroad—the United States, Abu Dhabi, Egypt, Saudi Arabia. They left. Of course, at times, in the height of the war I could have chosen to pack up and go to the States, for example. They asked me to, my family did. My parents even went to the States for a while. But I made the choice—this was my personal choice—to stay in my country. I wanted to stay and work here. And I am telling you today that I never have regretted this choice. The first time in my life that I have seriously thought about leaving the country is now, in this period, not during the war, the one we call the Civil War. Never. I'm thinking of leaving *now*? Yes, I am! If we have the choice, we'll leave.

Now, to go back to the war and the topic of what I was doing. Like I said, I'm the kind of person who is involved in politics. I would say that I worked in politics officially even; this was in about 1978. I was in my second year of university. But before that I worked for a nonprofit, Literature and Culture, in the cultural sector. We were establishing ways to create spaces for young people and promote cultural activities in Saida. We always put on plays, sponsored exhibitions and books, and worked on revitalizing Saida's cultural life. I have been around Literature and Culture since 1974. I gravitated toward it, at first, because my eldest brother was a member, as was another brother who was just a bit older than me. From there I got to know the group and the cultural sector more generally. I did this as a young person. To this day, I will never forget. . . . I mean, I remember vividly the first time I was asked to speak at the book fair. I was sixteen years old and so nervous—What could I stand up and say at sixteen years old? But really that day was one of the experiences that shaped who I was as a person—my capacities, my capabilities, my principles, everything that I have achieved today. It was a powerful and rich experience for me.

I really want to emphasize that I was raised and lived in a household that believed in freedom. It was liberated and democratic. Decisions on important questions—marriage, education, political activism, professional work—these were left to each of us children. My father and mother never once imposed a certain belief on us. I had no problem working in politics. But was this always so easily accepted? Yes, it was, but sometimes my father would joke and make fun of the work I was doing. It was always out of love and care for me, though.

If he'd ever told me not to go to Literature and Culture, I wouldn't have gone. But I was eighteen years old, and it was my decision to make. I began my experience in the struggle then. This experience was much like that in any political party. You have educational training you have to complete, weekly meetings in which you discuss political issues, and you're taught with materials about leftist political thought—this was very important. Then there was also training in the struggle. I began this work in Beirut because at that time I was still at university there. They asked me to go to one of the clinics out of which the party was running training camps. I used to go weekly—that is to say, twice a week—to a clinic in the Chiah area. I had so much fun when I went there. I would eagerly await the day when I went.

When I finished university, I went back to Saida. Of course, I worked under the auspices of Literature and Culture, and I completed my training and became one of the leaders of a women's section of the party. I had a position among both the women who'd joined the [People's Democratic] Party and also the wives and daughters of the male comrades. We had weekly sessions about political education and party thought as well as special sessions about "personal issues."

Looking back at this today, I would say it was a result of women's place in our society. Women are marginalized and weakened in our society; often they are not able to make their own decisions. We ran sessions in which they could share if they wanted to and think about our difficulties—Are they caused by our husbands, our brothers, our fathers, our neighbors? We talked about how to change our life situations. These were important sessions that provided me and all the women in the party with an opportunity to see what we could do to face up to our challenges.

Alongside the women's section of the party, I also worked in the cultural sector in the city of Saida. One of the male comrades and I were responsible for creating a union of cultural clubs and associations. We worked together to organize a series of events in Saida, tasked with revitalizing and planning nationalist events. For example, we commemorated the anniversary of the invasion and withdrawal, the martyrdom of Maarouf Saad, Palestinian Land Day, Jerusalem Day, and so on. We always had an annual calendar of events, so we could celebrate occasions and encourage activity in Saida's cultural sector. Though Saida is a city, it can have a closed-minded atmosphere, not like those big cities that have spaces that encourage cultural opportunities for the youth. This was part of my mission!

Challenges of a Being a Woman in Politics

The challenges I faced in doing this as a woman were not unique to me. I was a woman working in politics, but at the same time I was able to maintain "legitimate" relationships, if you want to call them that, with men. From time to time, you might hear someone say that the quote-unquote "ideal woman in political struggle" is the honorable woman, meaning someone who doesn't have multiple intimate relationships, though I am someone who doesn't have a problem with that. I consider this an individual choice for each person, whether a woman or a man. You can be there in political circles as the only woman present with no sexual connotations because you established relationships of fellowship and friendship, the highest form of human relations. You can be there and be respected.

How did I do this? Let me try to think about how. I would say that for my entire life the characteristic that distinguishes me is my honesty. I'm an honest person. I don't mind being in a group or any kind of meeting with others no matter how difficult. I always express my opinion very clearly and frankly. I don't know *how* I do it; I really don't.

You know, having someone like my husband, Majid, with me, as you can imagine, also gives me a lot of support. In so many crucial parts of my life in the struggle, Majid and I were there together. I always expressed my opinions and ideas and participated in everything related to the cause. For example, I can remember big occasions, like International Workers Day, for example. There used to always be a big celebration with, like, more than six hundred, seven hundred people there. And I would speak. I guess that shows you something.

Majid's presence—as a person, us sharing and being together in the struggle, me having my husband beside me—means I can openly mingle with whichever comrades I like. Him being there gives me a certain credibility, I suppose. Me being the secretary and later president of Literature and Culture, I guess, also gives me a certain kind of credibility. It's not just me; another woman could do this as well. A woman can really be a symbol of this kind of progress; I think that these three issues are what made me into a symbol.

Would things have gone the same way if my husband wasn't active in the party? We might say yes, or we might say no. Were he not active in the party but still open-minded, then it's possible. I mean, if he were supportive then, yes, it's possible. But you also should look back at how prepared women are for working on their own, making a work plan, and justifying their presence in the movement. And I should add something else here—this is also true of my job and my profession, not just politics or party work. Today if you're going to work in a professional environment, in a male-dominated context, you must justify your presence. You need to be able to do this.

I suppose my upbringing gave me the elements I needed to reach where I am. Being raised in a democratic, liberated home had a major impact on me. I remember we were always discussing things with our father—the Palestinian cause, the nationalist cause, and the resistance . . .

their achievements, their mistakes, abuses of power. This gave me a some-thing to build on. My involvement in the party and willingness to be edu-cated and see things from a revolutionary angle, this is what raised my consciousness and helped me understand things in a particular way.

But my professional and work experience helped as well. I consider myself one of the lucky folks who had the opportunity to work in the field of capacity building and training community and educational activists in Lebanon but also in Syria, Egypt, Yemen, and Sudan. I also met activ-ists from Palestine, but we had to meet in Cyprus because I was unable to go to Palestine. This was an extremely important life experience as well, exposing me to other people's experiences and allowing me to consolidate some of the skills and capacities that I already had. I traveled alone, mean-ing I left my children with Majid, who looked after them. This is another one of the factors that established me as a role model for others; I became "Rima who travels alone without her husband." He must truly trust me. "She goes, does her work, conducts herself appropriately, and goes home." Who's taking care of the children? Majid is taking care of the children. These are the factors that I believe helped establish me as a kind of symbol. Any woman could be a political party militant, an activist and community worker; she could really play this role for others and have an important role in her local community.

Beginning of the War

I was fourteen years old in 1974 when the war started. I remember the Is-raeli aggression in the region of ʿArqub in 1976. We also were immersed in Literature and Culture, doing social work—like visiting displaced people, gathering and redistributing clothing. Perhaps today if I stop and think about it, all of this helped pave the way for me. This work can help a person choose what kind of role they want to play in their society.

I can finish this story up with the year 1978, which is when I officially became a member of the People's Democratic Party. I started off as a mem-ber, but of course I was promoted through the ranks. Throughout this period, I had a lot of responsibilities. Of course, it's not just about being a political activist, but my biggest and primary concern was always about the community's well-being. I immersed myself in political life with the intention of creating real and genuine change—when I say "change," what I mean is improving people's lives. This is the first point.

The second point I would like to make is about a relationship with the Lebanese state. In that period—and I am speaking about the spirit of young people in that time, not only me and others like me, but all of us—we could see that the problem was the Lebanese state. We knew that we had to destroy it; it was our enemy. And in our lives, when we were working with people, we would present ourselves as an alternative to the state. Today we increasingly see that there can be no alternative to the state and state institutions. They are responsible for providing services to the people, and they are the ones who can ensure people's security, trust, and dignity. On the second principle, the issue of our relationship with the state, in the youth revolution [at the beginning of the Civil War in the mid-1970s], we were always against the state. We wanted to work under the slogan "We want change, we want to improve people's lives." If someone needed health care, we would send them to a clinic; we would guarantee they would be seen by a doctor, get medicine, food, clothing.

War, Armed Resistance, and the Use of Violence

The Israeli invasion began in 1982 and in Saida lasted until 1985 with everything that happened in Sharq Saida after the withdrawal of the Israelis. It was a period of turmoil, with clashes, and as a party we participated in those armed clashes against the Lebanese Forces' militia. There's something I should mention here—I didn't have a big role militarily.

If I were to analyze it today, I would say that I've never really been violent. My whole life long, I didn't believe in violence. Maybe someone reading this might think, "Even though you say you don't believe in violence, you were working with people who did violent things. The party that you were a member of engaged in violent actions. People carried weapons."

Yes, the party confronted Israel and its allies in Lebanon; there were battles, and of course I supported those battles—I wasn't against them, they were in self-defense. But I do want to say that I, deep down inside myself, reject violence and refuse to resort to the use of weapons. But for a period of time, we all had to agree that weapons were the only tools that would allow us to effect change and get to the place we were trying to go. Here I also want to make a distinction. I mean, if we are talking about the war with Israel, for example, of course it's impossible to go up against them in any way other than with an armed resistance.

It's impossible to imagine the Lebanese national resistance, which began after the occupation of the South and the war Israel has waged against it for dozens of years, could decline or surrender, as it has now returned as the Islamic resistance. The Islamic resistance is the culmination of something. No one today can say that only Hizbullah is responsible for resistance today or that it alone can defeat Israel. Not at all. It was the leftist, secularist, communist parties that first launched the National Resistance Front. It was them who let this legacy live on, who carried the torch and eventually forced Israel to withdraw from South Lebanon. Of course, Lebanon did also fight a fierce civil war, in which thousands were killed, injured, or wounded and in which seventeen thousand disappeared. Today the issue of the disappeared is still current.

In 1990, Rafic al-Hariri came and started talking about building state institutions. This is still an issue today, and it will stay relevant because it hasn't been dealt with yet. For me, though, there can be no reconciliation or end to the Civil War until the issue of the disappeared is solved, until the families of the disappeared learn what happened to their loved ones, their husbands, sons, daughters, mothers, fathers, and so on. We all have seen those mothers who are carrying on the struggle for the disappeared and keeping it alive. This is a humanitarian issue; I can't imagine that there is any issue more important than this one. There is a person, you have a person dear to you, and they disappear—you don't know where they are. But, unfortunately, today the warlords are the ones responsible for state institutions, so the issue will never be solved, and the case won't be closed.

Of course, the party I belonged to fought its fiercest battles in the Saida region and the mountains, in self-defense, for land defense, and to protect the regions in the service of the nation. Today I would tell you that I do ask myself if there wasn't another way. I don't know the answer, and it's not on me alone to find this answer. But for sure I would like to have the answer. So would everyone who lived through that era—those who were there then and still are here today. We'd like to be able to look back now: Was it a civil war that we fought? Was there an alternative? Could we have avoided it? Could we have achieved something? Because, in my opinion, the Civil War only brought loss and destruction to everyone living in Lebanon.

Now I'd like to say something more as well. . . . When you talk with people on the other side—areas controlled by Lebanese Forces militias— about the causes of the Civil War, they always say that the primary reason was that the Palestinians were in Lebanon.

This is incorrect. Palestinians being in Lebanon might be one of the factors that was manipulated and exploited—that is, they say that the Civil War broke out because of the Palestinian presence in Lebanon. But in the end, the Civil War was a war of political and economic interests. Every sect and group wanted to try to expand and increase their own share in it so as to strengthen their own existence. Today there is proof of this. All the main people who were symbols of these groups in the Civil War, they are the ones in power today. They control the country's resources and its destiny. And they're the ones who left the country in ruins.

Today we're not living through a war with security threats or military battles like during the Civil War. But if we're talking about our society, comparing where we were at in 1975 or 1980 or 1990 . . . we were much better off then, compared to the battle lines that have been drawn today. You can find this kind of social fragmentation today in every single home in the country.

I want to finish this off—this part of the story—by talking again about the issue of weapons and armed resistance. Even my children . . . of course, my husband and I, we are the kind of people who had a cause we believe in. We have principles, and these are for both life inside the home and also life outside the home and professional life—I mean, we live, eat, drink, sleep, and raise our children according to our principles. And we always talk about the cause and our struggle at home.

My son Rashid always asks me, "OK, so you say you didn't agree with all the things that were happening?! Don't say that you didn't support violence. You did support it." Many things Rashid says give me pause.

I reply, "Yes, you are right. Isn't that what a youth revolt is?" But I don't know. I don't want to claim that I know everything or that I have all the answers. But these thoughts preoccupy me, and I think that we need a new way forward.

The Israeli Invasion of 1982 and Occupation of Saida

I think about the Israeli invasion and the war in Saida and Sharq Saida in stages, as more than one historical moment. Let's start with the first stage, in 1975, and the martyrdom of Maarouf Saad. This happened during a demonstration against Protéine, a company that was coming to town, to try to get its hands on the port and control the fisherpeople working there. They wanted to set up a company and exploit the fisherpeople. At the time, the company targeted Maarouf Saad because he was a symbol of the people's cause, and he was killed for it. This was the spark that ignited the war.

This was the first confrontation with state power in Saida; I mean, it really led to civil disobedience. People closed their shops; the municipality building was turned into a meeting place for all kinds of political and community activities, for ordinary people, all the parties, as well as everyone studying what we wanted to do next. They asked the state to hand the murderer of Maarouf Saad over to us and so on. This was the first battle in 1975. Then the Syrian army entered the city, and there was another battle. The Syrians came so they could tighten their grip and control the city of Saida.

I was of course deeply impacted by the war and occupation of Saida, yes. I mean, when I look at any war, armed conflict, you are necessarily affected by it. One of the things that I remember the most is the reaction of one of my siblings when people started taking up arms to fight. I remember he came home in shock one day because he'd seen a Syrian tank, and one of the soldiers had his head cut off. He was in complete shock; this was a really big deal. You suffer from the things that you witness. This was at the beginning of the war, and that was nothing in comparison to 1982 and the Israeli invasion. It eventually reached Beirut, but on the way it passed through Saida, and it was incredibly harsh on us.

During the invasion, we had to live in a bomb shelter for more than a week because of shelling. Saida was targeted so that the Israeli occupation army could move through it and throughout the rest of the entire South. The first main battle was on the border of the city, at the Palestinian refugee camp Ain al-Hilweh. The Israeli aircraft bombers constantly shelled the Ain al-Hilweh camp for more than ten days in a row. The young men and trained fighters confronted them, shooting at their planes, bullets flying until the tenth day. That's when the Israelis occupied Saida. And after more than a week in the shelter, we were told to come out and go down to the beach on the shoreline. This is where the real tragedy happened. I will never be able to get it out of my mind.

I was staying at my family's house at the time. Though I was already married, I was with my parents, and we stayed in the bomb shelter with them. We lived near the coastline, where we were all required to go. It was only about 150 meters away. I remember when I walked out of the shelter; I don't know how to describe it. Total destruction. Everything was destroyed—every road, building, stone, electricity pole. The shelling destroyed the infrastructure. But even worse was the sight of the bodies of the martyred fighters, who'd died standing against Israeli tanks. It was a sight I don't know how I could possibly describe. But what I do want to say is that my tears were falling uncontrollably. We were all walking, tears were just falling, falling, falling. Because we were seeing not just the loss of bricks and stones but of people—human beings.

Imagine.

Today I can say that it was clear that we'd entered a new phase of the war. It was completely different when Israel arrived on the outskirts of Beirut. Today we know this, but we couldn't see it so clearly back then. I'm perhaps one of those people who works from the heart and not just the mind. For this reason, I believe that sometimes there's something inside us, like "common sense," as you say in English; there's a spontaneous feeling you just have from what's around you. At times, it simply tells you that something's not right, though you can't put your finger on it at the time.

But today I can see it—the repercussions of the Israeli war or the Israeli invasion of Lebanon, the departure of the Palestinian resistance, holding the Palestinians responsible for what happened.

I cannot help but connect the war in Lebanon, from its first phase as a civil war, to this phase we are in today, which I regret to say is controlled by sectarian forces who use religion and claim that they are defending people's interests in the name of religion, which they deem to be the absolute truth. For me, the repercussions of this phase of the war also include the failure of all of the secular, nationalist, leftist forces that had organized around the trust, dignity, and interests of the people. And when I talk about "the people," I'm talking about all people. I don't discriminate or make any religious distinctions. I'm not talking about Christians or Muslims, Shi'a or Druze. When I talk about all people, I'm not talking just about Lebanese people. I'm talking about Lebanese people and also Palestinians, Egyptians, Iraqis. . . . Lebanon is an open-minded country. It has attracted and welcomed all kinds of people who might have had troubles in their own countries. It was a kind of haven because it was, supposedly, "open-minded and democratic."

But our political activity today has nothing to do with democracy. Everyone who lives in Lebanon—poor people, needy people, marginalized and disempowered people—people are humiliated and have their dignity compromised perhaps sixty thousand times a day, unfortunately. These are the repercussions of the Israeli war on Lebanon. Frankly, the rebuilding and reconstruction that began immediately after the Israeli invasion was done by the dignitaries who today are in power in the Lebanese state. The people who destroyed us today are rebuilding. They say that they're building state institutions. But let's look and see. Are they building institutions? I'm sorry to say this, but they're not building institutions. This whole moment that we are living through now began with the Israeli invasion.

That day in 1982, the goal of the Israelis was to gather up everyone on the beach, and they ordered us down to the shoreline. We were thousands of people—men, women, and children—for example, my sister was married and had her two small children with her. They forced her to go even though her elder child was only three years old and the younger one was a year and a half. It was a tragedy to find yourself there on the beach. The Israelis made everyone stand on the shoreline. The first thing they did was separate the men from the women. They asked the men to stand in one place and the women in another. Obviously, I can't even describe the feelings you have at that moment. You are seeing your enemy—those whom you have considered your enemy your entire life—in a position of power. And they can tell you what you can and can't do in your own neighborhood, your own country, your own home.

It was truly difficult. I mean the feelings . . . I can't describe them. People couldn't accept this and didn't even believe it. They were stunned by disbelief. But at the same time, there was a feeling inside us that you could do what you wanted. I mean, what could the Israelis actually do about it? Would they kill all these people? There were these feelings of wanting to challenge them. Let me say that this was much more prevalent among the women than the men for the simple reason that Israel had started from the very first moment to round up men and boys in large numbers and sent them to detention centers—Ansar and Khiam. Israel detained them by the hundreds.

Women felt they wanted to challenge them, perhaps more than men, and ask, "What do you want?! What do you want to do to us?" But during the early days of the occupation, things were very difficult. It was a period of loss; we didn't know ourselves what we wanted to do. They left us there on the coast. They told us all to stay on the beach, but they allowed the people whose homes were right there on the coastline to go into their houses. We were able to go home; I mean, we went to our neighbors, who were from the Saad family. We were able to go to their place and sit with them. You would go to a house, and so every house—with no exaggeration—had more than forty or fifty people even if it was a small apartment. People opened up their places, all the rooms, and told folks that whoever wanted to could use them. Like anyone who had a small child or an elderly person with them could just go up and stay there.

Of course, after we'd just come out of a week in the shelters, there was no food, nothing to drink, no water or anything. There were many small children. I remember mothers who had babies washing them in seawater. They would do anything they could think of. How could we secure food and drink? My father was one of those people who had been a part of the struggle and played a role in support of Palestine to his utmost for his whole life. He worked in trade, but he was supportive of the Palestinian cause. He also had a certain position in the city. The next day, the local police began appearing on the beach. I remember that my father went up to one of these policemen and told him, "I want to leave." We were right near the co-op supermarket in front of our house. He told the police, "I want to open the co-op and bring people some food. If you want, you can come with me and keep track of everything I take. You can write it down and bill me for it. But I want to get milk and diapers because we have been here for some time, and there's nothing left."

And he actually did take a group of guys down to the co-op and opened it up. Two police officers went with them, with pen and paper, and they wrote down and calculated the price of everything they took. People started coming and taking cans. They had no choice but to let them because people needed food and water. We remained on the beach for more than a week, imagine that!

Later, whenever the Israelis saw us, they started talking to us—I mean to the whole group—using loudspeakers. The first thing they said was, "Oh people of Saida!" This is the first time I have ever repeated aloud the words that they said to us. This is the first time since 1982 that I am remembering these words and saying them aloud. This phrase alone struck fear in all of our hearts because when they said, "Oh people of Saida," moving through every residential area with loudspeakers, they would take all the men and the youth away so they could parade them in front of their hooded informants.

Returning Home

After about a week of this, we moved on to the next phase, when the Israelis let the people on the beach to return to their houses for good. We were allowed to go home. As I said before, it was only about 150 meters from the beach to our house, but before that we weren't allowed to enter our actual house. When we got home, of course everything inside was completely destroyed; things were scattered all over the floor, corpses were still lying there on the ground. Like all of the houses in the neighborhood, ours had been ransacked and vandalized, totally turned upside down. The Israelis had moved every single thing from its proper place. It was obvious to us that they'd been searching for something inside our houses—weapons, fighters who were hiding there. . . . I remember that they'd written a message in red marker on a large mirror in one of the bedrooms, in English: "Sorry, it's war." It seems that they were trying to apologize for all this destruction . . . excusing themselves by saying "but it's war."

So naturally we went back home; everyone did, not just us. There was no electricity, no water. Since the electricity had been cut for so long, everything in the refrigerator was spoiled. Everyone had to resort to cooking with canned foods. I want to emphasize something here: today you can read in books and documents that came out at the time that everyone back then was saying to expect an invasion—that it was clear that an Israeli invasion of the South was coming. Like in political circles, they were saying this.

But who on earth would have thought to prepare for an invasion by starting to stockpile supplies at home? I mean, did anyone plan for this and say, "Hmm, OK, the Israelis are coming, they're going to invade our country, what will we need? I'll start preparing by getting the food and water necessary to make it through this." No, of course not! In that period, people really did go hungry. Children, babies, they didn't have milk. There were no diapers to be had anywhere. People resorted to using pieces of clothing . . . I mean to make into diapers. People did all kinds of things to carry on and meet their basic needs.

Of course, at this time—I mean the day when we were able to go back home and the next day after—the Israelis had one main concern. They wanted to give us a certain image of themselves and what they were doing. "We've come to help you get the things you need." This is how they always talked to us, "We didn't come to fight against *you*." That's what they always said: "We're only fighting the armed combatants. We're fighting the Palestinians. They're the ones who ruined your lives and destroyed your country. Look what the Palestinians have done to you." They'd bring big containers of drinking water and say to people, "Come down and fill your water jugs."

I remember one incident very well. My sister was filling up a container with water, and one of them told her, "Come here, I'll fill up your water." He wanted to show her how nice the Israelis were. She told him,

"No. You're the ones who started the war." He told her that it wasn't them that started the war; it was the Palestinians. She told him, "No it's not." He then said, "Look around, we are giving you water." I remember that then she picked up the huge water jug that she'd filled and threw it in his face. She then got herself together and went home.

Challenges of Parenting in the War

The biggest challenge I had was indeed the issue of spending time with the children. Today when you look at my daughter, for example, she's married and has a child. You can see that my daughter, her husband, and son, they do things together that I didn't do. I can tell you today that this wasn't right. We didn't have time; perhaps this is because Majid and I both were in the party. We always had to have a division of labor. Before noon, the children were either at school or nursery or at their grandmother's house, where she looked after them. In the afternoon, we divided our time. Either Majid was with the kids, or I was because their grandmother couldn't have them both mornings and afternoons. We just didn't have time to have a social life where we could go out and about as a family. I'm not just speaking about having friends. I'm talking about going out as a family with the children. There are many things that I didn't do in my family life. And it's unfortunate that I have to say this, but it is a result of our twenty-four seven commitment to party life. This was the clearest challenge that I had to face.

We used to express our family problems in a very jokey way. My children always tease me and ask me both jokingly and seriously, "Really? Is it you who raised us?" It was something they said as a joke. It doesn't mean that they carry this around inside themselves, but it is an indication of something when they say, "Are you sure that it's you who raised us? Didn't Grandma raise us? What about Auntie Nadia? Maybe both of them together?!" I mean, there was a rotation, depending on when. There were times with Grandma Nemat, God rest her soul, and others, with Grandma Nawal, God rest her soul. Sometimes there was Auntie Nadia, who was also the wife of one of our comrades, helping us out. And there were consequences to this. I'm telling you that it's natural because at times we really worked for so many hours each day. This was a challenge; of course it was a challenge. I can't say that I regret it. But I think that if I could turn back time, I wish I could have given more time to my children. For sure. I would have given more time to the children. Maybe I feel this because now I'm a grandma myself, and I look at my grandchild. But I know that at the time I couldn't have given more time to my children.

War and Women's Empowerment

What can I tell you about the experience of war and women's empowerment and liberation? In my opinion, yes, for sure, the experience of the war was a path to women's liberation. But my experience in the party is not the same as in the religious parties. I am talking about within secular, leftist, nationalist thought. This is what fortifies people from the inside; I mean, this is truly what allows people to develop themselves. I believe that the party experience truly helps a person to build skills and capacities.

On the other hand, the parties that we see today—Hizbullah, AMAL, the Progressive Socialists—excepting the small parties, they used to have more space for women. But I do not see these parties building up liberatory thought in the context of women's empowerment, unfortunately.

I worked for three years—from 2012 to 2015—on a project called "Empowering and Serving Women Who Are the Most Vulnerable to Violence." We provided psychological and social support services to women who were exposed to violence. We managed to reach many women at home, not so much women who worked outside the home. Seriously, we were able to reach about two thousand women over the course of three years, which is a lot of women, an impressive number. And most of the women we reached were women who stayed home.

I'd like to share with you a testimony of one of the women who came to us to do a vocational training course in tailoring. She told me, "I'm thirty-two years old, married, and living at home with my children, whom I gave birth to and raised. This is the first time in my life that I am doing something for me. Doing the sewing course and the tailoring course was a real experience for me, and it will be something just for me."

I'm telling you that today we need more innovative projects to address the issue of women's empowerment and liberation. We need new and unconventional initiatives to achieve this. This is a cumulative process. We need to start working with women, with children, today so that in ten, twelve, fifteen years we can create generations of young women, teenage girls, who can and are willing to have liberated worldviews. Otherwise, unfortunately, it won't work. Especially now, as we were saying a few minutes ago, when the challenges are so daunting. Society today is really divided, and there are a lot of challenges.

After the War

Even if I don't like to say it this way, war does shape who you are. No one likes war, and no one wants there to be a war. But those difficult circumstances, of course they are what helped me today to be able to play the role I do in my local community. You know, I think that if there isn't justice in your society or community, there's a notion of justice in the world. Because it's not just me or you or people I think are like me or look like me who reject injustice. This was our slogan—"Refuse injustice." This is what prompted my personal quest for change.

I want change, and I think, What is the framework that will allow me to achieve it? I am not one of those people whose life stops at my own doorstep. I can't just go home, shut the door on the world, and forget. Till today I still put the word "family" in quotation marks; in our home we usually say "tyranny." For me, this sense of tyranny has increased with time. Especially as you grow older and have more life experience. At this point in my life, there are things I've seen that today I would simply say, "No, I don't accept it; I won't stay silent about these things," and I feel that it's our job to shed light on them.

I also want to tell you that this accumulation of things is what caused us—I'm speaking in the plural for myself and Majid—to find ourselves working in an association of civil society organizations in Saida, comprising more than sixty, seventy, eighty groups. Working in this framework is a kind of compensation for the party work that I did. I'm not saying anything about Majid here, but just about my work in the party.

When you're active in politics, and you've worked all your life in the service of the people, it's really hard to then just sit on the sidelines and say, "I don't want to do anything anymore." That's not me. My immersion in civic work and people's causes was a kind of moral compensation, if you want to call it that. It's what pushed me to develop some of the most important experiences in my career and professional life. But I didn't just do it to make money. I did this because I believed in the principle and the cause.

In addition to this professional work, I was also able to accomplish some modest achievements: I taught a course at Saint-Joseph University, for example. One of the things I was asked to do was to give a course called "Community Dynamics and Communication," to a group of professionals who worked in social services. I was one of the experts who participated in developing a national strategy for early childhood, meaning from birth to eight years of age. This is also something that I in all modesty consider an honor—that I was asked to participate in this. I was one of the people who worked with the Ministry of Education in Sudan around early-childhood issues as well. I did the same thing in Aswan, and I was working in coordination with the Ministry of Education in Lebanon. Today I am working within the Lebanese public-school system on a project devoted to peace building and acceptance of "the other," with the United Nations Development Program.

4

Arab Loutfi

"War is so much more than meets the eye"

Also active with the resistance in the South, especially in Saida, like Rima Z., Arab L. credits similar support from her family and upbringing with shaping her into the political person she became. A well-known filmmaker and activist on behalf of the Palestinian cause, Arab L. worked and continues to work between Lebanon and Cairo. Her detailed descriptions of her childhood and upbringing focus on her character and political conscientization from a young age as well as how she lived through a revolutionary moment. Also like Rima Z., Arab L. discusses her partnership with her husband, who was an activist and militant, but in her case they could not stay together and eventually split up. Differently than Rima and most other women in the book, Arab L. experienced and analyzes sexism within party ranks and the difficulties of acting as a woman within its hierarchies. She also echoes all of the women in the study in denouncing war and its terrible impact on people, while acknowledging how struggle and resistance allow for one's vision to become clearer. This is what she calls the "complexity of the war."

[b. Saida, 1953]

My father, Shafiq Loutfi, was a lawyer in the High Court, and he was really distinguished. He had progressive stances on many issues and was one of the first people who supported the idea of political change in Saida. He took a strong stand against nepotism in politics, and he supported Maarouf Saad when Saad first confronted the issue. There was something really nice about my dad; he was friends with different kinds of people. At home, you'd meet intellectuals who might be considered part of Arab popular heritage but also educated middle-class people who you might think of as more organic intellectuals. This opened us up to all kinds of thought—we could enjoy knowledge and ideas regardless of where they came from, not just logic from academia but knowledge of life in the world. He was always open to meeting new people and learning new things. Of course, all of this had a profound influence on me in my childhood. Moreover, because we lived in Saida, a city that was one of the first to receive Palestinian refugees in 1948, we were surrounded by an atmosphere that was always totally and consistently supportive of the Palestinian cause. This was a central issue in our lives. Palestine, Israel, the occupation, and the resistance were always there. My dad was special because he supported the fedayeen, Palestinian freedom fighters who at the time were operating outside the law, even at the peak of the control and repression by the Lebanese security and intelligence apparatus, the Deuxième bureau.

But when people say that we have strong personalities and good heads on our shoulders because we are our father's children, my sister, Maha, and I always tell them, "No! we're actually much more our mother's children." First of all, she had a very strong personality. She came from the Bizri family, but there was something about her that made her different from them. She had no interest in bourgeois life; she didn't care about it at all. In her eyes, a boy who worked at a drycleaner's was more important than a landowner or a representative in Parliament, like Adel Osseiran. She had very genuine relationships with people, and she was always very relaxed with everyone. She evaluated people based on how kind they were—or not—with no regard to their class or background. And she held onto this even though she knew that traditional people often had preconceived ideas about others: who was considered to be the "right sort of person" or not. . . . Social status just didn't matter to her. All she cared about was the person who was there with her.

Mama was a very strong woman, by the way. Even her brothers agree that she was the strongest sibling. They looked up to her and sought her guidance in everything they did. She grew up in an atmosphere where girls' opinions were always encouraged and listened to. There was no such thing as a "man of the house" in the sense that a man or boy could say or do more than a woman or girl. Everyone was equal, and she raised us with this mentality, too. This helped me out a lot in life because I didn't come from a home in which I'd been repressed, a home I wanted to rebel against. On the contrary, I came from a home that had shaped me into a woman who was very comfortable with the idea that I was an independent being in my own right.

The second lucky thing about my life is that I came up in a revolutionary moment. The general atmosphere was one that encouraged participation in liberation struggles. This gave me another push; it made me feel that I could do anything in the world. Then there was also a third thing that was encouraging: throughout my different experiences, I met people who really were up to the challenge of the times we were living through, the good and the bad. People weren't working against each other or trying to hurt each other; we were all experiencing everything together. Imagine if I had come up in a period when these Islamists were around—disaster. There are girls today who are very frustrated in their homes, with their families and siblings. There are girls fleeing to Cairo. . . . I mean, they go to Cairo with nothing just to live far from their families. There are girls who run away from home and never go back. Girls who truly hate their families. They've lived through truly harsh experiences. But we came up in a world that embraced you. In some ways, I was very lucky about the circumstances I grew up in: the general atmosphere was one that fostered strength, not weakness, and helped a person self-actualize. Of course, this takes root within you, so that when you grow up and face difficult moments in life, you find yourself ready—I mean, able to withstand these situations better.

Childhood, Young Adulthood, Politics, and Struggle

The first time in my life that I saw a fedayee was when I was young, back in the 1960s. It was before the disastrous defeat of the Arab armies in the 1967 War. This fedayee was from one of the first groups of freedom fighters. His name was Hojaij. When he was released after being tortured in a Lebanese prison, I remember people around him propping him up because he couldn't even walk on his own two feet. This fedayee's wife was Algerian. He'd met her when he was training in Algeria. His mother didn't know how to communicate or get along with his wife very well. There are so many stories like this in our collective memory, and they all played a role in shaping my consciousness.

I even remember when I was in the first year of primary school, and they held a competition for the best story written about Palestine. I took first prize for the South, and I also remember that Ghalib al-Turk, who was the governor of South Lebanon at the time, was the one who gave out the prizes. My point here is that my family was generally very much immersed in a political climate, one in which we freely discussed politics, culture, intellectual thought . . . but it wasn't an atmosphere of empty philosophizing, no! It was really an atmosphere of just enjoying life . . . it was normal for us to talk about things like that; I mean, I wasn't raised to believe that culture is something for the elite. Culture for us was a way of life, just like they say about knowledge and interaction. It's really no surprise that all of this contributed in important ways to forming my personality from the very beginning of my childhood.

I got into political work at a very young age. Later, the Deuxième bureau appeared as part of the Lebanese intelligence apparatus, and there was an Israeli attack on the Beirut airport in 1968. After a while, the resistance movement started gaining traction, and at a certain point there were even records kept about people's comings and goings, especially for people who were politically active. I remember that back then *Al-Hurriyya* magazine was being published, and several issues were censored. It was a daily magazine, and some days the issue would be published with missing excerpts. Those parts that they censored, I put them in my movie *The Upper Gate* [*Bawwabat al-fawqa*, 1991]. I documented issues that were meaningful to me.

It was during that period that organized political action began. For the first time in my life, I started going to the Palestinian camp in Ain al-Hilweh. It wasn't a normal camp, like for fun, or a scouts' camp. It was part of the resistance, and at the time the people in the camp were starting to affiliate themselves with different organizations. Palestinians still didn't have the right to do political work in Lebanese cities, but they really did start to have a presence within the camp.

All these transitional periods really shaped us and introduced us to political work and the movement, creating a passion for resistance within us. During that time, I met young Lebanese people from the [Organization of] Socialist Lebanon and the Organization of Lebanese Socialists before they merged and became the Communist Action Organization, in Lebanon. They contacted me despite how young I was since I came from a political family and background that were known to be politically inclined, too. I was so young that my presence was quite exceptional. Normally, I would have needed to be older to be able to join a political party. So I started truly experiencing political life then.

Since it was a Marxist group, discussions were mostly centered around the labor struggle, the student struggle, and demonstrations and strikes as a movement. One or two years later—I was fourteen or fifteen by that point—the strike of the Régie tobacco workers at the branch in Ghazieh began in the South. This was in 1970. There was a need for girls to go to the tobacco factories and speak to the women workers. Mariam Makki and I headed there. I even have a small photograph from there that I included in the movie. You can't see us in it, but we were next to the women workers at the factory entrance; someone took it as a souvenir. My point is that it was at that time that I met Umm Mahmoud, Nouhad al-Damr, Wardeh, and all the young people who were up there at the tobacco factory in Ghazieh. I definitely think that this experience impacted me and my beliefs.

As for my affiliation to a political party, the truth is that I've had a sense of political awareness from a very young age by virtue of the general atmosphere at home, at school, and in the city. I was always surrounded by people who were interested in understanding and debating politics; it was important that everyone have their own point of view. Many of my family members were affiliated with different political and national movements. I'm just trying to explain that I grew up in a political and politicized climate.

I was thirteen years old when the 1967 War erupted, and the Arab defeat was a defining moment that marked my drive for political action. My political experience started with my support for the Palestinian resistance.

We formed popular committees to collect donations for the resistance and to oppose Zionist aggression. My daily engagement with political work really started with this support for the Palestinian resistance, with all the debates I had about its importance as a revolutionary movement. There is no doubt that the general atmosphere in which I found myself from the very beginning of my political consciousness made me lean toward the left. I was deeply involved in the revolutionary left, with all its complexities. Everything around me—my family, my friends, the general climate I was raised in—was leftist, as I said.

The fact that I started working with the support committees of the Palestinian resistance drew me right into the core of the political struggles of the time. Then there were intensifying escalations and clashes with the Lebanese state because the police and security apparatus was hostile to the resistance back then. Organized revolutionary movements, both Lebanese and Palestinian, started to form. During that period, I contacted a group of people—the Arab Socialist Action Party—who afterward merged with another group and formed the Communist Action Organization in Lebanon. I started working with them at a very young age; I must have had just turned fourteen. I was mostly active in the popular committees, but I also participated in student activism as well as more general activism, and also I worked on labor issues. I was engaged in all kinds of political work.

I became more and more invested in becoming a revolutionary in all aspects of my life, and I worked toward that goal on a daily basis. I devoted a lot of my time to political struggles, even when I was still in high school. I always played one role or another in activism, in demonstrations, protests, meetings, in the student and labor movements, and with the tobacco farmers in our region of Saida and South Lebanon generally.

I came from a middle-class family, and I had a comfortable standard of living. My activism exposed me to real-life problems for the first time, problems I never could've imagined existed. This reshaped my morals and my values; my sensitivity to others was enhanced. I started understanding a lot of needs that I had never really thought about in depth. So that period of my life was an important part of my experience as a human being, and it deepened my political commitments. It also expanded my ways of thinking. And it gave me a true taste for life and deepened my love for people. This made me better able to see the true beauty in all kinds of ordinary people, in the small sacrifices we make every day, and in people's ability to give. My perception of many small things changed, not only through reading and discussion but through daily life, through the inspiring people I met—people who were extremely generous and kind despite their difficult circumstances.

This defining period of my life continued until the 1970s. At a certain point, as the conflict developed, a shift occurred in my own thinking and became increasingly close to that of the PFLP. I was very motivated by the idea of armed resistance and the overall conceptual project of resistance in its broadest sense. Then we lived through the experience of the Civil War. I went through many things; I won't go into all the details. I think it was a very important experience, honestly. It made me feel closer to people on a human level.

There is no doubt that community work and this connection to people's issues—a sense of belonging and a capacity for solidarity and empathy—these things definitely are enhanced by political work. This destroyed any individualistic mentality I previously had, and it heightened my sense of community. It made me more human. I am proud of my experiences, and I am proud of every militant, female and male, that I got to know, that I got to share these experiences with. I learned from them, and they learned from me, too. They are my whole world. I mean, this world—this world I belong to—it is my inner pride, it is my entire life, even in my work in cinema and other creative pursuits, including writing. I think that these people have inspired me in different ways and have influenced my values. And this is my compass, the moral compass that protects me from making any small—or big—compromises. It's what keeps me from feeling self-important and protects me from my ego.

The War and the Israeli Invasion of 1982

Truth be told, like I previously mentioned, the war has been ongoing ever since it started, and it changed people's priorities and the general structures of their lives. But the most violent thing that happened was the Israeli invasion of 1982. Our city, Saida, was subjected to extreme violence and aggression. In one day, no less than six thousand people were killed in enormous massacres carried out by Israeli air strikes. The city faced brutal destruction, and even though people resisted with force, the invasion was incredibly ferocious.

I had been in Cairo because I needed to see if I could enter Egypt, having been banned over my political stand against the 1978 Camp David Accords. I was also wanted because I was implicated in a case that had been brought against some organizations, including the Popular Front and the Dhofar Liberation Front. But I decided to return to Egypt anyway because there wasn't really a viable legal case against me. They allowed me to reenter Egypt because I was the wife of an Egyptian. But they did start calling me in for interrogations and stuff like that. . . . Anyway, I entered Egypt at the end of May. On June 5, 1982, around 4:00 or 5:00 p.m., when the invasion started, I was in Cairo. I returned to Lebanon in September.

Beirut had fallen. I entered through Syria, and that was a nightmare for me. It was so strange. I was trying to get to Saida through all these regions that I never would otherwise have passed through, areas that were crawling with Phalangists and the Lebanese Forces. I had to cross through a Lebanese Forces checkpoint. Then, when we made it to the Beirut-to-Saida road, Israeli checkpoints started popping up. You're entering your own city, but now it's filled with Israelis. It was a very strange experience.

To be honest, the reason I came back to Lebanon was my mother. . . . When I went to Cairo, I was planning on staying there for a year. But I returned to Lebanon because I needed the assurance that there was nothing standing in my way. The idea of the occupation was making me so anxious, I felt like I needed to return to Lebanon to prove to myself that I could indeed enter the country. I needed to break that barrier of fear. I stayed in Lebanon for two months.

At that time, I was meeting lots of people. Some had left; others had fled and were just returning. People were talking about what to do and what not to do. I witnessed a military operation against the Israeli army by chance. It was an important experience because it was the initial phase of these military operations, and people's mindsets were starting to change, even in how they discussed things.

That day of the military operation, I was with Fatima Ghandour, a friend of mine who's a philosophy professor. We were in Saida, and all of a sudden a young man showed up and detonated an explosive device. He was carrying out a military operation against an Israeli patrol. He fled right after. The Israelis surrounded the area, and I remember that Fatima told me that day that she envied this young man because he probably felt freer than any of the rest of us.

It was an important experience for me to witness firsthand how these operations against the Israeli forces were shaping up. At first, the Israelis were everywhere; the city was teeming with them. We'd even see them walking among us whenever we were out. Then, all of a sudden, the operations became more and more frequent. One time I was on my way to Beirut, and when we got to Nejmeh Square in Saida, there was an explosion near Cinéma Shahrazad. They blocked off the whole area. The Israelis were shaken up by that because they had started getting comfortable in Lebanon: they were out eating ice cream, window shopping. . . .

But after that the Israelis only moved around in their Jeeps, weapons out and visible to all. This was a good thing. When I started packing up to go back to Cairo, I had met many young people and had lots of discussions with them. The pace kept picking up. Emboldening the resistance. On my next visit to Lebanon, Beirut and Saida had already been liberated, and Nabatieh followed. I arrived when the Israelis had already left Saida. I started working on documenting the operations that had taken place to drive them out.

Popular Resistance

The popular resistance started to form. This resistance was what managed to liberate the region from occupation. That was the most dramatic period in the sense that . . . I mean, yes, war is continuous and ongoing. People always talk about killing and death and blood and massacres, and this is all real. People talk about displacement, about losing a sense of safety in a specific location, and this all happened to people, everyone experienced it. That's the main point.

The problem is that during wartime people reshape their entire lives; they revise all their choices because they can no longer follow the natural course of basic human life. Once this trajectory changes, they need to redefine how to think, how to plan. For example, you can no longer talk about your dreams to further your education or about where you'd like to work, where you'd like to live—because all of that is being affected by the ongoing state of war in the sense that choices were always being reoriented by the constant battles we were living through. This altered the course of so many of our lives.

The simplest example is how the war affected people's stability, their ability to continue their education or even to continue living with their families. Entire families were forced to separate and scatter, each person living in a different place, either to be able to survive the war or to be able to find work that would then help them keep themselves and the rest of their family afloat. So many people had to move more than once. There were homes that were completely demolished. People were forced to settle for living in worse conditions than before. This is what war does.

We experienced it—among our friends, within our families, everywhere. In my specific case, I can also say that a lot of things in my personal life changed, even my priorities. Like even my interest in the arts or my interest in certain other fields. I was constantly being pulled in new directions or forced to take another path altogether for extended periods of time.

I was always mostly involved in political work, in supporting the struggle, even though I am actually more interested in the creative arts. But at a certain point, you realize that creativity itself is something that needs to be used in struggle and resistance. But the struggle is always about people's choices, their passion, stamina, friendships, relationships . . . every single thing is reshaped by this context. There are so many things. . . . For example, I might imagine—if our countries had been in different circumstances—that I'd have studied at the University of Acre. But Acre was occupied. Thus, though it is so close to Saida, we can't go there. We can almost see it from Saida, but we just can't reach it.

These kinds of events uproot lives and make them veer offtrack. Suddenly you find yourself having to go abroad to study or stuff like that. You could have very well had your own dreams to pursue, but there comes a time where it hits you that if you were to pursue these dreams, you'd be giving up your principles and every one of your priorities. This leaves you no choice but to switch the course of your life.

What I am trying to say is that the effects of war are, of course, always the main focus: death and displacement are really very violent, very cruel, very dramatic. But there are some types of soft cruelty that aren't visible. That makes them no less suffocating, though; they stifle people's personalities, suppress their worlds, choke their relationships, even between the closest of friends. Take me, for instance: when I was very young, many of my friends had been martyred and so were already relegated to the past tense. You could say that my understanding of death started in my teenage years. And what an understanding to have! Usually, people get to grow old before they're confronted with losing their friends. They're in their sixties or even seventies when they begin losing their dearest friends.

But for our generation, death was an experience we became familiar with at a very young age. My best friends from childhood were martyred in their twenties, and before that we lost lots of other people, even schoolmates. We experienced loss at much too early an age. Death, too. . . . Sometimes your friends are all scattered. I mean, all the people who are supposed to be part of your daily life aren't—everyone is in a different place—these are all examples of the changes that really have violent effects on everyone's lives. In addition, there are problems of identity, of feeling like you're losing a sense of who you are, your memory of things, and on top of all that there's an attempt to destroy your memory as a whole, as if it were being reconfigured in different ways.

War is a very complex process. People always categorize war as being limited to death, blood, and killing. But the truth is that war is something infinitely more complex, and the wounds that people are left with are much deeper than death. Death is not the ultimate end. There are lots of things that end way before death comes. Death is one of these ends, of course, but there is so much more that ends, that is destroyed. Constant instability, a constant sense of feeling dislocated and displaced. All these details . . . to me, war is so much more than meets the eye. The deep human struggle to reject war in its greater sense remains, despite all these acts. It's not just that people don't have anything to eat or don't have anything to drink. I'm not taking away from how serious these problems are, but, to me, this topic is much more complex than that. The impact of war is a major issue. There's no one answer that can cover it all. . . .

The war really shaped my personality. Being confronted with danger or going through difficult moments has a way of making you discern what's real from what isn't, what matters from what's trivial and superficial. You start to really see the value of things, sometimes even their deepest meaning, and this can help to steer you away from trivialities, while making you more sensitive to exhaustion and fatigue and whatnot. This could explain how people are able to produce great works of literature, poetry, and cinema with a creativity that can only arise from those kinds of difficult times.

What I mean is that these experiences trigger human reflections that are wholly unconnected to how superficial society is. And this reaches even the lives of ordinary people. So many people have had to pull their courage out from deep within themselves. They've had to make real life-altering decisions to avoid being broken. And those who don't know how to adapt are hit the hardest. So, yes, the war was an element that pushed my personality to develop in specific ways. Especially when you don't intend to give up—I'm talking in the context of war—the ability to resist gives you extraordinary strength. Your ability to resist is what protects you, and it helps you move through life with more determination. It transforms all your internal defense mechanisms into elements of resistance.

Creativity itself is a tool of resistance. Music is a tool of resistance. Life, really, is resistance. The war really changed who I was and who I became. I'd hoped to live a normal life in a normal society. But the experience I went through did allow me to learn so many things that deepened my humanity.

War Experiences and Participation

I was mainly in Beirut during the war, at the Burj al-Barajneh camp. War is a formative experience. First, there were high hopes that the revolution would be victorious. What we wanted was a national, democratic Lebanon and an end to fascism. There was also the idea of confrontation with Israel and the possibility of real change. That was all at the top of our list at the beginning. And it gave people the momentum to carry on.

Of course, after the fall of the Tal al-Zaatar camp, it gradually became clearer and clearer that we were under siege, that we were going up against a powerful attack. In the face of all that, there was also a deep sense of being able to withstand the pressure. After a while, we reached the point of being convinced of our own steadfastness, but we could no longer tell where we were headed. Our prospects were getting dimmer and dimmer, especially after the Syrians entered Lebanon. It started to feel like our revolutionary project was under siege from all sides.

When Kamal Jumblatt was killed, it just confirmed this idea that Abu Ammar [Yasser Arafat] was participating in a sort of pragmatic collusion. There were a lot of conflicts and arguments. At first, the revolutionary project was working full-force, and there actually was a possibility of victory. People were really talking about the possibility of victory for the revolutionary project. But it was hit hard by the violent siege by the Arab regimes, Israel, and the Lebanese Forces. The Lebanese Forces weren't all that powerful at the beginning of the war. Practically speaking, they'd gotten to the point where they were completely surrounded, but the Syrians' entry into Lebanon breathed new life into them and allowed them to carry on.

There was a real conspiracy against the revolution in Lebanon. Naturally, all of us in Lebanon had faith in the possibility of victory, of building a national, democratic country. The people on the streets were awe-inspiring, in full solidarity with each other despite the fact that they all were strangers. You'd see people handing out copies of the Lebanese nationalist *Al-Watan* newspaper everywhere; everyone was clamoring to read it and wanted everyone else to read it, too. There were even publications being distributed at checkpoints! People had incredible momentum and were totally mobilized.

I remember that when I went to the Palestinian camp, everyone threw their doors open and welcomed me. I remember just how much these revolutionary moments helped open people's minds. I once turned up at a friend's house after midnight—he was a young man, and I didn't know his parents at all. When I knocked on the door, he called out to his mother, "Mom, that's my comrade." And his mother immediately started heating up some water for me because they barely had any hot water left, and they didn't want me to go to sleep without having the chance to wash up. They wanted me to be as comfortable as possible. Ordinarily, or traditionally, his mother would have admonished him for bringing a girl home at 1:00 a.m. All of these details reveal just how much people's spirits had changed. People stopped commenting on or caring about a lot of things they previously would have. People respected you and respected your work; they no longer cared if young men and women were working together. It was kind of a utopia. . . . And these were just ordinary, traditional people, not necessarily formally educated at all. That's why when people say we are "traditional" or "backward," it's just not true. Values change and mature over time. In any given revolutionary moment, people's minds are opened, and they are much more able to stand together in solidarity than they otherwise might be.

There isn't just one event or incident to talk about during the war, so many things happened! I've often seriously considered writing these stories down. There are times in life when things just click. All the little details of your experiences contribute to how you feel about things, and this leads you to a deeper contemplation of the complex issues around you. This doesn't happen all of a sudden; it's rather an accumulation of small flashes of consciousness. For example, I remember that there was a fourteen-year-old boy working with us. He was a Palestinian who had fled Jordan after the Black September massacres of 1969 and 1970. They escaped Jordan with the resistance. His family was in dire straits. He joined the resistance and became a fighter. He started getting extremely anxious, and I took him to the clinic run by one of the Swedish doctors who'd come to work with the resistance in the camp.

I asked the nurse how we could help him. She replied that he needed to drink milk, get more sleep, eat more healthily, and stop smoking. In a moment like that, you suddenly realize that he's just a child. What can you say to a child in these circumstances: "If you don't go to bed early, I'm going to shoot you"? How was I supposed to convince this boy in these circumstances to follow the same logic as you would use to convince a child who has lived a more protected life? The world around him was far from protected or normal. How could I be anything other than worried about him?

I remember that something strange happened to me that day, while I was walking back with him. I was thinking about how he really was just a boy and that he should be living a different kind of life. As we entered the camp, I saw a few young men just sitting there and listening to that song by Abdel Halim Hafez, "Ahwak." Suddenly, I saw the situation for what it was: I was surrounded by teenage boys, and I had an even younger boy with me. I remember that I wept a lot that day because I was overcome with the realization that these young men should be loving and living a more normal life, where they could dream and do what they wanted to. But nothing about their lives was normal because their country is occupied, and they were living in harsh circumstances. They were put there by a reality they had no control over.

And people just sit around philosophizing and wondering incredulously how these youth could be leading such violent lives—as if they themselves had anything to do with choosing their life circumstances! Reality thrust them into these vicious conditions and forced them to live under conditions that are themselves far from normal. What everyone forgets is that these young people would much rather live normal lives. Like everybody else, they dream of just living with their families.

It's very moving to hear people's stories, about their dreams and what they wish for. War has a way of helping people discover just how meaningful their life experiences are. The story I just told you, for example, really makes you think about different elements of these realities, things that reshape how you view the world around you. This pulls you farther and farther away from a middle-class mentality, from the rigid binary of right and wrong, and from outdated traditions. As a result, you start to realize more and more how absurd people's logic is. They flatten reality by making it seem like all conflict boils down to just a few principles that can solve everything—if only people could understand them. But when you become conscious of how complex life is—and experiencing war precipitates such a consciousness—you find yourself learning so much from people's own stories and life experiences. Sharing these things with others creates a very intimate bond between people.

I remember this young man I used to know from Gaza in occupied Palestine. We took the elevator together once, and it was his first time taking one. He was standing there looking so tense, and he said, "No, this isn't my first time in an elevator; I took one in Cairo when I was there . . . ha ha ha!" Can you imagine, he felt the need to justify that he had experience in riding elevators? Just that sentence is enough to jolt you back to the reality that this young man is a farmer, he's never lived in a city, and all at once his entire world changed. People have all kinds of challenges and issues to contend with; their whole worlds revolve around constantly discovering new things that shape their lives.

I'm going on and on about the human side of the story, not the political side or the actual revolutionary struggle. But these details are what push you to have a more comprehensive understanding of the world; they make it possible for you to see more clearly people's issues and shortcomings. This also can make you feel less anxious about your own fate because it helps you realize that your own circumstances are actually quite good compared to those of others.

Confronting Sexism and Patriarchal Values in Political Work

Of course, I confronted patriarchal values often in my political work. I was considered to be a valuable member of the party for various reasons. I stood out, perhaps, in the sense that people respected me and considered me a leader. They thought that I had important contributions to make, both intellectually and as an experienced participant in the struggle. But there was this thing that kept happening—the first time it happened, I didn't see it for what it was.

I didn't care about things like who had which jobs and positions in the party or who was assigned to what role. To be honest, I never cared about rank, like everyone else does, because I believe that your rank doesn't make you who you are; it's just the bureaucracy of the organization. What does make you is your relationship with people, with the world, with life. People are the ones who give you respect. I never cared about the organizational hierarchy of political parties unless it was somehow dangerous for my work.

But I discovered something strange back then. I learned that people could consider you to be the best person for a job and still suggest that a man do it. When this first started happening, I just thought that maybe there were some things they saw that I couldn't see; I tried to find any possible justification because it made no sense that these people could have something against me. They were all people who loved and respected me. After a while, though, you really learn that there is such a thing as patriarchal logic.

So many things like that happened. But in the long run, they became less frequent. Lots of people clashed over stories like these. And some people did change in the end. I tackled this in one of my films, the one with May Sayegh where I talked about women's experiences in the PLO. These women tried to create their own branch of the organization, and when they merged their women's organization with the PLO, they suddenly were faced with the fact that women who had occupied leading positions in their organization, like May Sayegh herself, were relegated to lower ranks within the party.

One woman who had been a leading member of the women's organization was given a mere basic role as a member of the PLO organizing committee. May talked to her, comparing the status of women in the Ba'ath Party and the PLO. The Ba'ath Party, as an organization, had more respect for women. The Arab Nationalist Movement faced some problems in its early stages as well, but those were later completely overcome within the Popular Front for the Liberation of Palestine. Relatively, at least. I mean, a number of women played key roles, but there was always this prevalent idea that the main leadership was to be reserved for men. These types of problems exist even in the best organizations, like the PFLP. Patriarchal hegemony was a constant, though it may have varied in degrees between one organization and another, in the way they dealt with women's issues. Often party members themselves are the ones who stir this up because they have their own problems of character. You can't change society if you yourself need to change, you know?

Al-Hakim, which is what we called George Habash, the leader of the PFLP, believed in women's emancipation, for instance. That was ingrained in his personality. It's just who he was. The best proof of this was his relationship with his children, especially his daughters, and his wife and female comrades. His stance on women's issues was deeply felt. But not everyone is the same. There are other types of people who may respect women militants and admire their strength. But this is all still based on patriarchal logic. They continue to assert their superiority and believe that by judging women in this way, they are giving them badges of honor by performatively granting them the status of men. That's the basic idea.

These problems exist in our society, even with men who consider themselves to be liberated. The contradiction between theory and practice was always a constant struggle at work. But I don't think that the war and my party work negatively affected my emotional well-being. On the contrary! I think that the experiences I've had profoundly enriched my character. They've enriched my emotional experiences as well in the sense that they've given me the space to reunderstand the way I feel about the people in my life. Sometimes I've even rediscovered people themselves.

There's something terrible about war, though—the way it really puts you to the test. But it's difficult for people to deceive you in times like this because in moments of such raw confrontation you're able to see things much more lucidly.

I've never regretted any of my choices. Even when my family and friends were constantly pointing fingers at me and calling me out for things, I'd always tell them that I would only do what I thought was best. That way, if I did something wrong, I'd be the only one responsible. I didn't want to be beholden to anyone or for them to have something to hold over my head if I made a bad decision. And if I ended up making a good one, I'd come out on top anyway.

If at any point I made some sort of concession to keep everybody happy, and I later felt the disastrous repercussions, that would just make me feel like I'd been used. I never wanted to feel taken advantage of. I wanted all my mistakes to be purely my own. I've always trusted my instincts throughout all my experiences in life, including my marriage. We separated over political disagreements. We just had different ways of thinking. But afterward I never regretted what I'd been through; I felt what I'd done was right at the time.

After the War

In the aftermath of the Arab Spring in Egypt, my husband and I decided to separate, and that was alright. I didn't feel like I had to compromise my dignity or my beliefs for our marriage to continue, especially since I didn't think it wasn't worth continuing. At a certain time, our relationship had been a manifestation of the force of life; it was a great experience, a successful one, and I'm glad it happened. I'll never regret getting involved with this person. But he changed. I'd married a person who wouldn't give me trouble, but when that was no longer the case, I ended our marriage. So, in a sense, I've always done what I felt was right for myself. This is very important because this is where self-esteem comes from, and this is what allows you to not feel like a victim. I really dislike this victimization complex.

There are times when I do think about things I did in the past—choices I made, things I refused, things I accepted. And sometimes I feel like my actions may have been exaggerated, or maybe a situation would've been better had I done something differently . . . but not once have I felt that I was being pressured to do something. It's very annoying to feel like you had to do something because you were under pressure. And on the flipside, when you do things because you want to, even if you were to realize in retrospect that something needed to be done differently, you'll implement that change with the same free will that made you act in the first place.

Suppose I was obstinate in my opinion of a person, and after a while I realize that my judgment was too rash because this person has a lot of redeeming qualities. When I feel that, when I feel in my heart that my perception is changing, I don't consider that to be a compromise. I mean, the fundamental problem in our society is that it thrives on terrible compromises and bargains, and this even seeps into personal relationships and the choices people make, their work, their lives, their housing situations . . . everything that people do and then claim they did only because they had to.

My experiences, the successful and the less successful, the ones I really enjoyed and the ones that were average—at the end of the day, they are all my own. And you know, this inner peace is reflected in your relationships with others because when you're free of all that internal nitpicking, your relationships with others become smoother, more genuine. You don't really get into arguments with the people around you because there is a certain degree of respect underpinning all your dealings with others and because you don't operate on the basis of manipulation.

I refuse to let anyone manipulate me. I can't say this enough. I never try to play on anyone's feelings, and I refuse to let anyone manipulate me. If I so much as suspect that someone's trying to use me like that, I cut them off completely, no questions asked. What I'm trying to say is that when a person has strong convictions, this really helps. They give you the space to just be OK with yourself. Again, though, I realize how fortunate I was on a lot of different levels. In my home life, there was always a great deal of respect for women. The environment around me allowed me to grow into myself as a woman without any trouble.

5

Batul Ali Hashem

*"Political action can help
women reach their full potential"*

*Like Arab L., Batul H. (a pseudonym) was active in the struggle for Pal-
estinian liberation and talks in some detail about how she worked within
the party framework of the Popular Front for the Liberation of Palestine.
She was similarly supported in her family setting in many ways, like all of
the other women in the book. Because Batul comes from a more modest
class background than any of the first three women, her consciousness as a
girl from South Lebanon growing up in the relatively disadvantaged neighborhood of Msaytbeh was shaped by seeing poverty firsthand, especially in
South Lebanon and in the Palestinian refugee camps—both of which were
areas where her family members resided. She is one of the few women in this
book who experienced open sexism and abuse as a child within her home;
moreover, her studies were limited because she was a girl. Like Wadad,
Arab, and Rima, Batul met her first and second husbands doing party work.
She split with her first husband, with whom she had a difficult and volatile
relationship, and had a major political falling out with her second husband
shortly before he passed away. For Batul, political action is a path to self-
fulfillment and empowerment for women.*
[b. Tebnine, 1949]

We're from the South, from a popular area down there, Tebnine, but I was
born in Beirut. I was doing my PhD, but I stopped. And today I'm a widow.

Ever since my childhood, my family has lived in a modest neighborhood in Beirut, Msaytbeh. Most people who lived there were from the

countryside, but there were also a few who were originally from Beirut. There were many residents in that neighborhood, like us, who originally came from the South. Lots of people worked in manual labor—for example, hauling things, collecting garbage—and, sorry to put it this way, but some of them weren't educated. My father was a plumber, and he also fixed bicycles and stuff like that. He could fix all kinds of equipment. We were four girls and a boy at home. That's who was left, anyway—the rest died. I'm the youngest in the family. They treated me a little differently than my sisters.

It was decided that only my eldest sister and I would be sent to school; the rest wouldn't. The neighbor's son used to follow my sister around when she'd be on her way there. This is why my mom decided to keep her home when she'd finished middle school. Once, my brother lured the young man out and hit him while wearing brass knuckles. There was a big fight. After this, my brother forbade my sister to go to school. Back then, barely any girls were allowed to go. Anyway, if the guy my brother had beaten up would have filed a complaint against him, everyone would've said that the guy had it coming. This is when all the rules started. Once we girls grew up, we were suddenly forbidden to do all sorts of things. We couldn't go out, we couldn't do this, we couldn't do that, we couldn't even go to our neighbors' houses. When I was a girl, we used to hear about all types of tragedies in the neighborhood. Some guy killed his sister and cut his own finger off, for example.

I didn't really care. I just used to love to read. There wasn't one Egyptian writer whose books I hadn't read. I read everything they published. I was different from the environment I grew up in. But I wasn't in conflict with the people around me. I was just different. For example, I'd talk to the neighborhood boys. I wouldn't dress in conservative clothes to go to school; I went to school, period! That was a feat in and of itself. I made it all the way to the philosophy baccalaureate track. My school was in Zarif. It didn't have any specific school uniform, nothing formal we had to wear . . . so I really stood out. People used to think I was Christian or Druze; they couldn't believe that I was Shi'i. That's how things were.

But the important part of this story is that I loved to read. It was so useful. I never used to watch any of those TV shows, *Abu Saleem* or *Abu*

Melhim. I'd go into the bathroom and put a chair or mat inside the bathtub and just sit there and read. One time my family didn't want to let me in because my brother wanted to take a shower. Instead, they just sat there and watched me read my book. At some points I'd cry, at others I'd laugh, and they just sat there watching me. They really did. My brother's wife said to him: "Look at your sister, she's losing it. She laughs and then cries, laughs and then cries." The stories I read really got to me. That's what books do. . . .

I witnessed so much injustice against women during the war, too. That really pushed me to rebel, even in the most basic stuff. That was one thing. I was also active by becoming the first female student to tutor the neighbors' kids. I got paid for it and everything, and I used to have my own spending money. My father influenced me a lot, of course. I was the youngest child at home, and he always used to sit me down on his lap and listen to the regional news and what was coming out of Palestine and the Arab countries.

My father really influenced me. And I was affected by the fact that he had a maternal cousin who'd gotten married to a Lebanese man living in Palestine. Her husband owned seven or eight stores. When he was expelled from Palestine, they told him to register as a Palestinian in Lebanon. He's Lebanese, and so is she, but he was registered as a Palestinian refugee. Before marrying my father's cousin, he'd been married to his own cousin, and she'd died. They'd had children together before she passed, and they were all Lebanese—both his first wife and the kids. But the children he had while he'd been in Palestine became Palestinian on paper. They got their status as "Lebanese with nationality under study" in 1975, or something like that. But they were considered to have a "nationality under study" and had no Lebanese ID cards or other papers or anything.

We used to visit my father's cousin regularly. He was very fond of her. The Palestinians who'd been displaced had been in Lebanon for around five or six years, barely that. At school, they used to teach us to wash up as soon as we woke up in the morning and got dressed. They taught us civics and basic health education. They taught us all that, but what use was it? When I'd go with my parents to visit our relatives from Palestine, I noticed that there was only one faucet, all the way at the entrance of the camp. The women would be crowded around it, yelling, and the policemen would be cursing at them. How else could it be when everyone had to get their water from a single tap? Seeing that really got to me. I also noticed that there were no toilets or showers, and the running water came out of the faucet dirty; this made me wonder about all they were teaching us at school. How are they making these people live like this?

If anyone needed to use the bathroom, there were kinds of makeshift outhouses set up, divided into separate stalls. To go to the bathroom, people had to walk a distance as far as that separating Burj al-Barajneh from the airport! And there was no water or anything. All of these things really got to me. What was that?! What kinds of living conditions were those?! They were living like the poor Shi'a in the South! Seeing this, coupled with the time I spent listening to my father, really shaped me.

Political Consciousness

Before 1958, I was reading books in earnest. I would eagerly anticipate every issue of the newspaper *Al-Anwar*, which was just a couple of pages long. There was a popular resistance movement that started in 1958. Saeb Salam led a mass uprising; Rashid Karami was promoting Arab nationalism. At the time, people turned the mosque into a makeshift infirmary for the wounded who'd been injured during the fighting. All the young men were armed at the time. Naim Moghabghab was against all of this—the 1958 revolution and the supporters of Camille Chamoun, who was the president of Lebanon at the time. The distance between Moghabghab's house and mine was only like thirty meters, and Sami al-Solh lived in Zoqaq al-Blat. So there were two pairs of men on opposite sides: Saeb Salam and Rashid Karami were supporters of the revolution, and Moghabghab and al-Solh were against it. Some revolutionaries robbed Sami al-Solh's house. I saw one of them with my own eyes go into his house and leave with a carpet. What kind of revolution is that?

Not long after 1952, [Gamal] Abdel Nasser became president of Egypt. I really admired him a lot. I also admired Abdel Halim Hafez, the Aswan High Dam project, and the songs of the time, like "We the People" ["Ihna al-Shaab"], as well as the Egyptian films that I used to watch on television.

My cousin used to project films. He would get a hold of a reel and adapt it so he could show it at our house or his, and even the neighbors would come over and watch.

I had some level of political consciousness. But what influenced me the most was what I learned at home and at work. I had a single brother, and my mother was sick. It was my brother who encouraged my interest in Arab nationalism in 1958. We had this female relative who was from our village but from another family. They gave out Qur'ans to mourners at the local cemetery. We used to visit the grave of my other brother, who'd died when he was eleven years old. Our relative had been married to a guy with whom she was always fighting, and they separated. Once, I was on my way to visit the cemetery and saw him sitting outside their house. He was very tall and handsome and was just sitting there outside, looking sad, holding a cigarette, which he didn't notice was burning too close to his finger. He used to just walk into the house and say hello; he loved them and really was a part of the family.

But I really began to hate them, and I refused to go into their house. I felt really angry with them but never actually fought with them. This intense anger came from how annoyed I was with my relative, the woman, and how she was behaving. I wasn't annoyed by the guy, this man, but I couldn't picture the upbringing you must have had to make you act like that. If you have a girl and a boy, why do you have to differentiate between them? Why should the boy hit the girl? I've asked these questions since I was a young girl, and I still ask them today.

Palestinian Resistance

When the Palestinian resistance really took off, I was in my second year of baccalaureate studies in the philosophy track. I left school and approached the PLO because I knew that they were sending people to Syria for military training. I asked them to send me, too. They told me that they had an agreement with the Lebanese government not to involve any Lebanese people. They wouldn't send me.

They had a sort of book fair at the time for Palestinian writing, and I bought everything I could get my hands on and read it all. I immersed myself in everything to do with the Palestinian cause. I lived through their ups and downs, their trials and tribulations. How could this happen to an entire people? This was on top of everything that I had seen in Burj al-Barajneh—it's etched in my mind forever. The cruelty and oppression I witnessed, added to what I had learned at home, pushed me to become a rebel . . . not to participate in the war but rather to rebel as a person.

It was after this phase of my life, which coincided with the Palestinian revolution, that I approached the PLO, and they said all of those things to me. Where else could I turn? I tried to support the uprising by gathering food and supplies: rice, sugar, clothes, everything really, especially during the 1967 War and after Abdel Nasser's defeat. Back then, there were young men undergoing military training at the Beirut Arab University. I joined them, and while I was undergoing this training myself, Abdel Nasser conceded his defeat and announced his resignation. This broke me.

Like I said, at the time I was collecting things to support the PLO. I would collect and deliver to Fatah. People told me: "Whatever you bring is gold," so I brought whatever I could get my hands on. Now after my father died and my brother married, my sisters got married and left home as well, which meant my mother didn't have anyone left but me. What was she supposed to do? I was tutoring the neighborhood kids, and she had to do something. So she set up a small stand to sell candy to the neighborhood children. I'd get her the sweets myself, making my way to the store in a shared service taxi, which cost fifteen piasters on the way there and twenty-five to get back home. I'd have to pay close attention to the bag I'd carry with me. I used one of those paper bags used for cement powder, and I'd fill it all the way to the top with candy. I carried them for her so I wouldn't have to use her money to pay for the journey.

One of the men who worked at the shop where I bought these things for my mother used to talk to me about Palestine a lot. He asked me, "Are you part of the resistance?" and I replied that I often gathered supplies and delivered them to Fatah. "No," he said, "you should help out with the Popular Front [for the Liberation of Palestine]. You'd be more of use there." The shop owner was from the Baba family, which supported the Popular Front. He said, "I'll give you . . ."— I had bought some things from the shop previously. . . . But wait, before I get to that, I'll talk about my training.

Military Training

When the PLO refused to train me in Syria, I knew there was a lot of action at the Beirut Arab University. They were training with wood shaped like machine guns. I asked my cousin if she knew someone from the Popular Front who would send people to get further military training in Syria. She said she did know someone, and I asked her to tell me where I could find him. She came over and brought him along. These people had an office in Azarieh, in downtown Beirut. I went there and told them I wanted to get military training. I'd been there before to collect record books, the ones where you write down the amounts of donations you receive when you're fundraising. The man she introduced me to said, "We can't send you unless you tell your parents first."

"How do you expect me to tell my parents? I'm a girl! I want to go," I replied. "They'll never let me go. I told my mom I was going to camp, which is true in a way. I just didn't tell her where it was. I'm not lying. I could always ask some other girl to come with me to talk to my family. What could she say to them that I haven't, though? I haven't told them where I'll be going."

"Tell your mother you're going to Jordan," the man in charge said. He had another girl accompany me to talk to my mother. I told her I was going to Jordan for military training. "Military training? What do you mean, military training?!" my mother shouted.

Then I went back to the Popular Front's office. There were a few girls there with makeup on. And there I was in a long, loose, long-sleeved dress, my hair up in a ponytail, with no lipstick or anything. The people in charge said to us, "You Lebanese, it's time to go." Then one of them said to me separately, "You're Lebanese—you can go to Syria, too. We'll tell you how to get there in a private car."

"I'll go the same way the rest of the girls are going," I replied.

"These girls are going via Baalbek and taking a really bumpy road to Syria."

I repeated that I'd go whichever way they were going. I ended up doing that, and there was this really funny girl with us; I'll tell you what we did in a minute. We all made our way to Syria together, and when we crossed the Lebanese border, that girl said, "Lebanese people are the worst!" I looked at her with sheer disgust when she said that, but she told me she'd explain later. It turned out that one of the women with us was Abu Maher al-Yamani's wife, on her way to see her husband, and the rest were other men's wives, with the exception of Salah Salah's sisters, and this other young woman who still works with the Popular Front to this day. Then there was me, husbandless, fatherless me. We crossed the border and headed to the camp. They hurried over to us and immediately gave my new friend and me each a Simonov rifle.

Her name was Khawla—I'm not sure about her last name. She was married to a Palestinian man, and she still does political work today. When we arrived at the camp, they told us to stay outside the tent; we were in charge of the night watch. They also told us not to be afraid: "The enemy isn't here—but there are wild animals, and it's night out."

I went in one direction, and Khawla went in another. As I was walking, I heard the clinking of cans that were strewn all around. Then I heard a clopping sound that kept getting louder, and suddenly I saw a man appear and hide behind a tree. "Who's there?" I asked, and I spotted someone from behind. I shot him. And where do you think the bullet hit him? On his bum! The man I shot must have been wearing some kind of noisy shoes. At first, I'd assumed that it might be a hyena. When all of this was happening, someone walked up to me and said, "I just came from over in the camp—I need to let you know that the password is George Habash al-Hakim."

But I was new there, so I obviously didn't know what the password was or even that there was one. I told him to come closer but to keep his hands up. Then all at once an entire group of men showed up out of thin air, all running in my direction to take the gun away from me. It was a whole ordeal. Khawla said to them, "She's Lebanese and spoke to it in a Lebanese accent. If she'd pronounced it in a local accent, the horse would have stopped!" It turned out that I'd shot a horse. When I saw it up close, I got really sad. This turned into a whole drama. They tricked me into believing that the horse belonged to some Bedouins a little farther away, which meant that they'd come and kill us at any moment unless we paid them what it was worth. I told them I'd pay the amount in installments. I kept paying those monthly installments of twenty-five liras for three years, and they never hinted that I was close to paying it off. For three whole years, I made these monthly payments.

When I arrived that first night, my brother, Muhammad, came to see me. I had my papers giving me permission to collect donations, my military-training ID, and my party membership card. If only you could have seen what happened next. Some journalists came to the camp, so I spoke with them because the rest of the girls didn't have anything worthwhile to say. What did they all decide to do then? They spread the rumor that I was an agent, collaborating with the enemy.

And in the meantime, Leila Khaled showed up and took me from the camp. She made a big deal out of it. She took me out of there. First, she took two other girls, then she took me. She asked me where I'd come from and what my role was. I had no idea what was going on. Later, Salah's sister told me, "They thought you were a spy because you knew how to answer all those journalists' questions, and we didn't." They were Palestinians from the camps, meaning it was their lived reality, and I'd only heard of such experiences from conversations and books. That was only the first drama they created.

The second drama came when they claimed that I was spending too much time in the men's section of the camp. What would I even be doing there? And you know what they did with the horse? They lay it down right where we used to train. Right in front of us. They have no morals at all! Plus, our training area got so much sun; we were dying from the stench and all the flies. That's it for the horse story.

Going back to what I said earlier—they made a fuss about me supposedly spending too much time in the men's section of the camp. But we did everything together, and we were in the Popular Front! They were supposed to be more liberated than that. I feel bad for them; they're still so ignorant.

Return to Lebanon

Anyway, after I got back from the training camp, I headed to another one in Burj al-Barajneh. That's where I trained young women and taught them how to use weapons. Abu Abed came to see me at one point; he was the one who'd received me in the downtown office that first time, when we were about to leave for the training camp. He said, "You know, when I first met you, I thought you were a loose woman."

"What is it about me exactly that gave you that impression? The fact that I have long hair and tie it back in a ponytail or the fact that I wear long dresses and don't put lipstick on?" I just meant to imply that I was a regular girl. He said, "You're Lebanese, and you left your home and family to get military training." And yet his impression wasn't that I was a Lebanese girl with a mission and a cause. He kept quiet after that, and everyone started to respect me. I had forced them to respect me.

But when I got back home, my brother beat me up. He really wore me down. He took away my military-training ID and my papers giving permission to do fundraising. When he took them from me, I told him I'd find a way to get them back. He was staying in a house in the mountains at the time. I went to visit him there one day, and I found out he was hiding my documents inside a dresser. So I took them. He got really angry and started to make a scene, so I told him I'd file a complaint against him if he didn't stop. He never laid a hand on me again after that.

Before that moment, he'd beat me up every time he got into an argument with his wife. He'd even take his anger out on his children. He was the reason my sisters left the house, one after the other. One of them ran away from this treatment they were all subjected to, and he married another sister off to an idiotic man from the camp, so he and his wife could live in the house. We were four sisters and one brother. One of my sisters died after burning herself badly. We had this uncle who lived in Australia. When he came to Lebanon and met this sister of mine who later passed away, he wanted to marry her off to his son. He told my family to make sure she got an education. He assured them he would cover all the costs of her schooling and clothing. But my family kept her stashed away at home so she could serve my brother's wife. And what happened, happened. . . .

The household I grew up in was the reason I rebelled the way I did. Thankfully, though, my rebellion was positive, not negative. Anyway, I was part of the Popular Front when the Arab Socialist Action Party was formed. I was well integrated in the Front, training women members and everything. I wrote articles for its official magazine, *Al-Hadaf*. I also worked with young people at the Arab Socialist Action Party and with the Popular Front in rural areas. They'd take me to neglected villages, and I'd write about each village, its current conditions, how people used to live during the Ottoman period, things like that. I also wrote political articles about the Arab cause. After a while, I got married.

Challenges of Family Life

Samir and I got married in 1972, my daughter was born in 1973, and we got divorced in 1975. We'd barely been married for two years. Samir is from the Chouf. He said that after he heard about me, he really wanted to meet me. He was in charge of the area up there. Then the flirting started, and we got married. I didn't even know a thing about his family. He used to work at the airport, but he left that job to join the resistance. And I don't care about any of that sectarian stuff—I couldn't care less about any sect at all. I don't discriminate because I've seen how badly people have been wronged by each other. In our house, there was no room for sectarianism. My father was a manual laborer, and we'd go wherever his work took him. In the summertime, he would take us along with him to work in the mountains, which meant we spent a lot of time in different regions of the country because we'd go to a different mountain each year. Our neighbors were Sunni, Christian, Shi'i, and Druze. We never found this strange or unusual.

I married Samir. We didn't get married the Shi'i way, but rather following Sunni traditions. What did I care? We got married and settled down together. His aunt gave us most of the furniture, and I brought some stuff from my family's house, too. Anyway, Sir Samir used to get up at noon, sit beside me and have his breakfast, and then he'd go out and wouldn't return until past midnight. That's just the life of a revolutionary—or so he claimed. Then we had a daughter. He didn't even pick her up and hold her once. That was my department.

I spent most of my time at home, and when Samir would return and find out that there was nothing to eat, he'd ask me, "Why haven't you cooked anything? What did you and the baby eat today?" And he'd throw out whatever he happened to have brought back with him—mind you, he hardly ever brought anything home with him at all. I never reacted when he'd make a scene like this. I'd simply ask him again why he'd hit me. Even if he tried to talk to me, I wouldn't answer but rather just ask him why he'd hit me. "Just because" would be his reply.

He stopped leaving money for me. But what should I care? He used to hang out at the La Ronda café in Baakline. That's where he spent his money. He'd give me one lone lira, but there he'd pay for everyone and even leave tips. All anyone had to do was say hello to him, and he'd tip them. But me, he only gave me one lira. At one point, he told me that all Shi'a girls are bitches. After this, it took me only fifteen days to make up my mind and leave. I took the baby and thought, "Maybe he'll follow me." He never did. So I went back to the house and left him a note that said: "Meet me in court on such-and-such day." He didn't show up. Our marriage lasted two years.

Our daughter, Yara, lived with me. Abu Sinan, the secretary-general of the party, used to give her piggyback rides everywhere. Yara used to swear to me that she loved Abu Sinan—whom I married after the divorce—more than she loved me. He'd take her everywhere on his back even when she was thirteen years old. He'd always give her a taste of the food on his plate before he started eating, and he wasn't even her biological father!

When I worked at *Al-Hadaf* and *Al-Thawri*, Abu Sinan was always alone, living in a house that had a printing press in it. He and some young men from the party who didn't have anywhere to live used to stay there, along with a family that lived there full time. After my divorce, Abu Sinan said I could stay in that house with my daughter and help to keep the printing press secure. I was in charge of Maroun Misk at the time—a military site belonging to the party during the Civil War. George Habash, who we called "al-Hakim," also suggested that I leave my daughter with Abu Sinan when I went to work. He would play with her while I was gone, and I would go pick her up when I was finished.

When my Samir was abroad, he was happy with this setup. And when young men from the party started coming more frequently to the house, which Abu Sinan had found, he suggested I stay there, too, so I could keep an eye on the printing press. I used to use the typewriter, they would work with the stencils, and Abu Sinan would take care of the transcriptions. They'd finish work and leave.

We had this Lebanese neighbor whose children were part of the Palestinian resistance. One day her husband told her, "I want to shoot that Batul." She asked him why he was saying that, and he said, "Because she always has men over at her place." She showed him, though. And when they found out that I was in charge of a military site, they started to fear me. My comrades in the party would tell me that some friend of theirs was interested in me or whatever, but I always said I didn't want to be with anyone back then.

Later, I started going to South Lebanon to photograph the villages and countryside down there, and I'd write reports on those areas for the party magazine. I used to take my daughter along with me. My daughter and I went anywhere and everywhere Israel bombed. Some days I would leave her with Abu Sinan. He'd been married previously but had also divorced, and at the time he lived alone. His children were adults by then. My neighbor and her husband went to visit my mother and told her that there was a man in the neighborhood who had his eye on me. She told them to speak to me directly. So they did. They told me that there was a decent man whom they'd noticed I left my daughter with often and asked, "Why don't you get married? We're willing to be your witnesses."

I told them I couldn't marry anyone. I was in charge of the Maroun Misk site, and I was on my way to go check it out. There was a cease-fire that day. But I knew how treacherous the Phalangist snipers on the opposite side were, so I carried my daughter on my side, shielding her with my body, and I ran, trying to cross a street that was known to sustain heavy sniping. Sure enough, as I was running, three shots were fired at me, but because the street was narrow, I managed to take cover in time. That's what they did back then.

When the neighbors talked to me about Abu Sinan, I thought I might as well marry him since I was leaving my daughter with him most days anyway, and my reputation had begun to suffer. I also liked that he was older than me. With Samir, it had been difficult for me to get away with not wanting kids. I was confused; I didn't care about getting married, but I liked that Abu Sinan was older, and I was never home anyway. So I agreed to marry him in the end.

I knew I was dealing with a mature man, someone organized, someone who would never ask me why I hadn't cooked. I swear I used to go in and turn off the lights so I could get some sleep. He would stay up and write alone in one room, while my daughter and I would sleep in another. Every time he traveled, he would bring her back stuff, and whenever he'd leave, she'd stay with him as long as she could inside the airport all the way to the Departures Hall, telling me: "I love him more than I love you." He used to tell her stories all the time. I know I did her wrong. I left her alone too often. But I made sure she continued her education, I gave her a desk, I enrolled her in summer camps . . . there was no activity related to drawing or movies that I didn't take her to.

Political Work with Women's Organizations

I was completely supportive of the women and women's associations that belonged to all the parties: the Communists, the nationalists, the religious parties, and the Beirutis. This was during the Civil War, back in 1976. We had formed a left-wing women's organization that I was in charge of. It included women from all regions to which the party was somehow linked. Sometimes I'd go to the Beqaa, sometimes to the Chouf, and we had officials from every region in Central Command. All these women were linked, in one way or another, to the party, so we gathered them and told them what our policies were. We called the organization the League for Democratic Feminist Action, and we started off with seminars and trips, those types of activities.

My sister's children are Palestinian because their father is, and they were part of a group of artists. They used to go to the Isaad al-Toufoula School for Palestinian orphans in Souq el-Gharb. My sister, Umm Jamil, lived nearby. They're in London now; her husband is over eighty-five years old and isn't doing too well. They went there because his children went to London. When his son got arrested, they paid smugglers to get him out of Lebanon. They're all married. One of them works in telecommunications;

another is really good at music—he studied to be an electrician, but he's also a musician; and the third is in business management. They all work here except for Jamil, the eldest, who left to work abroad. But their heart is still with the Palestinian cause.

They didn't suffer or behave badly or anything like that. They all got married, and then they helped their mother leave Lebanon. Their father is still in Burj al-Barajneh because a shell hit their house directly during the war between AMAL and the camps. The neighborhood youth who belonged to the AMAL movement used to hang out at their house all the time. How did he let that happen? How could the people they were fighting be at their house?

They're doing well now, and they've helped me a lot financially. The salaries in the party were hardly enough to live on. They helped me even more when we were renting a house. I worked at *Al-Shiraa* magazine for a while, and I saved up and bought a house that I paid for in two installments. Two sisters owned that house: one of them wanted to sell, but the other didn't. First, I bought the shares of the sister who wanted to sell. I paid her $600 a month. The first installment was $20,000, and the second was $47,000. My sister's children sent me money to cover some of it; they really helped me out. I eventually made the full payment for the second installment, and now I'm pretty stable. I'm living my life, and I'm even renting out a part of the house since I'm not working. I live off the money from the tenant, and I try my best to deal with the people around me. Al-hamdulillah.

We discussed many intellectual issues in the League for Democratic Feminist Action. Abu Sinan wrote a book about women's issues. We distributed it to the members, and I would give lectures and pass out copies of the book afterward. Women in the group were active in different ways. Remember when I told you that my nieces and nephews' musical group helped us? It's because we would enter the camps for displaced people, using their name to help get in. We'd go see the kids, play with them, sing for them, dance with them. My sister's children would play music and dance the *dabke*. We just gathered the boys and girls and made them into a musical group, and we established relations with other people and civil organizations. They started working with us, too. We didn't bring up the party because our work together was as a musical group. I used to go to the Lebanese Women's Council on behalf of the group; they appreciated our work a lot, and the feminist activist Linda Matar told us that we had a promising future. She'd never said that to anyone before, so it was a big deal for us.

There was a conference in 1998, an Arab women's conference at the Carlton Hotel. I was in charge of the Beirut conference-organizing committee and the other committee that led the League for Democratic Feminist Action. One thing that helped us at the time was that we were always visiting different regions of the country, and we also had the Students' Democratic Front with us. That group consisted of youth who used to visit Akkar and organize activities and camps for young people; they would do stuff for the villages there. Girls and boys would join, they'd bring their friends along, and they even organized events like book fairs. Wherever there were activities going on, they were probably in charge.

The Beirut leadership of the party was really ignorant about women's issues—educationally, I mean, not with regard to political consciousness. Those who weren't very educated tended to be more enthusiastic because they were more oppressed. This gave them a certain drive.

If I had to define "women's issues," I would say that women have a role in society, and therefore they are also political agents. Political action can help women reach their full potential. Every now and then, we used to research a specific topic and discuss it together within our association, the Feminist League. Then we would inform the party of what we were doing, and we would also tell them about the struggles women were facing throughout Lebanon, in all the different regions of the country. When we held a women's conference once, some participants turned out to be quite knowledgeable, but not everyone was on the same level. During the conference, we agreed that we would conduct a study about children in the country. Every organization conducted its own study, but none of them worked alone: members of the other organizations contributed to each other's studies. I made sure my comrades participated in every study, despite the fact that some of them didn't know how to write or do research. Whenever we, as the Feminist League, would meet, we would discuss in detail everything having to do with the study at hand. We made sure each of us knew the main points she was going to talk or write about, so that we could all go to the conference prepared. Lots of studies came out back then.

I took responsibility for one specific study—on working women. Like with the other studies, there were women from the different feminist organizations who joined me. Women from all the participating organizations worked on every study I participated in. When it was time for us to evaluate the work we'd done at the conference, it was clear that the men had nothing to do with it. One of these men, Bilal, tried to meddle, but he wasn't even connected to us; his connection was to a different organization, a different party. He wasn't in charge of us. In the organizational hierarchy of the party, after Abu Sinan came Hussein. Comrade Hussein Maroush. He was the one who would supervise us. I used to poke fun at him, which made them think that I didn't like him. But he used to show up and start giving us unsolicited advice and criticism: "This one can't read, this one can't write," stuff like that. We met with Hussein Maroush to present our report on the women's conference. I had already assigned the girls to different committees. After the conference ended, they all talked about what they'd done and what they'd said. My heart was beating so fast, I was so happy. Linda Matar even attended this conference. And not just her, but the wives of many comrades.

Party Splits, Personal Splits

The story that drove a rift between Abu Sinan and me just before he died also shows these kinds of rifts in the party and with attitudes toward women. The wife of that same man, Bilal, who'd interfered with the women's groups before, started saying things like "You weren't elected." I replied, "No problem, let's hold elections then." I called up the girls and the members of the movement, the Feminist League, telling them that we were going to hold elections so we could choose the people we wanted to be our leaders. Then Bilal started stating that we had to divide the Beirut leadership of the women's branch of the movement since one of us was a seamstress and the other was some type of worker . . . or whatever it was he was going on about. He said this and kept repeating that his wife and Sami's wife were both university graduates. I swear to you, he convinced Abu Sinan to divide the women in leadership positions. And Abu Sinan went right ahead and did this without even asking me.

Listen, Abu Sinan never did me wrong personally. He never did any actual harm. But after this incident, I decided I wanted a divorce. This was before he got sick. I went to see Bilal and asked him how he could divide the women and bypass me like that. What did Bilal have to do with any of this anyway?! What business was it of his what was happening in the women's movement? But Abu Sinan went along with him and agreed to divide the women into two categories: one group that was highly educated and one that was only more or less educated.

The point is, there was a woman I had chosen—she's a comrade and the wife of a comrade—who was a very hard worker. The only issue was that she didn't have a Lebanese ID because when the French conducted the census, her father's name wasn't recorded. They only took the names of those who were present in the house that day. If you weren't home, your name wasn't included. Her father, who was still a child back then, was outside playing, so they didn't register his name.

Later on, the Lebanese state gave them a status called "nationality under study." I wanted to suggest her name as someone to represent us within the women's organizations because the other women leaders in the running were a total mess. They were all the wives of someone or another, and they pushed the rest of us out because they wanted to become leaders. Linda Matar was their supervisor, and she suffered when dealing with them.

But let's go back to the story of Bilal. He and Abu Sinan agreed that it was necessary to separate the women into different groups. Remember that Lebanese woman I just told you about, the one who was married to a Palestinian and who had a "nationality under study"? I used to drop her off at meetings so that she could represent me when I couldn't make it myself or when I didn't want to go. Bilal was outraged and said, "How dare you take her there? She isn't Lebanese; she's Palestinian." I didn't even dignify that with a response.

But he convinced Abu Sinan to divide the women into two groups, and his next excuse was that the women were staying at meetings too late into the night. Abu Sinan told me one evening, "See, we held a meeting, and we didn't stay so late." I asked him what the meeting was, and he told me that he'd gone ahead and separated the women's group into two because they were staying out too late. But we'd already created our own committees; some of the women were offering literacy classes, and we had our own political-awareness committees, too. The women would go visit women farmers—everyone was working, everyone was part of the struggle.

Anyway, like I said, Bilal convinced Abu Sinan, and there Abu Sinan was, coming up to me so proudly and saying, "See! When you have those meetings, they go on forever. Look at me, I finished up in an hour and a half because I divided the women into the two groups." I had already raised this issue with the Central Committee, which included people from all over the country. They rejected this separation proposal, and I rejected it, too. One of our women comrades asked Bilal why he had separated her from the rest of the group, and she just quit the party right on the spot.

I was really upset, but I didn't speak to Abu Sinan about it—not at all, I didn't admonish him for having bypassed me like that. Some of my women comrades tried to talk to me about what had happened, but I would just change the subject and not really address why he'd done what he did. I don't even know what excuse Bilal gave them. In the end, I just extricated myself from the situation.

After the War

Had he not died, I probably wouldn't have actually left him. You know what he told me at the hospital when he was ill? I swear to God, I'm not just trying to talk about my troubles—everyone who knows me knows how much I've endured. We would go to meetings at someone's house, and all the young men would be there. They'd eat, drink, and leave everything on the table. And then the wife of whoever's house it was and I would put everything away and clean up, do the dishes. Why did I have to do that? Why didn't the men lift a finger or clean up after themselves? Would you accept that kind of treatment? The reason I helped was for the woman's sake; I couldn't leave her to do everything herself.

We spent some time in Damascus with two other men, one Iraqi and the other Saudi Arabian. They were the dirtiest people. Whenever Abu Sinan took me with him to Damascus, I'd spend three days just cleaning. I'd wash the furniture, wash the sheets. I started hating these trips to Damascus. I only grew to love it after he passed away, and I started visiting his grave there. All of these incidents made us hate the revolution and the revolutionaries, but at the time we thought it was all natural, normal. Had I spoken to Abu Sinan, I would've gotten through to him, but I never did because he never had the time. Whenever he was home, he'd be busy writing. Sometimes I would shut off the electricity. He would murmur, hamdillah, and throw himself on the bed.

He passed away in Damascus and is buried there. He died during the Aoun War in East Beirut, so we couldn't bring his body back to Lebanon. Fatah al-Intifada gave us forty-five Syrian pounds to bury him. The Intifada paid, not the party. He never used to agree to being paid any extras; he wasn't interested in a life of luxury, like other party leaders were.

6

Elissar Zein

"I can't see someone in need and do nothing"

Elissar Z. describes in some detail her work in a variety of social service roles within a political party and outside it, particularly in organizing women. She shares this political party experience with many of the other women here and found a role for herself within the organized structure of the party even while at times resisting it. She describes how her marriage to a party comrade ended in divorce, as happened to Batul and Arab, though she remains on good terms with her former husband, whom she eventually left because of gambling. Like many of the other women, Elissar hails from a supportive, politically active family who encouraged her militancy. She describes in some detail being pushed into her role as an activist and militant by force of circumstances. She echoes the common theme running throughout these stories in stating how she felt she could not simply sit still and do nothing with the war raging around her. Her brother had died, her children were out of school, and she felt compelled to put her skills to use for social good. Also important to her stories are a firm antisectarianism and pride in her mixed-community family.

[b. Kaifun, 1956]

When the war started, we were in Chiyah, on Maroun Misk Street, which was the dividing line during the war. We lived on the part of the street that was close to the Old Saida Road. That's where the war started, between Ain al-Remmaneh and Chiyah. We were still students back then, pursuing our educations. I'd just started my first year studying physical education—before the war started, that is.

Back then—I'm talking about 1976, during the two-year war between 1975 and 1976—my brother died here; he was martyred right near the house. . . . He was active in the Syrian Social Nationalist Party [SSNP].

At that time, schools had been closed for a while, all of them. So some of us volunteered to get some kids from one of the schools together and teach them, and that's how our organizing and activism started. . . . Why leave our youth idle when we could get them together and teach them something? We started with groups of students, and then more people approached us to volunteer, too. We put them all in one class—I mean, we joined sets of two different classes together, grouping every two years of students into one class. We wanted to offer these youth something, to keep them off the streets, to give them something to do other than sit at home listening to war stories . . . that was the first phase.

But things shifted when the clashes spread and became more violent. I was a volunteer with the Red Cross at that point. As people started to be forced to leave their homes, we began storing supplies in the school we'd been using. We collected these supplies, like clothes and stuff, from our neighbors in the area because there was bombing all around us. This meant that people could only move around within their own neighbor-hoods. We would wait for the shelling to subside and then go around with things we had at home and distribute them, door to door, going around to people's houses with things to eat and drink. We'd pack these things up and take them around to others.

It was a very difficult time, so difficult that . . . let me tell you about something that happened back then. We were going—we'd just finished giving a training session to a group; we'd already done that training our-selves and had learned everything, and there was another round of people training after us. . . . This was training with the Red Cross.

Anyway, we were on our way to pick up the food and distribute it to the neighborhood. We had told others what time we were going to do this, and we even left a note stuck on the school door in case anyone wanted to come help. I'd almost reached the school when I heard a loud bang. I'd gotten there early, before the time we were supposed to start. It seemed that a rumor had reached the other side that the place where we were pre-paring the food was also being used to launch shells. I saw a van and ran over to it—it looked like Abu Sobhi's van. The door was hanging off it, and when I looked inside . . . there were decapitated bodies! Even the hair had been torn out of their heads.

That was the first horrific murder scene I'd ever witnessed . . . but I reacted immediately. I ran into the school because I was focused on the fact that I knew there was a stretcher inside. I ran in with some man, I had no idea who he was or where he'd turned up from. I don't think any-body could see straight! We looked around, trying to figure out where to begin. We started by stopping the cars driving by and filling them up with the wounded—it was almost as if we were piling sandbags on top of each other! We were helping people injured in the shelling get to the American University Hospital.

It was my first time experiencing such a thing. I walked in with the doctor. I'd completed my first-aid training sessions, which had been meant to prepare us for these kinds of situations. But that day, the scene was so horrific, so awful . . . I couldn't even tell if I'd been injured or not! I checked quickly and noticed that the pocket of my jeans jacket was torn, and there was a piece of shrapnel inside. We always dressed in light clothes because we knew we might have to start running suddenly. I didn't even react when I saw the shrapnel. Why? Because we were so busy. We were on autopilot. We had to keep moving, we couldn't stop. I must have gone pale in the ER because the doctor slapped me and told me to step outside. I told him I wanted to stay, but he ordered me to leave.

This was the first really harsh situation I experienced. It taught me a lot, though, and, afterward, it's like we totally blocked out our surround-ings—like everyone else, we had to run around and do things, we had to just act. But this made us stronger, in a way, to cope with these kinds of situations. Even now, I can't see someone in need and do nothing. I just can't. I really can't . . . it's not in my nature. My parents weren't support-ers, and they just thought I was strong or whatever. The two-year war was very hard on me. It put me through so much and really prepared me for stuff, and then that day and the bombing, this is what that two-year war was like.

I spent the whole two years working with the Red Cross in Chiyah, distributing food and drink, visiting schools and helping them clean, mopping and scrubbing and everything. We taught the women whose families had sought shelter in the schools how to work with us; we showed them how we organized tasks and taught them how they could organize themselves while they were staying there. This was all work done by volunteers. I guess I could say this was a key experience. When people put their minds to something, they will do it, no matter what. They'll do anything. External conditions can't dictate what they do—once their mind is set, that's that!

Family Background

My parents didn't object to me working in the Red Cross, and I came home every night to them. They didn't mind me working with men; they don't think this way. And my character is different than my siblings'. My father, may he rest in peace, used to tell my mother that he wasn't worried about me and that he knew he could depend on me for anything. This made me feel supported. My father used to work for the Internal Security Forces. My brother was a Syrian nationalist, he had those sympathies . . . but he wasn't a fighter.

My father was the kind of person who encouraged women to do what they wanted to do. He always used to say that he admired me because I knew exactly what I wanted. We used to have so many conversations. He was an educated man, always with a book in hand. He really was very cultivated, and he would always tell me about the things he was reading. We had so many discussions, him and me—and he only had them with me! I was the middle child: neither the eldest nor the youngest. I have one older brother and one younger, other than my brother who was martyred.

Both of my parents were very open-minded. I hate to talk in such terms, but let me say that we also didn't care about the differences between religions. My parents used to wish everyone happy holidays, no matter their religion, and we'd celebrate with them no matter the holiday. We never asked what or why or how—these questions didn't exist for us. They didn't even occur to us.

I mean, when we used to go to my grandfather's house, the rest of our family always found this strange. My parents used to tell them that "these kids don't care what religion they are." My father—and my mother, too, may she rest in peace—didn't care about sectarian belonging at all. And everybody loved them. We were used to the fact that my parents were the kind of people you'd call believers, or religious. We weren't, but we didn't fight them on it. You know what I mean? We just didn't fight them on it.

I met my husband in the SSNP, and we got married in 1982. We were passionately in love and had been engaged for about a year and a half, and we decided we just wanted to get married. I'm trying to remember what year that was specifically. In 1981, we decided to move into this house here in Bchamoun, and that was it.

My husband was a religious person—and his beliefs carried over into his party work. We both were on the same kind of life path, if you know what I mean, headed in the same direction . . . similar faith and convictions. But not blind or rigid faith. We aren't rigid in that way; it was more about how we lived out our daily lives with people, whoever they were. We weren't bigots. We were simply people committed to a cause, and we wanted to work on it. I mean, you can't say you're all for the struggle and then sit it out. You can't just philosophize about it. I'm very oriented to doing the work on the ground. It's just the way I operate.

We chose to stay here in Bchamoun because practically everyone was fleeing Beirut, rent was getting so high. You couldn't rent an apartment there. Some people from the party suggested that instead of renting, we stay in the house of a displaced Christian family. They said we were crazy to rent a house. But I wanted a legitimate household. I wanted to rent a place that would be my own. I didn't want to live in a displaced person's house. It's not like there was a shortage of houses or anything. . . .

I chose Bchamoun because so many of my friends lived here. And back then, this area was mixed. The Mountain War made it less so. During the war, people took sides. But us, we weren't on anyone's side. My husband and I belong to different sects. And as long as we're on this, I should say that my daughter, my son, my husband, and I all belong to different sects officially. Each one of us is free to choose. My daughter chose the man she wanted to marry and opted for a civil marriage. See what I'm trying to say?

There's a story about my son, too. A bit of background: my husband is of Assyrian origin and so is Christian, and I'm Sunni—fine. Neither my parents nor his had any objection to our marriage. Both of our families are nationalists. We got married and had children, and our daughter and son took on their father's sect. At a certain point, the question of inheritance was raised because with an Assyrian father and a Sunni mother, who inherits what? Because their parents are different sects, the children can't inherit. Their mother would have her own inheritance from her family, as a Sunni Beiruti, but because she married outside her sect, she can't pass it on. So then the kids protested and decided to convert to the Sunni sect so that they could eventually claim their inheritance. In the Sunni tradition, boys inherit, so people advised my son to convert to Sunnism so he could inherit from his mother. After this, my husband was forced to let our kids convert, and he did as well. And my daughter eventually chose to marry a Greek Orthodox man. At the end of the day, my daughter turned out a Greek Orthodox, my son converted again and is now a Maronite, and their father remained a Sunni!

We got married in 1982, but we didn't have a ceremony or anything because the airport was hit on June 5. Our wedding was on June 10. So we canceled the whole thing and said we'd be better off without any of the fuss. We packed ourselves up and moved to this house together. The Israelis had invaded and were on our doorstep when we arrived.

Political Activism and Organizing

I started doing activist work in an association. We tackled things logically—I mean, Antoun Saadeh's ideology teaches us that we exist to serve the community. I didn't want to limit myself to a purely partisan understanding of this, so we created an association that we called the Renaissance Women's Gathering. To give women the space to rise!

We started with that notion, and we worked on a lot of projects. We were a group of Syrian nationalists, but I really did want to help society develop—and not just because Saadeh said so! Now, how could we do this? We needed a specific methodology to follow. I couldn't just walk around echoing Saadeh's ideas. That wasn't the way to go. The issue was social and not merely ideological. At the time that I was thinking about these things, we were a group of women working together, all nationalist women. At the end of the day, you need to do the work on the ground.

Because the SSNP has a widespread presence—there were also some women with us in the party who maybe weren't fully into the idea of . . . the party as a partisan ideological thing. For them, their commitment to this group was more based on community belonging and support as a Syrian nationalist group. Do you see what I mean?

Anyway, I was saying, at some point during my work with the party they put me in charge of the entire upper western region. . . . I was responsible for the whole upper western region. In the village, I'd meet with a group of women, and I'd introduce myself to them as a Syrian nationalist—but I always made it clear that my work with them had nothing to do with the party itself. I framed what I was doing as work that would help us set up a framework for ourselves because women needed to have a role in society.

The most complicated area to work in was here, with the Druzes . . . I'm not kidding! It was the most complicated. Still, though, you can go to any village around here, and you won't meet anyone who doesn't know my name and who I am. See what I'm getting at? I don't let people get away with telling me that they don't deal with person X or person Z. I have my own way of making them open up to a different perspective; I use different tactics . . . so that they don't work against us. I talk to people calmly.

People here were always in some sort of disagreement with each other. There was this one time when the non–Syrian nationalist women objected to working with the nationalist women. They saw the groups as separate, and they felt they didn't have anything in common with the Syrian nationalist perspective. I decided to start a joint project with the SSNP—with the Syrian nationalist women in the village. You know? The other women weren't pleased with this, so they had their leader speak with me.

She thought that I was recruiting women from other parties. I told her that wasn't what was going on. The last thing I wanted was to rile up the village and its different communities—neither the Syrian nationalists nor the Jumblatti socialists! I told her again that this was not my goal. She took me aside and closed the door to the room; she wanted to speak to me in private, just us two. . . . There are always these kinds of bigoted tendencies in village families, you know?

But I pierced through all that. I did it in my own way and for their own good! With this woman, Intissar, for example, I told her that she was a well-known figure in the village from a well-known family—and well-off, too! As for myself, I didn't have any money, and we didn't have any at the Renaissance Women's Gathering, either. She asked me how I'd brought all the women together, given that I didn't have any money. How had I managed to gather all these women?

I told her that they'd gravitated toward me because I was offering them something different. I didn't want to, nor had I ever ordered any of the women around. I wanted to hear their suggestions, their own ideas stemming from the land they live on, from the people they know. At the end of the day, they know their own communities much better than I ever could. . . .

I told Intissar that because they had money, people would automatically reach out to them whenever they did something. But they weren't *building* anything. What had they done, really? What had they helped develop? I was really, genuinely asking her these questions. They hadn't developed a thing! I also told her that Bchamoun had been the most difficult area to work in. It had given me a lot of trouble. And I'd worked in all of the other villages around us, every last one! Even Ain Anoub, for example, had been more welcoming.

As part of the Renaissance Women's Gathering, I was able to bring the women in charge of every region together to meet once a month. I held three of these kinds of meetings in my house. When the women who were leaders in the Renaissance Women's Gathering from the neighboring villages came over, I'd be ready: I would've either baked a cake or made some juice or tea, depending on the weather. I'd have it all laid out on the table there, with plates and everything.

I always gave them a warm welcome. We'd talk a bit, then take a break, and they'd help themselves to whatever I'd prepared. I never put things in a tray and walked around, serving them. Not once. I wanted them to get up and help themselves to whatever they wanted! Why? Because I wanted them to feel at home.

I held these meetings at my house three times. Then I told them that from that point on we'd have the meetings at their houses, in the villages that represented different branches of our association. We'd go to a different village each time. And when the meeting was in Bchamoun, all the women from the upper western region would come to Bchamoun. But to the house of the woman in charge of Bchamoun, not to my place. I was no longer in charge of things on the ground; it had fallen to me to organize everyone's work. You know? You have to think about how you're going to effect change.

When the meeting was held at the representative for Bchamoun's house—remember we had a meeting, a work meeting, and yet she never sat down, she kept coming and going, the woman who was hosting us! I let it slide the first time. But when we went to a meeting in another village, the same thing happened. Our host kept bringing stuff in and taking it away, serving people. That meant she barely attended the meeting that was being held in her own house. And the same thing happened during the next meeting. I didn't know what was going on or how to deal with it. And all these women were older than me!

When that third meeting ended, I told them that this would be the last time something like this happened. I reminded them that they'd been to my house three times and that I hadn't ever gotten up to serve anyone. I'd put everything on the table and had them help themselves. It was more efficient, timewise, for people to help themselves to whatever they wanted and then sit back down.

I asked them, "Did you ever see me go to the kitchen when you were at my house?" We were gathering because we had a meeting, and the point of gathering was to actually have the meeting! The point wasn't to compete over who had prepared what foods, what was offered on the table, who did it better. What is all this fuss? Each woman trying to one-up the other?

They were shocked to hear me say that. And it had a certain impact. But they got used to it eventually. You have to make change happen; you have to start with yourself and not just tell people what to do. You have to do it first, in front of them! That's what I did.

I started to notice the change in their behavior during the first meeting in Aytat. The woman hosting there had really gotten it, and that's when it became clear to me that all the women had actually heard what I'd said to them. The next step for us was to bring local women from whatever village we were meeting in to the meeting—anyone from there, whoever they were. We just wanted them to come and listen. I was supposed to be the one speaking, so I left it to the others to invite people.

During our first meeting of that kind, about thirty-two women came. While I was speaking, describing the goals of our association, telling them what we wanted to work on and all of that, for some of them there it was their first time hearing such things! They asked me for another meeting because they knew that a lot of women would be interested in hearing what I had to say and doing this kind of work. I asked them to set a date and time, and I'd be there.

At the second meeting, there were ninety-two women—no exaggeration. We rocked that entire region. In that hall, in Aytat! Aytat . . . ninety-two women sitting there listening to me, Elissar! And we worked hard.

Women Organizing Women

To work in women's groups, you have to think about how to organize. Because the women I worked with had not received any formal education, you couldn't use an academic approach. You had to talk to them about hands-on community work—which is what I did. I talked to them about practical ideas that they had direct knowledge of. And I did this with every village, individually. Depending on the specific circumstances of each village, I set a work plan for them all. I liked for things to come from them . . . I didn't want to stand there giving orders! I'd ask them questions in a way that would help them develop an idea themselves, through their answers.

They determined the topics they were interested in. All I did was remind them that they were the ones who knew what their needs were. I would help them with everything, but only they could tell me what they needed. Truth be told, we did good work. But who did all of this bother? A local leader's wife. You know who I'm talking about. She says she is interested in activism, but . . .

I'd set a meeting for the ladies. I told them that we'd be operating from the school in Bchamoun since it was a big school, and I'd be in charge of organizing a summer camp for the kids. I said they could bring in kids from all the nearby villages. But before this, I had announced that I would need a pair of young people from each of the villages involved to give them a one-week training. I'd gotten permission from the government and everything.

We then started going to the Bchamoun Secondary School. I ran training sessions for the young people for a full week, so they'd know how to help me out once the real work started. They had to be ready to work hard because we were going to be dealing with a big group of children at the summer camp. And these kids would be showing up at 8:00 a.m. and leaving at 2:30 p.m.

We kept the kids busy drawing, doing sports, playing ping pong, studying, writing, dancing—we offered them all of this. The day of their graduation from summer camp, we divided ourselves into groups and laid out everyone's specific tasks. I had the volunteers rehearse the graduation ceremony, instead of the kids, so that everything would go smoothly on the day. Then each of us went back to our respective villages and invited people to attend. People showed up from all around the area!

I wanted to know ahead of time an estimate of how many people would attend, so that we could organize everything. I also told the volunteers that each of them had to bring at least ten kids from each village. At least ten kids each. We'd ended up with 150 children! This was happening when my own child was five or six years old, so in 1995. I had no idea that anyone was upset about it. All I'd done was invite the parents to attend their kids' celebration. So many people showed up! We'd worked hard to organize this graduation party. The summer camp was twenty days long, so it ran for about three weeks.

Balancing Work and Childcare

I raised my children while keeping up with activist, political, educational, and social work. Like I said earlier, whenever I was working on children's activities in the village, I brought my own kids along. They grew up in this type of setting, knowing that we aren't idle people. . . . I mean, I'm the kind of person—whenever we'd organize something like a children's book fair—who'd take my own kids along. I'd give each of them some money so they could pick whatever books they wanted. I'd tell them that I was going to do the same; we'd all pick our own books and meet back at a certain spot forty-five minutes later. Then I set them loose! And they'd each pick out whatever they wanted. These kinds of things need to be ingrained in kids from a very young age, not all at once when they're older! It has to happen gradually.

So about cultural activities, I can say that—be it with my daughter or with my son—we'd have conversations about whatever we were reading, when they were old enough. We even held discussion sessions at home. It was so much fun! I'd ask them how the story they read had ended, what they thought it meant, what point in the book they'd reached. My son still likes to buy books to this day; now he reads in foreign languages. . . . I told him once that I wouldn't be able to discuss the books he read in English with him since I only knew Arabic and French. I used to wait for those English books to come out in Arabic. Why? Because my kids are used to discussing every book they read with me and have been since they were little. I read *The Da Vinci Code* in Arabic, for example. My son and I spend hours deep in these kinds of conversations! And whenever he reads an English book, he always lets me know as soon as the Arabic translation comes out. And he tells me that he won't say a thing about the story, not even if I ask him. I always promise him that I won't ask. This is the kind of relationship I have with my kids. I'm more like their friend than their mother.

I was responsible for childrearing, and it was a shared effort for all of us at home—their dad, them, and me . . . we made it through things together! There were things that we simply just had to do. I'd leave the house in the morning with my kids, and we'd come back home together, around midday. Their dad used to come home late.

We liked to go out on weekends, to do barbecues, all of that stuff . . . and their dad was always involved. It's so sad how things panned out; I don't know what happened to him . . . I feel bad, but I . . . I don't harbor any resentment toward him. I don't hold grudges. We were able to raise our kids in a peaceful home environment—I was always there with them, and we were at peace, and that was enough.

But at the end of the day, I couldn't stay with him. You can't stay in a situation like that. Everything would've been a mess. I lived with him for twenty years, but the gambling got to be too much. I spent four years trying to help him figure out his problems, what his debts were, what he owed, but at the end of the day, with kids in the picture, life has to go on! Even his own mother told him that I was more than capable of raising our kids and that he simply wasn't up to the job, especially with the way his life was going back then. She knew me well. She told him to leave the kids with me and figure out his life. He was a grown man and needed to sort himself out.

And even back then, I never stopped the kids from visiting their grandparents on their father's side. It goes against what I believe in. I wanted my kids to grow up without the kind of psychological turmoil of being caught in the middle. I'm not the type of person to encourage a rift, so I'd always hand them the phone, so they could talk to their father. I'm not small-minded like that. It wouldn't make sense for me to be such a socially active and engaged person and not to know how to raise my kids right. It's just not what I stand for. . . .

After the War: People's Associations, the Grassroots Women's Associations

There's a lot of associations in Lebanon—every region has its own. Some represent villages, and others have a wider scope. The ones that represent villages only deal with their local issues. And if everything is going well in those places, then the work is being done right. But when it comes to women being in charge in such units, they are only called upon when there's some sort of problem. That's where I'd come in, to clean up someone else's mess or to help out in some way. But women need to have a bigger role.

This is where I started, but where am I now? And then I've had all these experiences, and I'd like to pave the way, so the largest possible number of women can do similar things. That's also part of my experience . . . this isn't theory!

I think that social and community work definitely should come before political activity because social and community work is what helps elevate people. I would ask my fellow women: Were you able to train a group of women and change them for the better, to move forward? If you can do this successfully, then you can make it to the top. But if you aren't able to, then you're still at square one.

Women who want to enter the political sphere must be able to effect change. And I don't mean to imply that this is only a woman's duty. It's also a man's duty! Men can't just parachute in out of nowhere, without any experience of being part of a struggle, and become political leaders just because of their last names. Inheriting political positions because of their names—that's nepotism. Men also need to work on the ground to know what it means to work with people. That's why politicians' children who inherit their parents' positions mess up so much. They flail around uselessly and do nothing to improve society—actually, they seem to not care about society at all. They couldn't care less whether society improves or not . . . what matters is that they inherited the throne.

We created our association because we were having many meetings organized through several different associations, and because they were all sectarian, obviously it wasn't viable for us to work with them. And also because of the nature of our work, we weren't a good fit for them either. So there was no way we could effect any change even if we did work with them. We worked instead with groups that had community goals, that operated across all segments of society—the ones through which we could bring about change. Let me give you an example. I'll tell you about something I went through with a group of women, about what we experienced when we were first launching our association—it's really an example to follow.

When we started out, we were a team of twelve women, and we were penniless; we didn't have any money. We'd been influenced by the ideology of the Renaissance Women's Gathering, but we didn't want anything to do with politics. We wanted to do community work. Does that make sense?

The association was completely independent from the SSNP. It had absolutely no connection to the party, either directly or indirectly. None at all. What we'd been thinking about was how women could take up a role in society. That's where we had to start. So at first our team was made mostly of teachers. I mean, out of the twelve members, eight were teachers.

They all taught in schools, but with students of different levels. We knew that we needed to check in with people to do our part and help out . . . and we knew that the kids enrolled in private schools were doing alright—there was money to go around, and even if they were lazy students, their parents would be able to hire tutors for the kids to get better grades.

But what about the less fortunate kids, those whose parents could barely afford to keep them in school? They were all getting to a point where they were leaving school; the dropout rates were really on the rise, and these kids' parents usually weren't able to help them study. On top of that, the kids themselves were often weak students, struggling to keep up. And so they were leaving school and finding other things to do.

We wanted to support them so they could pass their classes and not drop out. I mean, that way, even if students were really struggling to keep up, they could at least go to vocational schools. We based everything on this idea. We sent a proposal to the Ministry of Education, explaining our association's work, and they gave us the green light. We started working with a specific school, and the ministry supervised us. We had good results to share with them. The ministry gave us a good review, which made it possible for us to work with any school we wanted. And so our work started to expand to more and more schools.

Now, on another note, university students are required to do community work. So we decided to send a delegation up to the American University of Beirut to discuss a project with them. We told them that we were working with fifteen schools in Beirut and that we needed more people to help out, to work with us as teachers. Since the university had a similar system in place, we wanted to see if we could work together. They liked the idea. The work would be done between us, the association, and the American University.

We set up tents, several tents, each devoted to a different topic. The students who want to come teach with us go to the tent corresponding to what they want to teach. For example, they go to the civics tent—they just have to walk in; we talk to them a little bit, and if they like the idea, they give us their name, and we draft a contract with them. The contract has to be signed by us and our contact at the university, and after that the students are able to start their volunteering. . . .

We participated in these kinds of job fairs because we would always have university students sign up. We even used to ask the students in the schools what subjects they needed help in most, and we could recruit tutors for math or physics or chemistry or anything else.

Once the university students sign up to volunteer, we send them to one of the schools we work with. We also have other kinds of activities too, like on Teachers' Day. We gather everyone who works with us by district—so a group for Beirut, another for the mountain, all in their respective regions. At this point, the scope of our work has expanded a lot—we've been operating for six years! This was bound to happen. We've reached Rashayya, the South. We even got to the border towns there—the Beqaa, we have people in West Beqaa—really all over. This is the system we set up.

In West Beqaa, for example, we tried something out for the ninth-grade students passing their official Brevet exams. Because I used to be an exam monitor for these official examinations, I know how they get organized, how the schedules are set and everything, including how the monitors are spread across the different exam rooms. So we did a trial Brevet examination in West Beqaa. There were supposed to be eight participating schools, but when all was said and done, there turned out to be twelve. We did this in a local school that was large enough to fit us all. This took three days. The association is called the MMKN organization. It's doing pretty serious work.

Let me tell you how we funded it. There was a group of women who needed to raise money in multiple regions. We gave them some money at first, but then they'd need to find a way to sustain themselves. We started producing sweets. They'd make them themselves. We have a small factory in the Chouf and another one near Bhamdoun, too. Well, it's not a factory exactly, just the women making these sweets in their own homes. They'd make the things that we were known for.

We sold a lot of these sweets; the sales were so good that people even started asking us for them . . . they knew that the money we were making was funding the work we were doing teaching the kids who needed help. We decided we wanted to start a sponsorship program; we felt we'd moved on to the next stage and wanted to create this kind of collaboration with institutions that would support our work and provide the products we needed to make the sweets.

When we first started, we were paying out of pocket. It was just us twelve, using our own money. We'd meet in our homes, print some flyers, and put on fairs to sell some of the things we'd made, like handicrafts, household items, jams, and preserves. And the women who were starting to make the sweets were also benefiting from this: we'd helped them come out of their bubbles a little bit because when we organized those fairs, they'd want to participate, too; they didn't want to just stay at home, confined to the kitchen. They wanted to leave their houses, meet people, and have a role in society. And they were also making money. So we had secured them an income, eased them out of their home environment, and gotten them engaged with a larger community.

We supported some plays that we thought would benefit our students by giving some financial support. This was making us a lot of money. We highlighted some movies that we felt were important, that were being shown in cinemas, too. This helped us establish a network of relationships with people. People sought us out. You'd have to see it to believe it—we were just a group of twelve women, but the things we pulled off! We all had different political and sectarian leanings and came from different places, but it didn't matter. And we were also working with multiple other associations, affiliated to different political parties. We were really open to everyone.

Had the core twelve women not believed in this cause, things wouldn't have happened this way. You have to believe in a cause. We made helping the less fortunate students our cause, our own! And this is the work that we do. We even hold sessions to discuss how the association's work is developing as we move forward.

We do these in all of the different regions we operate in, considering that every area has its own specific set of conditions. You have to bring something to the table wherever you are, so that people get on board with what you have to offer. You have to teach women how to go around all of these regions, how to reach larger segments of society. In Aley, for example, I asked a group of women to gather as many other women as they could, and I'd just stand there and talk to them—just talk to them! At first, we were five, then we were seven, ten, twenty-five, and it kept increasing. You just need to find the key; each region has its own. It could just be a person who knows how to deliver a message!

MMKN Trips to the Olive Orchards

Once a year, we take a trip to the olive orchards. It's organized by MMKN, and we go to the olive press once per season. The idea is that we need to offer something to the farmer because it costs him so much to maintain and invest the land to grow the olive trees in. Why not help out by picking the olives? That way, the farmer wouldn't need to hire workers, who'd then take a cut of his earnings, which are already so low. We volunteer to do that work for him ourselves.

We gather a group of university students, and all twelve of us go on this trip with them. We all go together, to pick olives, get to know the land and its people as well as how they work. Whoever wants to buy some olive oil can do that, too. Then the farmer takes us to the press, and we can buy the oil of the olives we helped him pick. Even though we helped pick the olives, we still pay for the oil. We have to support the farmer . . . that's the whole idea.

We've also liked to all eat lunch together there—so we go early, and it's on him to provide lunch for everyone working. It's not a big expense for him because when you think about it, the farmer usually pays each worker $40 a day, and we send him sixty volunteers in one day! So we are still saving him a lot of money. But he also needs to have a role, too. He needs to be engaged with us and the students. We don't want to just go there and pick the olives for him, no . . . we want to all have lunch together on the land, too.

We spread sheets out on the ground, and we sit on them and eat all together, you know? And then in the afternoon—I'd have already looked up the area we're in, to see what we could show the students, if there's any particular landmark or ruins, so we can go around the area, too, get to know it. That way the students would also be discovering parts of Lebanon they didn't know. So that's what we do on our olive trips.

There's this family here in Bchamoun who was struggling a lot. People asked me if I'd purposely favored Bchamoun to send the students to, and I told them, no, it's just that there was a family who was in a difficult situation there. This specific family wasn't doing very well because the father had died of cancer. He left behind four kids and the mother. I decided to send the students to work in that olive grove that belonged to the family in Bchamoun because the kids were practically orphans. Even if we were going to end up working in more than one orchard, I wasn't going to miss out on this opportunity to help this family.

I spoke to my colleagues in the MMKN organization and went to survey the land, to see how big it was. I told everybody not to expect the family to provide lunch for us, the way the farmers usually did, because I didn't want to burden them in any way. The kids were practically orphans, and, I mean, the eldest sister was only twenty-two, and the mom . . . their situation was difficult, financially speaking.

We brought our lunch ourselves. The kids helped us out as we worked—the young woman, who's a friend of my daughter, and her three siblings. We picked the olives on their land, and when we were done, we all took a picture together with the bags full of the olives we'd picked.

Before going, we held a meeting at the organization for me to explain why I'd picked that specific grove. Everyone was on board. And they all showed up to volunteer on the day. As we picked the olives, the mother of the family kept bringing us some biscuits and *raha*, little snacks like that. She'd hand them out to us herself. When we finished, we gathered the olives we'd picked and stood beside them to take a picture together. I couldn't look up into the camera, I just looked down. I was crying because of how touched the mother had been and how warmly she thanked us. . . .

Later we all had a meal together and took some more photos, you know? The father had passed away a while ago, and he'd been the one who generally managed things. This is an example of our community work.

7

Umm Ziad Adnan

"If people let themselves be ruled by fear,
they end up doing nothing"

Umm Ziad lives in a mountain village not far from where Elissar Z. is based in Bchamoun. As becomes clear from her story, Umm Ziad hails from an older generation. She credits her family background—in particular her charismatic and open-minded father—for helping her get involved in politics, but most of her generation of village women did not attend school. From a religious family in a region where women and girls also did not engage in many activities outside of the house and family sphere, she discusses her activism and organizing in this context. The mother of a martyr, Umm Ziad has engaged in militant actions out of a necessity to fight the occupation. Facing tough circumstances, she has demonstrated bravery and courage in her actions, all described in a straightforward way—from military training to cooking to tending to the wounded and dead on the battlefield. According to her, you must confront your fear and carry on; otherwise, you will never manage to do anything.

[b. Abadiyeh 1936]

My name is Maliha Abu Said, Umm Ziad Adnan. Of course, I was top of my class at school, and my father always helped me out when I needed it. He'd been both the head of the municipality and the local mayor. He was a social man, a really good man. I'm the mother of a martyr—my son Ziad was killed during the war in 1986. When I was a child, my father always used to sit with us and help us study. I was so young back then, and I used to recite speeches or poetry at school. My father would teach me how to pronounce and enunciate words clearly and speak in public.

And I was always very open to learning. The schoolteacher would give us a few simple lines of poetry to learn by heart, which I loved to do. I liked the poems so much that I ended up memorizing them all. I'd stand up in front of everyone at school and start reciting them. I have an excellent memory, and my late father did too. There was this young girl I used to compete with over who got better grades—there was never more than half a point between us. Whoever got the better grade would get to sit at the front of the class. As of today, I've been here in Dhour al-Abadiyeh for sixty-three years.

You know, girls weren't allowed to go to school back then. My grandmother said, "It's a shame, why would you send her there? The Christians could see her, and. . . ." But in the end, I did go to school. It was called Zahrat al-Fatat, in Abadiyeh, a primary school. I got the Certificate diploma [equivalent of fifth grade], which was a big deal at the time. I've often been asked by women of different backgrounds whether I've been to university, and I tell them I haven't but that the way I see it, education is a gateway to knowledge. It's not about whether or not someone's been to university—you could very well spend some time talking to a university student only to realize their thinking is limited, they have a narrow perspective on things. People are responsible for broadening their own knowledge, their own minds, themselves. They just need to know how to read. Anyway, I got married in 1956. I wasn't even twenty years old. My husband died young, and I insisted on pursuing an education because my mother-in-law owned lots of property, lots of lands in the area.

Life was tiring for me. The area here in Dhour al-Abadiyeh had very few homes. People who came to our house were always so surprised and asked us how we could live like this, practically in the wild. It was totally empty around us, but the area developed after the Gulf states opened up for travel and work, and people started coming here to spend their holidays. We built new houses to rent out, and we even sold land for people to build on. My husband's mother raised her children alone because she'd lost her husband. They cultivated their lands and lived off them. When I left my family to get married, there was a popular old saying that went, "Choose your daughters-in-law by their wealth and your sons-in-law by their lineage." I used to hear that all the time in the village.

A person really does get shaped by their fate, and it's the cruelty of fate that pushes people to open certain doors over others—if they're destined to, that is. If they aren't, then nothing changes, and the situation remains the same. I'm the type of person who loves to learn, and I was taken out of school against my will.

I have three sons. When I was around twenty-eight years old, all my children were in school, and I asked to go back to school myself. But my husband and his family didn't approve. I tried very hard to get them to change their minds, but it was out of the question: in my day, it just wasn't acceptable for a woman to come and go, to move around a lot . . . especially keeping in mind that transportation was not readily available. All these circumstances are different now.

My husband died in a car crash in 1975, at the beginning of the Civil War. There were only eleven months between his passing and that of my father. Anyway, long story short, I really needed to work at that point. I had to do something; it was time for me to take on some responsibility.

Community Work and Activism

You can't succeed at anything without communicating with other people. You really have to be loving and forgiving with others. The most important thing, for me, is that I like people, not that people like me. I want to treat all people well. This is the model I've adopted, and it's worked for me. I'm speaking from experience. Taking care of people is the most important thing. It was after my husband passed that I started to do community work.

My mother-in-law got so angry; she blamed me for giving people something to use as gossip about our family. She claimed I was doing all sorts of things. At that point, my father had not yet been martyred, and she called him and repeated everything she'd said to me, that I was going to fuel people's gossip about us, that I was going to be spending too much time outside the house, and all that stuff. Again, back then, it wasn't allowed for a woman to go anywhere unless she was accompanied by her husband or her mother-in-law.

Before the Civil War, when my husband was still alive, I'd learned how to give injections. There was this woman who'd come from Australia;

she'd come to my house to give my son the injections he needed—he was seven months old and needed the shots because he was sick. I didn't want to keep inconveniencing her, so I asked her if she could teach me how to administer the shot myself. She did, and I started giving my son the injections on my own. And even when our neighbors had the flu or a cold, I'd help them out. I became the neighborhood nurse but worked without getting anything in return.

It took strong nerves to do that kind of work, and I did put a lot of thought into it. People have accused me of having been too much of a risk taker during the war, but I really wasn't. There was a first-aid class that I took, and I was nervous about taking it, but I've always been inclined to take up social or humanitarian work—knowing that I had to be able to rise to the challenge. If people let themselves be ruled by fear, they end up doing nothing. This was kind of how people started to know that I was working.

Political Awakening

My brother wanted to get involved in politics, so he started training with the Palestinian resistance. We didn't really know where he went to train, maybe Jordan. He would disappear for periods of time, but we had no idea what he was up to. One day he started talking to me about all these things. People in the mountains where we lived are so closed-minded, so he couldn't really tell me much. My husband's parents were unwavering supporters of Kamal Jumblatt, to an extreme degree. I lived among them, yes, but I was different. But there was no escaping because of the kids.

Whenever my brother tried to tell me about his political work, it was only when we were alone, and he only talked in broad strokes. He didn't talk in front of everyone; when he came, there were always people around, the kids, my mother-in-law . . . it was difficult to get a chance to sit down with someone in private. And the war had already started in Beirut.

In 1975 or 1976, I explored my brother's bookcase and read works by Mao Zedong—my brother was still alive at that point. We didn't talk a lot, for around six months or so, and that's when the war broke out. I didn't have any time to read anymore, and I really missed it. At first, I sided with the Arab Communists. I mean, I'd read Marx and Lenin and Mao Zedong. My late son Ziad, may he rest in peace, was communicating with the Chinese Communists by post—they sent letters back and forth, and they even sent us magazines all the way from China. It was a really special time. When Israel invaded Lebanon, we burned them all. We should have kept them, but where were we going to hide them?

That's when I started reading more philosophy. I told myself that philosophy could solve humanity's problems—I mean, realizing that people are equal and especially that women are equal to men in every way. I tried to think in this way and test if the theory held, but after much life experience I realized that it was incorrect. There are differences between women and men. I mean, Marxists say that women shouldn't work in mines or jobs that require manual labor because of the nature of a woman, the nature of a mother—the way God made her. Because of this, it would be wrong for women to have to do certain jobs that aren't compatible with their biological makeup, knowing that they are biologically different. I came to this conclusion after participating in the war, as a woman. There's nothing women didn't do during the war, but I did notice differences.

During the Civil War

When the war broke out, I started training with the resistance—my children and me. They were with me full time by then. The youngest was thirteen years old. We trained at Radar in Baysour with a rough Palestinian man. We trained for twenty-one days with the Palestinian resistance. There was a Palestinian man there who was very scary. He was from Upper Egypt or something like that, and he looked like someone who'd lived in difficult conditions. He was such a big man—he had a big build. I started training with my children. We'd come and go there together. That's how I raised them.

It was when the war broke out that I really came into my role, in the village of Chouit. My father died, and my brother was martyred. When I started training, my brother Nassim was still alive. Once, there was a big battle with lots of casualties and injured. My role was to help out at the small makeshift dispensary. I had a lot of tasks to take care of there.

The war was what thrust me into my role. When I fired my first round of bullets into a trench, Nassim warned me to be aware that there could be a Phalangist ambush ahead. He explained that the militia used moving ambushes: it always advanced at night and retreated during the day. I had to know where the night ambush was.

The leftist and national forces had dug trenches in our orchard, facing Aaraya. There was a direct line of fire from there, approximately five hundred meters away. It was very close. My brother first told me I had to know where the enemy ambush was located, then I could aim at it and shoot. I fired all the bullets I had. The Phalangists shot flares back at us along with actual shells—they landed on the ground, and there was dirt and stones flying everywhere. We were almost buried underneath it.

I was afraid for my brother. He told me to keep my head down to avoid the dirt flying at us from every direction. When things calmed down, we were able to leave, but only after the clashes eased up. That was my first battle. I was thirty-nine years old. We'd been trained on how to plant mines, and they even taught us how to use medium-size weapons. The training was tough.

After that training camp in Baysour, it was time to apply what we'd learned. The leader of the organization of the National Committees, Mounir Shafiq, whom we also called "Abu Fadi," asked us women militants and me specifically what we thought about being positioned as snipers in a specific location. That way if any of the enemy forces was passing through, we women would be on the lookout for them. Officials used to ask for my opinion, but I didn't know a thing about military action! I'd just agree with whatever they said. This was around the time Syria wanted to enter Lebanon in 1976. They didn't end up making us snipers, but they instead positioned us at an elevated site among the houses. We were equipped with 3.5-inch missiles that were ready to be fired when needed. They taught us how to fire them.

That site was for women militants only. We'd stay up through the night and take turns keeping watch. Two of us would have to stay awake, and the rest could sleep. There was usually four or five of us there each night. A group. Some women were from Baysour, like Suad Ml'aeb and her sister. I know a lot of women from that town, but I can't remember their names anymore. There were also some women from Abadiyeh, but now they're all socialists, with Jumblatt. Back then, though, they were on our side. Some members of the Zahr family, four or five or maybe more, were also with us. Again, this was before the wave of Jumblatti socialism.

As the war went on, I started cooking meals for the fighters. I was the oldest of the women around. They were all still practically children! I'd make them help and asked them to bring me ingredients, to peel some vegetables, or do specific tasks. The fighters really put a lot of responsibility on my shoulders. They'd show up, for example, and just hand me their weapons to keep safe while they were off doing something. It's like all these different responsibilities were following me everywhere. So much was expected of me, but I managed it all.

People used to say that I was ready for action at the front in Chouit twenty-four seven. I was fully dressed at all times, ready to respond to anything. Whenever a bomb fell, I'd immediately rush outside to see if anyone had been hurt. And I'd tend to the young men who'd been hit by snipers: that meant that whenever anyone died, I was there. After a while, the Druze shaykhs would come—you know, I didn't wear a white scarf on my head, like religious women; I used to wear a kaffiyeh.

Once, a young man was martyred, and he was taken to a *khalwa* so they could pray for him. The shaykhs started asking where I was; they wanted me to be there. All of them were shaykhs. What was I supposed to do there with them? I don't know how to pray for the dead or anything. What did they expect me to do? I couldn't understand why they were asking for me, but I still showed up; I looked at the martyred man in the *khalwa*, and I said things like "May God have mercy on his soul" and "May God keep you all in good health." That's all I could think of doing. That was my role. Then I left.

Dalal Mughrabi, the Fatah fighter who was martyred in 1978, once came here, to this house. She used to work with us. We would all sleep in that middle house over there. The last house there, we built it, too; we used to store missiles in it. That's what we had to work with. So we used to cook here and then deliver the food to our fighters setting up ambushes in the region. A lot of people were showing up to support the Palestinian resistance: some were from Egypt, some were elderly. . . . Those who wanted to contribute to the resistance would show up here, especially considering that the war had taken on an anti-Palestinian tenor around that time.

The resistance funded all this cooking—they brought us meat and vegetables, and no one was left wanting. We'd then distribute the leftovers among the people here, to those in need, keeping in mind that a lot of folks lost their jobs during the war. But there were also expats coming in, which was very useful because the money coming from abroad helped a lot. The state collapsed, unlike what is happening now in Syria with the Arab Spring and the civil war, which didn't cause the state to collapse.

Sectarianism, the War, and Fighting

So . . . back then, during the Civil War, my son was thirteen and a half years old. When the war broke out, we didn't want him to take part in it because he was still too young. But when my brother Nassim died, I couldn't hold him back anymore. It's not that I couldn't hold him back—I'm tough, and I'm a tough parent, too, and I get what I ask. I mean, I'm hard on my children, but I'm hard on myself above all.

At that time, he really insisted on going to the front to take part in the fighting, but I refused to let him go. When my brother was alive, he never let him go, either. The battle was a decisive one, and the front was dangerous. The demarcation line extended from Dahr al-Wahsh to Aaraya, up to the mountains in Monte Verde, and all the way to Beit Meri. Chouit is located in the valley between them all, and those regions all overlook it. So you can imagine the sniping that was going on there. A lot of young men died from sniper fire.

There wasn't a house left for us to cook the meals in. We'd cook here in Dhour al-Abadiyeh and in Abadiyeh too. And we'd take the food from there. There was nowhere left for us to stay, no house. All the upper regions were too exposed to sniper fire, so we ended up in the lower towns, in the displaced Christians' homes. There wasn't really much room there either, though. They were all getting bombed. There was a house in which two young Christian men had been killed—they had nothing to do with the

Phalangists, those poor men . . . we knew them well. They just weren't able to escape the violence. They were easygoing people. The Jumblattis killed them.

Those Jumblatti socialists working with him called themselves "militants in struggle." What a joke! Is that what struggle looks like to them? What did those two young men do to deserve what happened to them? They'd been living in Chouit for ages. They weren't originally from that town, but they'd moved there and were working at the carpet factory. I don't know if they had any sensitive information. They were shot and buried, covered with dirt. They must have been taken by surprise; this all happened at night.

When my father was martyred, some Jumblatti socialist guy started accusing the Christians in Chouit of having killed him. He threatened that they would "pay the price for killing Abu Na'im," warning them to watch out. They ran off. Into the wilderness. They left their fridges full of food and just ran off under the cover of darkness. Some people had even left the dough they'd been kneading in their mixers. Their homes were left wide open. Then there was chaos, robberies, people taking whatever they could get their hands on. I used to overhear fighters with Jumblatt's party saying they were just waiting for the end of the month. . . . What? Were they in that party just to make money? Instead of to protect their lands and their people?

Before he passed away, my father tried to protect the Christians in our town. He let two Christian families live on the ground floor of our building. He wasn't fazed by the threat of bombs—he'd say, "If they're going to bomb us, let them. We lived together, and we'll die together." Two Christian families from Chouit, he let them live on the ground floor. My father had a very good relationship with the Christians. People used to joke that he liked Christians more than he liked Druzes. We had so many friends. But they're all gone now; they've all fled.

The place where they buried those two Christian men—they just dumped them there. Because of the smell, the area had to be covered over really well to be used. But even the concrete absorbed the stench of death. I would call one of the fighters and tell him that we needed to put a table there, because there was no more room for us to even stand. We needed to have a table, even though it smelled so bad. I would call them, over and over again, and then one guy came and said to me that they couldn't stand the smell anymore. It just stank of death.

My brother Nassim, may he rest in peace, was only twenty-seven years old back then, but he was widely respected by people in the village because the majority didn't have access to education, so they didn't have any clear political awareness. The day he was martyred—I mean, on the night we found out what had happened—we waited. I thought maybe some of our fighters had been injured, some even withdrew, and a cease-fire was eventually announced. By the end of the night, though, I told everyone that our men were dead. It was over. I knew there was no hope. We waited five months to retrieve the bodies of our deceased fighters; they were still in the battlefield, and we couldn't get near them. Abu Fadi used to come tell me that he was trying to set up an exchange to get their bodies back and all sorts of things like that, just to try to calm me down. But I mean, I . . . I had raised Nassim, my brother. I'm thirteen years older than him—he was like my son and my brother all in one, my companion in life. He was the light of everything I did in life. So you can imagine how much this impacted me.

At home, our family exchanged knowledge and culture and trained for military action. But when Nassim first started training, none of us was aware. Jumblatt's Progressive Socialist Party didn't have any members in Chouit, so they recruited Nassim to be in charge of the military front in Aaraya. The Chouit–Aaraya axis was a big one; it included villages in our region: Chouit, Abadiyeh, al-Hilaliyah, Roueisset el-Ballout, and Baalchmay. This was the region that led to Ras el-Matn, to the top of the mountain. If the Phalangists managed to overtake this route, they would've taken control over the entire area. And this was the axis that Nassim had to take charge of. He became responsible for it. He boarded up the Christian homes: he got planks of wood, and with the help of some young men they all boarded up the doors leading inside. Whenever any door was going to be opened, they wanted to know who was entering. He even stationed some young men he trusted at the entrance to the village. So if anyone was trying to bring something in, he would stop them. He had to monitor this, of course.

When Nassim died, the Christian part of the village was ransacked. Doors were thrust open, things broken; people caused a lot of destruction. And even though I only officially worked with my brother for four months, everyone knew that we were practically one person, so they really latched onto me after Nassim passed away. People didn't necessarily have any political or militant experience, but they'd found that kind of awareness and understanding in Nassim. They saw him as genuinely human, someone with a sound opinion who was ready to share it.

One day a shaykh showed up, a hardcore Jumblatti socialist. We sat outside on the balcony. I set up some chairs for us. He asked me what we were going to do about all the robberies that were going on in the village. I told him we had to bring back the checkpoint, like in Nassim's day. He got emotional at that and said that back when Nassim was alive, we always somehow landed on our feet. "Now who's going to help us up?" he asked, tearing up, I swear.

Later, another shaykh showed up with four or five young men. They gathered around a table outside, near my father's house. They told me that they wouldn't let me sit out the rest of the war. Their exact words were: "You're going to take Nassim's place." I said that we'd do our best by the grace of God. But, actually, I had no idea what I'd do—I knew nothing about war! I did have people with me, standing by me, though, may they rest in peace . . . Abu Mahmoud, Abu Fadi, other young people who supported the resistance, people I trusted a lot. They really were my main support. I had good men by my side.

I used to attend gatherings where people discussed all kinds of things I had never heard about before. Some were organized around intellectual, literary, or cultural issues, and still others on militancy and the struggle. I had so much trust in these people. I'd really listen to what they said and try to implement the ideas we discussed in practice, which I was able to do because there was no one left for me to take care of at home. My brothers and sisters were all abroad. There was just me. My father was gone, and so was my brother—there was no one at home or even in the country.

The Siege of the Tal al-Zaatar Refugee Camp

During the siege of Tal al-Zaatar, the road leading to the refugee camp was stormed by the Phalangist militias. Many Palestinians were lost—I mean, the Phalangists killed so many of them. And they killed our people, too—the joint Palestinian–Lebanese forces lost more than seventeen or eighteen people when they were trying to break the Phalangists' siege on the camp. Of course, there were also many people injured and everything else that comes along with a siege. Our people weren't used to this, to this kind of fighting. I mean, these things require lots of training.

There was someone with Jumblatt's socialists who was firing a cannon, aimed at the men who were storming the camp. A member of the Popular Front was hit in the back, and Amin al-Andari's brother was also hit. We took care of his foot injury. His entire heel was gone, just blown off, right here. In his case, it's not like he had a lack of knowledge or training, but he was the one driving back the Phalangists when he was hit.

Anyway, that raid . . . we did everything to try and support the people in Tal al-Zaatar, to make them feel less isolated. But at the end of the day, the camp was done for. I mean, whoever was left there under siege was just left to die. There was a man we knew from Abadiyeh, Amin al-Andari, Abu Wajih. He set up a route from Abadiyeh through a road in the valley so that aid could be delivered to people stuck in the camp under siege. When Tal al-Zaatar fell, we heard that that people had started leaving the camp. Abu Wajih confirmed it. They were being liquidated. What a shame, it was such a sad situation. Heartbreaking. All those children . . .

There was nothing left in the camp for people to eat. Nothing at all. They had some lentils, but barely any. They'd ground them up and baked them into a sort of bread. It was so crunchy, barely edible. They'd brought it with them, but it was so dry. Basically inedible. And those kids! I swear, in Abadiyeh we had to prepare so much milk for them, pots and pots of it. We'd dissolve the powdered milk in water and heat it up for the kids, then we'd bring it here, to my house in Dhour al-Abadiyeh. These two buildings were open to everyone; they were like rest stops. The Palestinian resistance provided us with the food we needed, but people coming from the camp didn't stay long—they moved on to Damour.

Resisting the Israeli Occupation of 1982

Anyway, when Israel invaded in 1982, the markets and sidewalks were teeming with Israeli soldiers and products. I'd be on my way to work and had to drive very carefully to avoid bumping into them—that's how many there were, and they were all armed. Later they started walking around without their weapons! They were *that* convinced that the resistance didn't exist. They thought they were safe.

Back to my point. When the Palestinian fighters left Beirut in 1982, we went to Saadnayel in the Beqaa Valley. Abu Mahmoud had passed away, so some guy had taken charge of the National Committees' budget in his place. That guy had lost all his credibility: nobody in the town trusted him, not the youth, not his family, no one. He's from here, from our town; he's one of us. But he got greedy after Abu Mahmoud died, and he was in charge of the budget. He started going to Tripoli to collect money from the resistance, the allocations that would have to be distributed among the fighters. So all that money was in his hands. And sure enough, lots of young people started complaining because when he'd show up again, there was no money to be distributed. He used to claim that it was because the situation had calmed down, so there was no more money to go around. But he was still collecting that money, and the rest of the guys knew it. Because some of them had accompanied him to Tripoli the first and second time he went there. So they knew for a fact that the money was still coming in. And that allowance continued to be offered for some time. . . .

The guys transported all of the injured during the siege of Beirut—they'd pack them up in the car and transport them to safety, and all the while the Israeli jets were still bombing them, with all those young men out there fighting. I found out that a young man from the Hatoum family, from Kfar Silwan in the Matn, had been hit in the foot during the battle in Bhamdoun against the Israelis. That young man was like my son—he was my son's age. He was always around our house, and I was like a second mother to him, really, just like I was to all those young men who were my son's age. I was like a mother to them. They'd come sleep here—excuse these details, but let me explain it to you. You see that set of sofas in there? They used to move them all to the side, take the pillows off, set them on the floor and sleep on them. The bedrooms were already full, so they'd sleep on the floor, on those pillows. My house was known to be that place: where young people could always find somewhere to sleep.

So back to my point, I told that guy—the one who looked after the budgets and accounts after Abu Mahmoud—that I needed to go to Syria to check on one of our men. He was very dear to us. I told him I needed money because I had to go see him and needed to give him at least one thousand liras [approx. US$300]. I tried so hard to get my hands on that money, but the guy told me that there had to be someone to nurse him back to health in Syria. He was trying to get me to change my mind, but I insisted that I needed to go see him and that I wanted to take him some money. I told him again that I wouldn't go with less than one thousand liras in my pocket for him. He managed to get his hands on the sum. I don't care how. But that's the kind of person I was. He gave me the thousand liras, and I went to Syria. Obviously, I paid for my own expenses; back then I was working at the medical lab making three thousand liras [approx. US$1,000] a month, and during that lull between the events of the Civil War and the Israeli invasion, I was managing to put some money aside.

In 1981–82, I was able to put gas in my car and buy enough cheese, *labneh*, meat, and vegetables to fill the fridge. This would cost me around fifteen or twenty liras. I'd really splurge, you know? During that time, my mother-in-law couldn't stand it when I was in the house. I wanted to leave really badly. We were living together here, in this house. The things you'd hear if this room could talk! Eventually I got too annoyed. She wouldn't let up, and I couldn't stand hearing her yell and argue and curse anymore. She didn't curse, exactly, but she wouldn't stop calling down misfortune upon me, you know, old lady talk. She'd really say bad things; you know how older women can get.

When I'd finally had enough, I told the kids that I'd decided to look for another house that we'd live in together. I hoped God would make it easy for us; we'd see. I got in touch with Halim Zahr's family; they're good people, those young men were also on our side, Halim's kids. Anyway, I told them that the situation at home had become unbearable for both me and my mother-in-law, really just too unbearable, so I was looking for a place I could move to and settle down. He was very helpful and told me that there was a house that belonged to a Christian family who'd left—they were their neighbors, and they'd left them the key. They'd been neighbors, but the Christians were displaced, so Halim Zahr and his family were keeping an eye out on their house in their absence. They called them to get their approval—they were keeping in touch. So they called them to tell them that they were going to open up their house for me and that I was a good person and so on.

We opened up the house in 1981. Just before Israel invaded. We moved out because my mother-in-law couldn't stand the dynamic anymore. We'd hold meetings that young people would attend; they were always coming and going. There were meetings all the time. And my mother-in-law was a very religious old woman who spent all her time reading the Druze holy book, the Kitab al-Hikma. So the situation at home was too much; it was time for us to leave. She used to go around the town saying nasty stuff about me, but nobody gave her the time of day. Nobody in all of Abadiyeh. The entire Zahr family was on our side because their children were working with us. They spent all their time with us; they became like my own children.

Israel invaded Lebanon in June 1982. The Israeli soldiers stayed in Kayfoun for a month, digging trenches. There was a small resistance force building up there. We were in Abadiyeh at the time, and the withdrawing Palestinian–Lebanese–Syrian joint forces started showing up, one after the other, as they were retreating back to Ras el-Matn, escaping Israeli shelling. When they'd get to Abadiyeh, they'd ask us for directions to Ras el-Matn; there was a road that took you straight there from Abadiyeh, and they needed help finding it. Everyone would tell them to come to my house for help. I had no idea who these fighters were, and they didn't know me, either—people from Jordan, from Syria, from everywhere. Everybody who felt some sort of patriotism, everybody who had love for Palestine and wanted to fight against Israel, showed up at my house at one point or another. Some people even came all the way from Egypt.

There were three or four fighters from Jordan who were martyred down there in the fields below our house. They died from Israeli bombing, and the townspeople buried them here. Their own families never found out.

Like I said, everybody passing through Abadiyeh who was withdrawing from the front would come here, to my house. My son Said had a van
he used to transport vegetables and stuff like that—remember I told you
earlier that we had an orchard, my father's family's orchard, that we'd
planted stuff in. It was a very large orchard, spread all over Chouit. Said
was taking care of it. He'd load the fighters into his van and take them to
Ras el-Matn. They were so exhausted that they would even leave their B-7
weapons behind. He would go back and forth delivering fighters.

My son Wajdi and other young men would spend entire nights picking up those discarded weapons and burying them. I remember he came
home once and fell asleep immediately, just like that, he was so exhausted.
He'd been up all night with the guys, burying those weapons. They were
so afraid.

The house we were in had a basement, and whenever I'd see him lying
down like that, so tired, I'd ask him repeatedly to go lie down in the basement before the shelling started. I didn't want him to fall asleep before he
went downstairs. He'd tell me he'd go down in a minute, lift his head for
a moment, and then fall back asleep. This happened over and over. Then
a shell fell right next to our house—the house was street level. The shell
hit the field just adjacent to the house. Fragments of it scattered inside the
house as a result—that's when he finally got up, picked up his shoes, and
went down to the basement. We went down there together.

The second shell hit the large window all along one side of the house
directly. All of Abadiyeh turned against me and my children because we
supported the Palestinian resistance, making our house a target. So the
shell hit, and the house burned down. The sofas, the apartment on the floor
above us, everything burned to the ground. Six people were martyred that
day from the shelling. A jet fighter bombed a house that collapsed on top
of the people still inside—they'd gone there to hide because they thought
it was safe. But the building completely collapsed. The people who died
were all from Abadiyeh. Another house that was hit by the shelling was
right next door to Dr. Amin Zahr's. Two people died there, and another
woman who was getting treatment for the injuries she sustained in that
attack also eventually passed away. Fouad al-Najjar's daughter was on her
way to the Zahrs' house when her husband, Khalil, was hit by the shelling.

Everybody in the building rushed to hide together downstairs. They crowded together down there. Khalil's leg had been broken, and he was screaming in pain. His wife kept saying that she was fine, she hadn't been hit, and telling everyone to check on him, to see what was wrong. They were still newlyweds. My son and some other young men carried her to Halim Zahr's house, which was right next to where they were. He started to perform CPR on her. Meanwhile, we were getting violently shelled.

We were sitting there, facing the hills of Monte Verde and Beit Meri, which meant we were fully exposed to the shelling. Everything was coming from that side. A shell hit right in front of the house that we were in in Abadiyeh, and it brought down the entire staircase. The shells were being launched from planes—they kept hovering above us, and then a bomb would hit. Abadiyeh was completely destroyed. It's not like Israel needs a reason to bomb a place.

Some people died the very day of the shelling, but others had to be hospitalized for different periods of time. It was only once the violence had subsided that people were able to go around looking for their loved ones and checking on their houses. A woman from the Makarem family just died from injuries she sustained back then, when she was still a young girl. She'd lost her two feet from Israeli shelling. Her funeral was yesterday.

We took charge of helping out people who'd gone to seek shelter on the ground floor of a stone building used to house livestock. It was a large, fortified structure, with arched ceilings, and therefore protected. People ran there seeking shelter. There was a young boy from the Najjar family— mind you, that entire family is against me today—I carried him because his mother was badly injured on one side of her body. They carried her out on a stretcher and took her to get medical help. Her treatment took a really long time, but God healed her, and she fully recovered. She's the principal of a school in Abadiyeh.

Anyway, at that point, the entire town rose up against us: they all said that my children and me were the reason the town was destroyed. It was easy to blame us because everyone else who was on our side, those who had some money, was afraid for themselves and their families, and so they'd all left for the Beqaa, for Saadnayel, before this. All of them. Everybody who was on our side had already gone to Saadnayel. But I stayed in that house with my children. Where was I supposed to run? Anyway, the house burned down, and I decided then that I didn't want to go back. I moved some stuff that was in the bedrooms—mattresses that had been a little out of the way had survived. I moved these things to Chouit, to my parents' house, where there was a safe place to stay on the ground floor. We set up our stuff and slept there for a few nights as we continued to look for a more permanent house.

After the chaos in Abadiyeh calmed down, and once all the injured were moved to hospitals and the shelling subsided, guess what I did? I went to visit them. I went from hospital to hospital to check on every-one who'd been injured. The National Hospital and the Shepherd Hotel in Bhamdoun, too, because it had a large hospital. I visited everybody in hospital, all of them. The people from Abadiyeh were forced to receive me. They thought that I was the reason the Israelis had shelled Abadiyeh, as if I'd called Israel myself and told them where I was. I mean, had my family and I been living abroad, maybe I'd understand their suspicions about me—but we were there, living among them, we helped them all to safety . . . and yet whenever they saw me, they'd turn the other way.

After the War

I was one of the founders of the Women of the Mountain Association, which was a collective launched in 1994. I played a major role in the as-sociation because I really enjoy planning events: we used to rent out halls and hold seminars. Most of the women who participated were from the al-Khair Association; the majority of them were Lebanese expats in Kuwait who used to send aid from there. I took up a job until the Women of the Mountain Association really took off. Some of our members would show up here—if only this room could talk! We were sitting right here, in the winter, when they told me that they didn't think the association would manage to accomplish anything. But I've been a social and community activist since 1976; I have a lot of experience, a lot of patience when it comes to these things. I have it all stored up here, in my memory. The other women were very chic, elite women; they didn't have experience in this field, and they didn't want to bother with something taking so long.

They then came here and told me we should probably stop the work altogether. But I told them to be patient.

During the July War in 2006, three families fleeing Israeli bombings were living here. Most families helped out to make the schools available to the displaced. The less tolerant people didn't open their homes to the displaced, but they did offer them food and other things. You know, even among the Shi'a, people were saying that had Nasrallah not hit the Israelis, they wouldn't have hit us. We can't blame our people—I mean the Druzes—when they talk like this. But the way I do things, I'd rather talk about the positives than the negatives.

Another thing we do is host lunches. Last winter, I hosted eighty women here. Each one of us cooks a dish in her own house. The proceeds from this home-cooked lunch were over two million liras. Instead of selling tickets, I just open up my home and host a lunch and the proceeds go to the Women of the Mountain. The money goes toward helping students out, 130 students this year. I'm always present at the events where we distribute support, whether they like it or not. Students walk up and receive their aid in envelopes.

I became acquainted with the Islamic resistance in 1996. We created an association in 2006 and then another again that same year. I used to know some friends of my children's at the American University in Beirut back when we were part of the resistance in the National Committees, but I don't know what they're up to now—whether they're with the Islamic resistance or not. Back in 1996, we set up another association that we called the Committee for Resistance Support. This was after we started knitting. At first, it was just a group of us doing the knitting; they'd give us the wool, and we would then distribute it around the whole region, even the most remote areas of it, in the Matn, in the West. We knitted sweaters for the resistance.

After 2008, people became less tolerant of the resistance; a lot of hatred started to grow. After the Jumblattists clashed with the Islamic resistance on May 7, 2008, they stopped offering us that venue. We also no longer knew where to distribute the aid. The situation forced you to think twice before supporting someone. The basis of our work was that we were supporting the resistance that was fighting against Israel, especially after the 1996 war and the Qana massacre, when a lot of people came here from the South and the southern suburbs of Beirut. After 2008, whenever we wanted to do any charity or auxiliary work for the resistance, it felt like we were navigating a minefield.

The resistance asked me later on if I could collect the names of all the young people who were martyred during the battles with Israel back then. So that became my task. I went to Aabey, to the Hamza family's house. That family had lost Enaam Hamza. I also went to Charoun and Ras el-Matn, and I met with someone from the Gharz al-Din family there—the brother of the martyr Rajeh Gharz al-Din. He told me that they didn't want anything, and they didn't want to talk about him at all. I said that a martyr's memory does not belong to one person alone but to an entire nation. A martyr's memory lives on in the entire country. Still, he didn't accept, and he even said that he didn't want his name mentioned from the podium during the celebration commemorating the martyrs that fell fighting against Israel.

During Israel's war on Lebanon in 2006, we were handing out sweaters in a *hussainiya*, a mosque at the outer border of Bchamoun. We knitted the sweaters. And in 2010, we went to the resistance outposts at the border in South Lebanon, to spots that nobody ever goes to. I asked to do that back then; I told Hajj Bilal, the Islamic resistance official in the mountain, that we'd knitted a lot of sweaters and wanted to offer them to people on Liberation Day. I brought him one of the sweaters, and I told him that we'd gotten very good-quality wool, and all the sweaters were handmade—they'd keep the men waiting in the trenches warm. I also told him that we'd like to go see the men at the border. We did, and we delivered a small speech there . . . it was a really good trip.

8

Hajjeh Zahra Abdel Latif Sh'ayb

"I could never sit still: I was always on the move"

Hajjeh Zahra is from a rural area, though a different one than Umm Ziad, and is also from a religiously oriented family background. Unlike Umm Ziad and the other women who tell their stories here, however, Hajjeh Zahra found her path to militancy and activism through religion. As her narration emphasizes from the very beginning, she is very much a part of an Islamic resistance, mentioned by others at times in disparaging ways. Much like the other women, Hajjeh Zahra also emphasizes in her stories that she does not identify as sectarian. She is careful to assert that she does not believe in fighting against other Lebanese women and people committed to liberation, even if she doesn't agree with them or their ideologies. Her struggle is against those who have occupied and oppressed Palestine and Lebanon. The Islamic path defined by Hajjeh Zahra is closely linked to her belonging in her community in South Lebanon, and like the other women in the study—secular and religious—she credits her family support and upbringing with her empowerment as a woman. She also notes that although war, occupation, and especially her imprisonment in Lebanon and occupied Palestine are terrible experiences that no one should have to suffer or repeat, they also bring a person awareness and clarity on issues. Her story emphasizes women's solidarity across difference and being someone "always on the move," themes repeated throughout the chapters of the book.

[b. Jabal Amil, 1947]

In the name of God, the Most Gracious, the Most Merciful. God bless Muhammad and His pure family. Praise be to God, the Lord of all worlds.

156

I'm from the village of Sharqia in the Nabatieh District. Let me tell you about my childhood. I'm a village girl, and I'm proud of where I come from. We were like all those other folks who migrated to Beirut from the South, and I grew up between Beirut and my village. Our household was very religious, especially my father. People used to refer to him as "mullah" because of how well versed he was in Islamic law and jurisprudence. He was neither a shaykh nor a scholar, but he knew so much about our religion that people just naturally called him "mullah." He was a devout Muslim, and he was devoted to the family of the Prophet Muhammad, peace be upon Him. He even used to hold the gatherings at our house to commemorate the death of the Prophet's family members. These gatherings really helped shape my character. Sayyidah Zaynab, peace be upon her, was my role model.

We were committed to this path—that of total resistance. It's not what people at the time were calling civil resistance—that was just child's play masquerading as resistance. You think we could defeat Israel with that? My opinions stem from my convictions, and my convictions are rooted in my beliefs. Nothing could make them waver despite all the time that has passed and the parties and people I've known. But in opposition to a completely civil resistance, we believe in Islam as the starting point. This is the path that Imam Khomeini, may God sanctify him, set for us. He reminded us that Islam began with the era of the Prophet Muhammad, peace be upon Him, and His family.

It's hard to achieve anything if you have a specific ideology but no ability to defend it. And on the flipside, the use of weapons without a specific ideology to guide you could backfire, as people might turn against each other or even against themselves. There would be nothing steering them in the right direction or toward the right goal. Imam Khomeini, may God sanctify him, led us to a good path, a way to live an authentic Islamic life; we believe in and are committed to this. He brushed off the dust that had been concealing it and made it shine, a Qur'an in one hand and a rifle in the other. They protect each other. The rifle protects ideology, and ideology protects the rifle, making sure it is only used in the right way. From this standpoint, our resistance is not civil, Arab, or secular.

I spent my childhood between my village, Sharqia, and Beirut, where we lived in the Nabaa neighborhood. I remember we were in Nabaa in

1958 when people revolted against Chamoun. We had been in Nabaa for some time but had to leave to return to our village; we kept going back and forth. And the same went for my schooling: I was enrolled in the village school and then in Beirut, always moving between them. I'm illiterate. I'm telling you the truth! I haven't been to university—I only completed the third grade. I didn't even finish that grade since the war in 1958 forced us to flee to the village, which meant I had to leave school again.

Lying is haram, it's forbidden, and so is pretension. I won't lie to you and pretend I've been to university, nor will I claim I've completed high school or any other formal education. No, I started the third grade, but we were forced to flee Nabaa at the beginning of the school year. We packed up and left. I made it only through the first semester of the third grade, hamdillah. But if God, the Most High, wants to bestow gifts and light upon someone, no one can stand in His way. Between you and me, with all due respect to university students, and I've met many—men and women—who've studied physics, math, and chemistry, letters, and equations but who know nothing about life. Life is what I call culture. I may be wrong, but, to me, culture is about society, and life isn't about memorizing words and alphabets and science and algebra.

We were four sisters and six brothers. Some of them got married, some of them left the country. My brothers moved around from one place to another, depending on where their work took them. But we girls were the younger ones—I'm the youngest of all my siblings. When the 1958 revolution was happening, my father was supportive of everything going on because Ahmad al-Assaad was the leader of that revolution. During the events in 1958, Ahmad al-Assaad was in Syria, and he was sending weapons to Lebanon. My father was a contemporary of Imam Khomeini, may God sanctify him, and he admired him very much. He adhered fully to the path the Imam set out for us. My father thought in political terms and had a vision. He wasn't a traditional man, religiously or politically speaking, but saw things clearly. He believed that Ahmad al-Assaad was the best politician in Lebanon, the least likely to steal from or oppress the people. That was my father's opinion back then. I was still young, and I didn't really know if he'd joined the revolution, but I know that Ahmad al-Assaad was its leader.

The Outbreak of the War

We didn't directly witness the outbreak of the war in 1975. We used to live in Nabaa, Beirut, and had returned to the South. From the South we went to Dahieh, the southern suburbs of Beirut, and became residents of Dahieh. While we were in Dahieh, the events of 1975 broke out. We had left the South around a year before, and because of the war we had to leave Dahieh and go down South again. Our large family was scattered around; the majority were married, even me. Our own nuclear families became our primary families. I spent a large part of the war here in Dahieh, between Bir al-Abed and Chiyah. But I got married before the war. I used to pick up my children from Aamiliyeh in the thick of the shelling. Bombs would fall right in front of me or just behind me during Aoun's so-called War of Liberation in 1989. I have five children: three girls and two boys.

We Islamists didn't participate in the war at the time, but we supported the nationalist cause. The way we saw it, if we were to join the fighting, we'd only fight under the banner of *wilayat al-faqih*. That was the only legitimate banner for us. I would see people shooting toward Ain al-Remmaneh; then they'd start shooting at each other.

There were small groups of young men, four or five, or maybe even ten, who had their own bases. They'd be in Hayy Madi or Ain al-Remmaneh, somewhere like that. But they had their own fronts—you could have a common enemy at one moment, but then they could turn on you at any given time. But we believed in protecting and directing our actions with legitimate means, and for us this meant the use of weapons was guided by our religion. We couldn't take part in the fighting without this kind of legitimation.

At that time, we Islamists didn't have any essential role on the ground. We weren't organized in a political party, but we were present in groups. In that sense, I was doing social and political work from 1968 onward. Politically, we were butting heads with the different parties, joining in their discussions and debates, and doing our best to prevent them from taking advantage of our young women and men.

The parties used to hold meetings in people's homes, and they'd just register people in the Communist Action Party of Lebanon, the Ba'ath

Party, the Communist Party, the PLO . . . but none of this meant a thing to us. AMAL [the Movement of the Dispossessed] was established in 1973, and it was exposed as hypocritical in 1974 when there was an explosion in a training camp. We had our reservations about the establishment of the AMAL movement. I mean, they considered Musa al-Sadr, may he rest in peace, to have mysteriously disappeared, but actually he was martyred on the second or third day.

They kept using his name to garner attention, though. Let them! He wanted to do something for the Shi'a, so he amassed as many people as he could, but we weren't operating like that. Our idea was to start something off slowly. We even told him back then that combining all those people into one party wouldn't work since they were so different: there were members of the Communist Action Organization, Syrian Ba'athists, Iraqi Ba'athists . . . How could they all be lumped together like that? But al-Sadr said that's who was available. Some stories say that in thirteen years in Mecca, the Prophet, peace be upon Him, only converted thirteen people to Islam, who became his companions. And these people in the end represented the whole *umma*.

We divided ourselves into groups, which we called Islamic committees and later were renamed the Islamic Action Committees. We started operating in the '60s, the late '60s. We launched from the Association of Shaykh Muhammad Mahdi. But today we criticize that association because it called for civil not military resistance against the Israeli occupation.

Back then, we gathered as a group of young women; we'd go out, meet, and work together according to the social and political climate. We did everything that was needed at the time, but we always saw our main calling to be bringing people back to Islam. We'd discuss religion with Muslims, trying to prevent them from leaving the fold and joining political parties and all that stuff. We helped as many people as possible; we did the best we could. Our goal was to protect young women and men from the secular left parties. Right-wing parties such as the Phalangists and the National Liberal Party weren't even part of our world.

When we were living in Nabaa, I was very young, about ten years old. It was in the '60s, in Bir al-Abed, that we started our religious work.

Shaykh Muhammad Mahdi had an association that we launched our work from, and some ulama working there gave us lectures on religion. But I personally distanced myself from Shaykh Muhammad Mahdi in 1972. I could tell he was the type of man who wanted to get ahead no matter what; he'd do anything to make himself more important. He became the vice president of the Supreme Islamic Shi'a Council, and Almighty God brought me back to the path of Imam Khomeini.

At the beginning, we operated in secret cells; we didn't even know who else was working with us. I received an envelope at first: a greeting card with the Imam's photo and some of his sayings printed on it was slid under my door. Then I started to meet some of the other people involved, and things gradually became clearer.

We members of the Islamic Committees started operating out in the open after the Islamic Revolution in Iran in 1978. Sayyid Mustafa, the son of Sayyid Khomeini, was martyred. He was killed by the SAVAK. Later, the Imam declared a revolution. After Sayyid Mustafa was martyred, the idea of revolution really ripened, and the Imam declared it so.

Our role was to tell people about the Islamic Revolution in Iran and explain its goals. We went out, and people viewed us as strange, in every sense of the word. We were even strangers to our own people—the Shi'a—to our relatives, our shaykhs, and our ulama. Everyone was surprised at what was going on; some people knew of Khomeini. I remember there was an Islamic holy book dedicated to him that was being circulated by the Islamic Committees at the time. There was also one they brought us that was called *Lessons in Jihad and Sacrifice*, which discussed the Palestinian resistance. At the same time, it also gave religiously sanctioned permission to legitimately join the resistance forces and partake in militant actions inside Palestine. We were very much separate from those uncontrollable PLO fighters who continued to provoke Israel at the border, prompting the Israelis to rain missiles down upon us all.

The Israeli Invasion of 1982

About a week after the invasion or even less, I headed to the South. Back then it took you a day or a day and a half to get there from Beirut; there were Israeli checkpoints everywhere. Israeli tanks were advancing toward the city. They would simply drive over and crush any cars in their way. I was probably the only one who managed to complete that route in four hours. I didn't care what the Israelis said or what their rules were. I drove with my son, who was about five years old at the time. Whenever I was required to stop the car at an Israeli checkpoint, I'd tell the soldier that my car was overheating, and I couldn't stop. They'd motion to each other to explain that my car was overheating, but I didn't even acknowledge them or look them in the face. The men at the checkpoints were all Israelis. There weren't any of Lahad's men from the South Lebanon Army.

The work on the ground really started when we arrived in the South. That's where the resistance was thriving. The people down there were different. The world down there was different. It was as if we were in Israeli territory. There were even Israeli goods in the markets. Of course, Israeli soldiers were everywhere, roaming freely in the streets and on the beaches. It got to a point where they would go to the beach in Sour completely naked! They'd go into shops, walk through the souqs, enter houses, and even frequented the Friday market in Abbasiyya, the Monday market in Nabatieh—you get the gist. They were crawling around all the souqs in the region. You'd find Israeli goods sold in the market out in the open. I asked a merchant for eggs once, and he asked me which kind I wanted: the Israeli or the Lebanese? And the local stuff was more expensive! Even the bread, the watermelon. . . . Everything was such a mess.

This is where we started boycotting Israeli products as part of the resistance. Something happened once that's worth recounting. I'd been put in charge of the South, from Ghazieh to Chakra and Bra'chit, and my job was to talk to the people down there about Islam and our resistance work. I'd spend two or three days in each town, spreading awareness. At first, our resistance was nonviolent because we couldn't go full steam ahead from the get-go. Had we done that, we'd have been fighting our own people. The first step for us was to liberate people's minds. So many people had been really beaten down and couldn't tell who the enemy was anymore—they saw Israel as the savior that helped them get rid of the Palestinians.

The AMAL movement and others had brainwashed them to believe these things, and the Israelis and Palestinians helped the process along.

They did really terrible things, things that even history is ashamed of, to the point that the inhabitants of southern Lebanon truly believed that the Palestinians were worse than the Israelis and that Abu Ammar wanted to create a Palestinian state down there. Our main concern was to remove this idea from people's minds, to clarify so they could see the truth of their reality: this is what Israel is. What they did to the Palestinians they will do to us. Where will we be displaced to? Israel's goal is to get its hands on our land and our water.

Anyway, back to my story. I was heading to a region way down south, near the border strip. This was during the first months of the invasion. I was passing through the town of Chehabiye, and I saw a small shop in front of which the owner had piled up a mountain of watermelons. People were rushing to get their hands on them, and everyone was buying two or three. Obviously, they were being sold for cheap. That's how I knew that the watermelons must have been from inside Israel. I parked by the side of the road and walked toward the shop. I said hello to the owner, and we exchanged pleasantries. I asked him how much he was selling watermelon for, and his answer confirmed my suspicions. "I hope they're not Israeli watermelons," I said. I wasn't looking to buy anything; I just wanted the people in the shop to overhear what I was saying. He confirmed that it was an Israeli watermelon, and I told him I wouldn't buy any Israeli product because it would be haram. I said out loud that nobody should buy any Israeli goods.

There was an old lady in the shop, carrying a watermelon and waiting to pay for it. This was all happening during the month of Ramadan, by the way. I respectfully asked her what she was doing, and she said she was buying that watermelon so she could eat it to break her fast. I told her that would be haram, and she shouldn't break her fast with it because it came from Israel. She assured me that she'd clean and purify it, but I told her that the watermelon itself wasn't impure—she could take it for free and eat and enjoy it. I clarified that the problem was paying for it. By paying for that watermelon, we would be funding the Israelis and enabling them to buy more weapons to attack us. In the end, she left it, and everyone in the shop started looking at each other. The vendor asked me if there was anything I did want from the shop, and I told him that I'd wanted to buy some watermelon, but I'd changed my mind because it was haram to pay for it, and so on and so forth. . . . I was sure that he was going to kick me out of his shop anyway, so I said everything that was on my mind without holding back.

In a nutshell, that's what the situation in the South was like. We had meetings in every village; we had formed a sort of secret committee for women. I was working with both men and women, separately. Sometimes I'd take the fighters where they were going in my car, stuff like that. We started our work with the late Shaykh Ragheb Harb, may he rest in peace. I worked with him during the first months of the resistance. Shaykh Ragheb, may God be pleased with him, believed in individual initiative. There was no organized work per se in our circles.

The AMAL movement had all supported Lahad's army—like I said earlier, they didn't have an ideology to guide and protect their actions. AMAL started protecting Lahad's checkpoints with armed fighters, and we hid from them. We may not have been organized formally or officially, but we followed our spiritual guide. This meant that, ultimately, we were organized, but we just didn't have any organizational framework. Our connection was to our spiritual guide, to the people who adhered to that guide's decisions on the ground.

Shaykh Ragheb, may God be pleased with him, was one of the people who emulated Imam Khomeini, may God bless him, and in the end AMAL sold him out. Anyway, everything we did started with Shaykh Ragheb. One of the things we focused on the most in our operations was targeting the villages where the Israelis had taken and detained people. When we knew that there was a specific village that the Israelis had detained young people from, we'd approach Shaykh Ragheb and ask him what to do, whether we should stage a protest.

People only had to be religious or come under any kind of suspicion to be arrested. When that happened, we'd mount protests and give locals different tasks to carry out. We did this in one village after another. Sometimes, when we would be planning protests for two or three neighboring villages from which young people had been arrested, we would hold a collective protest and invite local shaykhs to speak. This really bothered the Israelis.

There was also a group of young people we knew through Shaykh Ragheb, may God be pleased with him, who were aligned with the Communists. They really, truly believed in communism, in the revolution of the workers and the farmers and whatnot. And so when they saw what was going on, how the Israeli army was invading Lebanon, they were very disappointed.

They just dropped their weapons when the going got tough. But how were we supposed to get our hands on weapons to join the armed resistance? We had no access to any whatsoever. We started collecting the weapons that PLO fighters had to leave behind while they were withdrawing from positions seized by the Israeli army. We grabbed what we found; there was always someone who knew the hiding places to look in, where the storehouses abandoned by the Palestinian resistance were.

The young people returned to us! They had fulfilled their religious requirements to fast and pray; they came back to the faith. They were committed. They would set up ambushes at night with Shaykh Ragheb. An ambush was really the most you could do at the time. That was how the resistance started.

Lead-Up to Arrest and Detention

I was arrested in late 1983, about five months before Shaykh Ragheb was martyred. Things were like this when I left, but I'm not sure how the situation developed after my arrest. All I know is that Shaykh Ragheb, may God be pleased with him, was martyred. He wasn't killed directly by the Israelis. But they planned it, that's for sure. It was an Israeli decision to take him out, but the ones who carried out the dirty work were AMAL. You think the Israelis would have ambushed him right near his house? They never would've dared.

I was arrested in December 1983, supposedly on charges of political incitement and mobilization and for assisting Shaykh Ragheb, may God be pleased with him, in military action. I had the honor of visiting Palestine in my arrest: I prayed on its land and knelt on its soil in worship. I was imprisoned in the Ramleh prison, but they barely kept me there for a year.

I was about to unleash a revolution from within the prison, and they just wanted to get rid of me.

There are so many things that happened in 1982, in the phase leading up to my arrest. For example, I was headed to Saida one day when the Israelis set up their checkpoint at the Awwali bridge. They controlled people completely: they'd choked traffic such that it was completely blocked from the Awwali bridge, at the northern entrance to Saida, all the way back to the town of Ghazieh. They deliberately took their time letting people through. I started to overtake other cars whenever I got the chance to, and I eventually got very close to the Awwali checkpoint. A soldier spotted me and approached my car, but I didn't even look his way. He asked me in broken Arabic why I was overtaking people. I didn't answer. He ordered me to move back in the line, but I ignored him. Then I turned to him and said, "You're an oppressor and an occupier." He told me not to use those words, so I repeated the same sentence, "You're an oppressor and an occupier."

He had his Kalashnikov at the ready, and he started loading it. I told him to go ahead and shoot. My young children were in the car with me, frightened, and they started crying. I turned and asked them, "Why are you crying? Don't cry. When we go to heaven, we'll be martyrs, let him shoot." Then I turned back to him and said the same words I'd said before: "You're an oppressor and an occupier." He pushed his rifle against my chest, and I challenged him to shoot, repeating once again that he was an oppressor and an occupier. Then I said, "I'm going to tell you one last thing before I go to heaven a martyr. Remember it well and spread it to others: since you came here, you've only encountered those who've surrendered. But you haven't seen anything of the Muslims yet. They're coming for you."

Unfortunately, the Lebanese police were also operating the Awwali checkpoint before the bridge with them—the Lebanese police worked alongside the Israelis at all checkpoints. The presence of Israelis had simply become part of our reality. The state, the population, the law, everyone acknowledged their presence as a given. May God sanctify the soul of Imam Khomeini. All of those Lebanese who supported the Palestinian resistance and waved the Palestinian flag high, chanting "Long Live Palestine" and "Long Live the Revolution" and whatever else, where are they now? The Palestinians went to Tripoli, and Abu Ammar left from there by sea, in a hurry. And their Lebanese supporters? They dropped their weapons, packed themselves up, and that was that.

Anyway, back to my story. The officer in charge of the checkpoint came up to us and asked the soldier why he had stopped me. He said that I was overtaking other cars and that, on top of that, I was cursing at him. The officer then told me to continue on my way, in a thick Hebrew accent. I said I wasn't going anywhere, so the policeman turned back to me and said, "Hajjeh, just go." I repeated myself once more, "I said I'm not going anywhere, got it? I won't follow the orders of this officer. He doesn't tell me what to do. I'll leave when I decide to." The policeman told me to take a breath, say a prayer to the Prophet, and calm down. But I wasn't taking any of it. "No, no, no," I answered, "and you'd better wash your mouth out with soap before *you tell me to pray* to the Prophet. If you cared about the Prophet at all, you wouldn't stand alongside these impure people. And those guns you all carry? They're a disgrace, and you're a joke. And you take orders from these people instead of firing your gun straight into their heads." They told the officer that I wasn't going to budge. He said to me, "Fine, if you want to stay here, stay here." I turned the car back on and continued on my way.

I always got into trouble at checkpoints. Another time, I was driving toward the town of Jwaya when I was stopped at another checkpoint. The soldier asked me for my ID, but I didn't acknowledge him. My son knew the routine, though, so he reached into the dashboard, took out my passport, and handed it to the soldier, who then asked for our travel permit, the paper granting people access to the Occupied Territories—the system put in place with the invasion in 1982. I barely looked at him and, not at all hiding my disgust, asked him, "What travel permit would that be?" He said, "The one from the Israeli army." I replied, "You're telling me I need a permit from the Israeli army? Go get one yourself! This is the land of *my* ancestors, *my* forefathers. I'm on *my* land. You're the occupier. You're the aggressor. You're the one who is in my country without permission. You're the invader," and continued, "I'm not the one who needs a permit. *You should* be telling *me who* gave you the right, who gave you permission, to enter my country."

The soldier then said he wasn't going to return my passport to me. I told him that was fine by me; he could keep it for all I cared. At that point, there was a queue of about two hundred cars behind me. No one dared try to just drive past that checkpoint. The Israeli soldier didn't know how to react and clearly looked uncomfortable. He held my passport up in the air and said he was going to give it back to me—not for my sake but for my son's. I assured him that I wasn't asking him for any favors, nor did I need any favors from him—I made sure he knew that my dignity didn't depend on him. Driving off, I turned too sharply, and the car lost traction for a second, stirring up the dirt on the road. My tires were spinning uncontrollably.

Before I drove off, people had started getting out of their cars and telling me to just leave it and get out of there so they could cross the checkpoint themselves and get on with their lives. I told them to go back to their cars and take a moment to revel in our collective humiliation: "Go back to your car. You see this? This is Israel, the same one who's here to set you free. Go back to your car." That was when the soldier handed me back my passport. After I accelerated and drove off, I looked in my rearview mirror to see the soldier and checkpoint. But I couldn't make them out for a good few seconds because the air was so dusty from my spinning tires. I got into these kinds of problems at checkpoints all the time.

Interrogation in Prison

They took me to my first interrogation session. They already knew the basics, so they started off strong. The officer asked me where the weapons were, but I pretended I didn't know what he was talking about. He repeated the same question, so I told him the only weapons were with them; we didn't have any. In broken Arabic, the Israeli asked me again where our weapons were, calling us "subversives" who carry out operations against the Israeli Defense Forces. I told him I didn't know who was carrying out these operations and that I had nothing to do with that—I said we were religious and didn't go anywhere near weapons.

"What *do* you do, then," he asked, "since you're in a different town every day, and you're always moving around? Plotting to kill Aql Hashem,

Husayn Abdel-Nabi, and Saad Haddad?" This was twenty days before Saad Haddad died. "I wish I could," I replied, "but unfortunately I don't have any weapons." He asked me again what else I could be up to, and I repeated that our group was strictly religious, operating in mosques and *hussainiyas*. "What do you do there?" he continued. Whenever I spoke to him, I did so submissively and in very simple terms to make him think I was slow. Sometimes you need to make them feel that they are superior in their intelligence, that way you can more easily figure out what they're fishing for.

He kept asking for more details, so I tried to get my point across in my own way, pretending to be naive: "It's our job to tell people that Israel didn't come here to kick the Palestinians out but to occupy our homes and our land. At first, we were told that the Israelis were here to expel the Palestinians, which sounded good to us, a relief. But it seems that you want to occupy our homes and our land just like you did to the Palestinians. That's it."

In the cell, you're isolated. You start to conjure up scenarios that the interrogator has planted in your head—"Talk and you're free." I tried to come up with a plan and thought about giving them any name, even if that person wasn't with us, part of the Islamic resistance. But even if I made up a name, a person with that name would still have to pay the price, and so would his parents, his town, and his whole family. I thought up different scenarios, and in the end—in Islam, we have something called the Istikhara prayer. All along the exterior wall of the building, they had set up dividers to create individual cells, one of which was mine. These types of walls are spray-painted, but little pieces of rock jut out all around. I collected some of those little rocks and used them to perform the Istikhara prayer in the only way I could, given the situation I was in. It seemed to me, from how it went, that things were going to go my way.

I knocked on the door, and the guard appeared. I told him to take me to the interrogation room. He said he couldn't do that since it was up to the prison administration to call people into questioning. I told him to tell the captain that I'd decided I wanted to confess and get out of there. That did the trick. They thought that I'd had enough, that they had broken me.

I'd been on a hunger strike for about a month—every time they brought me that tray of food, they'd find it untouched when they came back to take it away.

Obviously, if I could have gotten out of prison, I wouldn't have hesitated—it's not like I was having such a great stay inside. But I didn't want to cause harm to anyone, not even the Communists. I knew lots of Communists, and I knew that they had nothing to do with the occupation or the resistance; they'd extracted themselves from that equation. Still, it was against my religion to cause anyone harm, whoever they may be. The only reason I was acting out a charade to the Israelis was that I'd made sure there was no chance for them to actually make anything of it.

I made up a story of who was running the resistance cell, giving them three fake names, including saying the leader was Abu al-Fadl al-Abbas, like from Islamic history. One of the names I took from my former work as a tailor. To put it briefly, there was this salesman that used to bring me cloth, a very polite, good man. In the story I told the Israelis, I changed this man's last name. I picked a family name that didn't exist in the South because I knew that whatever name I gave, the family would be dragged into interrogations. I wouldn't do that, not even to a Communist. I'd never cause harm to another person. Whatever the Communists are, they don't come close to the evil of the Israelis. You can't even compare. The differences we have with Communists are ideological, but with Israel our issue is with their very existence as a state.

Communists can face up to whoever they have to answer to when the time comes. That's their problem. I try to talk to them, to discuss things with them, and if I manage to convince them, then great, and if I don't, that's fine, too—not my problem. At the end of the day, we belong to Allah and to Him we shall return. Suppose, for example, that I'm having a discussion with a Christian. We believe in completely different things. Christians believe that Jesus is both God and the son of God—*astaghfarallah*. But for us Muslims, God has no partner, no child, and that's final. And God sent to Lady Mary, peace be upon her, an angel, who breathed the divine spirit into her and bore her Jesus, the spirit of God, a prophet sent from God. God Almighty bestowed upon him the ability to perform miracles: he spoke in the cradle, healed the blind, the mute, the deaf, and the leper, and with the will of God he revived the dead.

On to the Ramleh Women's Prison

One random day, the guard opened the cell door and told me to get up. I asked where to, and he said, "To Israel, inshallah." They tied my hands and blindfolded me. They had some Peugeot pickup trucks, their cargo beds covered, and they loaded me into one. I was afraid my fellow resistance fighters would carry out some operation against the Israelis, and I'd get caught in the crossfire. We arrived at the border—I was still blindfolded, of course. They were taking me into Palestine. The border guards took over from there. I swear to God, they were terrified of me. Two female officers sat me in between them, and there was also the driver and another officer. On the way, the blindfold loosened a bit, and the sun appeared to me like a red dot through the cloth. I could tell it was almost sunset, which meant I wouldn't be able to perform the noon and afternoon prayers.

Such vast lands, such large orchards . . . the soil was so dark and rich, it looked like it was dyed with henna, and there were oranges everywhere. It was peak orange season. Anyway, we have our own ways to perform our prayers no matter the circumstances—it's important to never miss a prayer. In my specific case, all I had to do was set an intention and start to pray. So I immediately set an intention for my prayer and started to recite: "Bismillah al-Rahman al-Raheem." I made a slight motion to mimic bowing, another to mimic kneeling. It was a prayer in gestures. When they saw me moving like that, they went nuts. They started mumbling things to each other and didn't stop until we arrived at the Ramleh prison. The ride took about an hour and a half. We got to Ramleh, and they took me inside the prison.

We went through the prison gate. It had a high wall. They took me to the administrative section, and as I looked around, I knew that I was now in totally unfamiliar territory. I started crying. They made me take off my abaya and my hijab, and I was screaming, shouting, and fighting with them. The female guards were in military uniforms, and they all had very short hair, like boys. I lost it. They were all women; no men were allowed there. I really lost it and started to weep. I'd been through so much before I finally broke down. I hadn't shed a tear until then. But still I refused to allow them the satisfaction of knowing I felt humiliated. Up until that moment, I'd been constantly manipulating them by either picking fights or acting simple-minded; I was trying to get my point across however I could. But I never, ever let them feel that I was humiliated or weak—God forbid. Taking away my hijab, though, that went too far.

Still holding me by the hands and shoulders, they carried me out of that room crying, shouting, and cursing at them. I was thrashing around, trying to free myself from their grasp, and screaming out for my clothes. They kept saying they were forbidden and took me to the prison dispensary. There was this Jewish woman prisoner who kept slipping away from the guards, and when she saw me, she immediately headed over to the Palestinian prisoners and told them that "one of you all" had been brought to the prison: an Arab, "and she's terrified—screaming and crying!" What did she know about why I was crying?

They took my blood pressure and did some basic medical checks. I heard a Palestinian prisoner trying to make an excuse to go to the dispensary; she said she needed some Panadol. She made it in and tried to reassure me not to be afraid, that they were Arab like me. I told her to leave me alone and not to speak to me again: "I'm not afraid. No one talk to me!" I was getting increasingly worried about spies and informants. The guards took me to a cell, one they claimed was reserved for women who were detained but not convicted. This meant that I was still considered under detention, in an administrative holding category that was renewed every six months. No ruling had been issued against me yet. There were two other women in the cell with me who were in the same situation.

They asked me why I was crying, what I was afraid of. "Who told you I was afraid?" I replied, "In the South, they used to push their Kalashnikovs against my chest, and even then I wasn't afraid. I'm not scared, I'm infuriated. I'm upset that they took away my abaya and hijab." They reassured me that there were no men there. "None at all?" I asked, and they confirmed that there weren't any, that the guards were all women and that no men were allowed inside the prison. That helped me relax a little. But

I was still cautious because I knew that informants were always planted among the prisoners. No matter what the Palestinians said or asked about, I didn't respond.

When I finally found out what situation they were in, I learned that they'd been sprayed with pesticides two weeks before I was brought there. The prison that I'd been taken to was apparently the finest in all of Palestine. It was specifically designed to display to foreign visitors, to show them the "democratic face of Israel." The cells were tidy, with bunk beds and that sort of thing. Anyway, the prisoners I was with had physically confronted the prison warden: they'd hit her, yelled at her, and spit in her face. Palestinian women are no joke. They were being punished for this. Otherwise, they were normally allowed to move around inside the prison. Their cells were always open, and they could leave them whenever they wanted. Some of them even worked in the prison. The Ramleh women's prison is considered the finest in all of Palestine, and the Ramleh men's prison is not far away.

Like I said, they had sprayed the women prisoners with pesticides. The cell doors there had small windows, around ten-by-twenty centimeters, that the guards used to give you your food or a cup of tea or Nescafe. They had locks on them. Anyway, they'd sprayed the prisoners with pesticides to punish them; and now they couldn't leave their cells except for one hour per day, each individual cell at a time. They were collectively forbidden from leaving their cells. Each cell held three or four women. The women from one cell would be let out for one hour; then they'd be taken back to their cell, and the women from the next would get their turn. They started throwing up because of the pesticides; they really were in bad shape. I developed an allergy then that I still suffer from today because of the toxins that I breathed in. They permanently damaged my windpipe.

It took me about four or five days to get comfortable around the Palestinian prisoners. They were divided: they'd separated themselves into left- and right-wing groups, which represented the nationalists and Marxists on the one hand and Fatah on the other. They felt they couldn't wait any longer—both the Left and Right wanted to meet separately, but they were all mixed together in the cells. The only time they were able to see each other was when it was time to eat. They'd designated one table for each group. Incredulous, I asked them where they thought they were. Each camp started trying to pull me into their fold, trying to get close to me and tempt me by doing me favors. I told them not to bother: "I'm neither left- nor right-wing. I firmly believe in the good of the middle way. I'm an Islamic resistance fighter, neither Lebanese nor Palestinian, neither Eastern nor Western. My leader is Imam Khomeini, and I represent female Muslim resistance fighters everywhere in the world, not just Lebanon. I stand for the path of resistance that led me here, the path laid out by Imam Khomeini, and I am ready to unite with you against our shared enemy. I have my own beliefs and my own convictions. And you have yours. You sit there arguing about left and right, about communism and the PLO—none of this means anything to me. All I care about is our shared enemy. If you want me to unite with you against this enemy, I'm ready to do anything, I'll go as far as it takes." They were even arguing about who I would sit with at mealtimes. I told them I'd have lunch with the left wing and dinner with the right wing—every meal at a different table. I broke my hunger strike there. You didn't really have a choice—you needed to eat.

That's what the prison in Palestine was like. These women drove the Israelis crazy, and the guards even asked me if I wanted another table to sit at by myself. I said it wouldn't be necessary. The guards kept trying to pry me away from the rest of the prisoners, the Palestinian women: "What business do you have with them anyway? They've been convicted, and they're being punished. But you can leave whenever you want. Their punishment doesn't include you." I told them that the other prisoners and I were one.

The way I managed the prisoners was by spending time with each group individually outside our cells, especially when I received the news that Shaykh Ragheb, may God be pleased with him, had been martyred. It was very shocking, and I found out through the Red Cross. It was the first time they visited me in prison, and I learned about his martyrdom through our conversation. I started wailing so loudly that my voice flooded the entire prison. I started explaining to the Palestinian women, one by one, how the leaders of the Palestinian resistance in the South just threw down their weapons and fled. "What a waste of your struggles and sacrifices that was! Be it the Left or Right—each was worse than the other," I said to the

Palestinian prisoners. They got emotional at the news. There's so much to say, too many details to rehash.

Release from Prison

When I was released, they took me to the El-Buss Palestinian refugee camp in Sour. It was around 2:00 a.m. Back then, curfew was enforced with an iron fist: nobody could be on the street past 7:00 p.m. They just left me there by the side of the road at 2:00 a.m. The entire area was nothing but shops—What would be open at that time of night? There was absolutely no one around; the nearest house was about one kilometer away. Remember, this is thirty-five years ago. El-Buss was completely different then. There were no roads or anything connecting it to Sour.

I turned in the direction of Sour, but it was a ghost town. Not even a stray cat roaming around. They opened the car door and ordered me to get out. So I did. Then they drove off. They just left me there. Even if there had been a house nearby, who would let you in at that hour? Knowing the circumstances. . . . Not only was it extremely late, but there was also the curfew. I was most worried about two things: that there would be some resistance operation or that the Israelis would change their minds and come back for me.

I stayed on the road for an hour or two, praying to God Almighty. I suddenly noticed vast lands behind me, agricultural fields. I heard some noise, as if something had moved in the dirt. To be honest, I froze—I was holding onto a pole, just standing there, leaning on it. I was rooted in place. I wanted to turn and see what was going on behind me, but I didn't dare, so I just froze . . . moments of pure terror. A dog walked up to me and started barking. I was so afraid—What was I supposed to do? The funny part is that four or five other dogs showed up because they heard this one barking, and they all surrounded me. All I could see was their mouths opening and closing. I didn't dare move or try to shoo them away. I was afraid even to breathe. They barked at me for about ten or fifteen minutes, and I didn't move a muscle. I had no idea what to do.

But then I saw headlights in the distance, coming from up ahead. I got even more scared. Alone in the dead of night, what were they going to do to me? I had no idea who it was: it could've been collaborators or some bad type. . . . I was a woman alone. How could I defend myself? Two or three o'clock in the morning, in the dead of night like that. All I could see was a black fog all the way to Sour. No light or anything. I kept watching those headlights getting closer and closer. I didn't dare move a muscle. When it got closer, I could tell it was a truck by the sound, and I started wondering who would dare drive in the night like that. I thought it must be an Israeli truck, what else? I was wearing my abaya; I must've looked like a black pillar. And the sound of the Israeli truck kept getting closer.

When it was right beside me, I could make out that it was civilian. I shouted for the driver to stop. The truck had already passed me, but the driver must have heard or noticed that there was something there in the dark. Fortunately, he didn't ignore me: he backed up to where I was standing. "What are you doing out here at this hour, Hajjeh?" he asked. I begged him to get me out of there, explaining I'd just been released from prison, the Israelis had just left me there. It turned out that he was from Sarafand. Anyway, he let me into his truck, and I asked him to take me wherever he was headed.

I got into the truck and was finally able to breathe because the driver was from my region. To be honest, it was a terrifying night, but I made it through, all thanks to God. The driver even offered to let me sleep the night at his family's house, with his mother and sister. It turned out that I used to know his parents. But I declined and asked him to drop me off at the entrance to the town of Akbiyeh to find a ride to my daughter's house in Baisariyeh.

Later Years

Those were the good old days of the resistance. They recurred again for a while after 1985; we fought a lot back then. Most of my battles were with the Israelis. I never stopped being active in the resistance. And after 1985, Hizbullah used to carry out resistance operations that the AMAL movement would take credit for. Hizbullah hadn't made a name for itself in the South; they weren't part of the scene there yet. But after 1985, when Israel withdrew to the security belt area, we started to make ourselves known.

That's when the skirmishes with the AMAL movement started, too, leading to our major battle with them. May God help them, and may He for-
give Shaykh Subhi al-Tufayli and Nabih Berri. Anyway, we continued our
resistance work and followed the Israelis as they were withdrawing; the
farther back they retreated, the farther ahead we moved. There was a long
line of cars. Members of AMAL even shot at me. They shot each of the four
wheels of my car. I had a huge fight with them.

I also worked with the Martyrs Foundation, with the families of people
who had been martyred. In 1985, I headed a delegation of martyrs' families on a visit to the president: I'd received an invitation from him and was
told that it was an open invitation—I could visit whenever I wanted. They
did, however, also say that a delegation of martyrs' families was going to
the Presidential Palace at 10:00 a.m., and they asked if I would head that
delegation. I agreed. I also founded the al-Rasoul al-Aazam Center for Industry and Commerce—this was before the hospital was established. [The
hospital] was in its early stages, still a field hospital set up when Dahieh
was surrounded during the clashes with the AMAL movement because
before this our wounded would quickly end up martyrs. This was when
AMAL and the Syrians carried out the Fathallah barracks massacre. The
Syrians had completely surrounded and besieged Dahieh, which meant
we had to treat our wounded inside buildings and homes, removing bullets and performing minor surgeries. But some wounded were in worse
shape—they needed actual hospitals, and the Martyrs Foundation was established in response to that.

9

Sanaa Ali Ahmad

"You do what you have to do"

In telling about her imprisonment in chapter 8, Hajjeh Zahra talks about how she would not harm anyone, "even a Communist," as they have a shared struggle against a common enemy. One of the Communist women she is referring to, Sanaa A., was also imprisoned in the notorious Khiam prison in South Lebanon. From a similar class and geographical background as Zahra, Sanaa grew up in a military family in the South. After two of her brothers were killed in a military operation against the occupation, Sanaa became active in the Lebanese Communist Party. She is a lifelong activist and organizer, deeply engaged in her community, and propelled to action by witnessing the pain of her family upon her brothers' death. Also like many of the others in this book, Sanaa was encouraged by and worked closely with family members, especially her only surviving brother, in her political work as a militant with the resistance. Her courage and bravery shine through her narrative, as does the recurring theme of war providing a terrible experience that paradoxically opens up new horizons. Like all of the other women included in this book, Sanaa emphasizes how her participation was something that she felt she "had to do" because of her circumstances.

[b. Blat, 1966]

I am from Blat in the Marjaayoun District in South Lebanon. We were three boys and eight girls in my family growing up.

I was six years old when two of my brothers were martyred. They were in the Lebanese army barracks in Marjaayoun. My father was a retired soldier. When the Israelis attacked the South for the first time in 1978, my brothers went face to face with them. The Israelis surrounded their barracks and ordered them to surrender. They refused. A battle then ensued, and my brothers were martyred. The Israelis took their bodies; they weren't returned to us until the liberation of the South.

I remember that our family fled to the Beqaa when those battles started. We went down to the Litani River and followed it to the Beqaa. We lived in the town of Riyaq from 1978 to 1983, and at the time of the invasion we were still there. My siblings and I went to the Riyaq school. I was very young when we fled Blat. I studied in Riyaq until high school. When you're living under occupation and have lost two brothers as martyrs, and the occupation forces impose themselves on you, you do what you have to do. If your only option is to leave your village, then that's the option you go with.

I have a third brother who was affiliated with the Communist Party and carried out operations against the occupation forces. He would provide the parts that were needed for the other young men to make explosives and bombs. This is the atmosphere I grew up in. I witnessed how devastated my mother was about my martyred brothers. It was very difficult, and the occupiers used to show up at our house all the time. Lahad's lackeys were always making a show of their power. My mother would've filled our kitchen cupboards with food, and they'd throw it all over the ground and stomp on it. But we weren't defeated, and we never surrendered.

Growing up, I witnessed firsthand what the Israelis and Lahad's guys were doing to us, to our families. This creates a drive in a person to defend your country, your dignity, and your honor, even if it is just with words. I began working with my brother in secret, and when they started the Lebanese National Resistance Front [LNRF] groups, I coordinated with them and helped my brother out.

Resistance Work

We returned to Blat during the invasion, in 1982. The resistance was increasingly strong, and people were full of energy. The Lebanese Communist Party asked me to bring uniforms that looked like the Israelis' uniforms, so that our men could carry out operations unnoticed, without being killed. I smuggled some into the occupied zone for them through an officer in Lahad's South Lebanon Army. I told him I needed several uniforms to pass on to our guys. That officer was also one of ours; he was a mole we'd planted in Lahad's army. I got the uniforms and put them in a bag, and I crossed through one of the Israeli checkpoints. They didn't catch me. Our guys showed up wearing uniforms that looked like Israeli army uniforms, and clashes broke out. The Israelis thought they were their own soldiers. After a while, they held another meeting, and our men infiltrated it and gathered intelligence. Then they carried out an operation on al-Rihan Mountain and in the village of Sojod, which is across from Blat. A man from Lahad's army was on watch, and he saw them, so he reported that so-and-so had shown up and helped the people who had carried out the operation. Then our mole in Lahad's army confessed. Once a spy, always a spy.

Lahad's army had planted their own spies in the Communist Party and were plotting with them. But our operation succeeded nonetheless. The person working for Lahad who had been surveilling meeting spots reported on the house where a meeting had been held. The woman whose house the meeting had taken place in told her brother, and her brother informed Lahad's security forces. He assumed that the LNRF group would return and meet in the same house. But I found out about this and told people not to go back to there because the Israelis had people's names.

The leadership within Lahad's army asked our mole, "Can you help us get them?" He said yes. And then this officer started asking one of the young men when they were coming back. This aroused his suspicions, and he let the rest know not to return. My brother was among them. Had they gone back, they would've killed them. They wouldn't have even arrested them or anything. It's unfortunate that such a despicable person like that mole, who then collaborated with the Zionists against us, has been left to roam free by the Lebanese state even after liberation.

The mole who was planted by the Communist Party was the officer who had reported which house the LNRF was meeting in. But this officer was following the party's every move, gathering information, and reporting it back to his fellow collaborators. After that incident, our mole got caught, the questioning led back to me, and I was arrested and taken to prison.

Under interrogation, they asked him if he knew me, and he said, "Yes, she's the one I give the intelligence to." I was beaten badly. He's a coward; he confessed after the first slap. I endured severe beatings. Even now, I do a lot of interviews, but I still to this day don't mention the names of my contacts in the LNRF in case they're wanted by Israel. Whenever I'm asked, I just say that people used to help me. I never name them at all. But our mole got slapped once, and he confessed straight away. When I was arrested, and they put us in a room together, I told him, "You're a liar." He said, "No, you're the liar." Why did the party even choose him? He drinks, he uses drugs—he's never sober. Pick someone who's up to the job! When you're up against an enemy, an occupier, you have to man up . . . whether you're a man or a woman. You need to have the strength to stand up to them without flinching.

Arrest

Anyway, they arrested me, and the following day I still hadn't confessed. There were others who were part of the operation, too, and I wanted to give them the chance to flee because I knew that once the word was out, everyone would find out what was going on. Once they found out that I'd been arrested, they'd have a chance to spread the word and escape.

They arrested me to make me confess. But what information did they actually have? They had nothing on me. Israel has its dogs sniffing out information and reporting back. That's what Israel does. I had a lot of information, but I didn't tell them a thing. Despite the torture, I didn't say a word. I only repeated what our mole had already confessed. His role was only to get the uniforms. He didn't know what my role was. My relationship with him was limited to "Hello, get the uniforms." That was it. He had nothing to do with anything else. I was the one who had relationships with the rest, but he didn't know that. He knew some things, but I knew others.

They put us face to face with each other, and I told the interrogators that he was lying. He started saying, "Confess, Sanaa, they know everything." I told them it was true that I'd taken the uniforms from him.

The interrogator asked me, "Where did you smuggle it through?"

I said I smuggled it through the checkpoint.

"Which checkpoint?"

"Right in front of your lackeys. Why didn't you search me?" I swore as well.

He said, "You're a rude one."

I replied, "I'm not rude. You asked me where I smuggled the uniform through, and I'm telling you I smuggled it right under your dogs' noses. If you're so good at patrolling, how come you didn't catch it?"

"Who helped you?"

"I forget. I don't know." I didn't want the others to get caught. I was trying to give them the chance to escape.

"Who?" he asked again. I was being beaten up really badly, and I just said, "I forget. There were people . . . they came and took the uniforms from me."

"Who were the people who took them from you?" I kept telling him I didn't know them.

The threats kept coming, rape threats too. It was all to pressure me to speak, but I told him, "I've said what I have to say. What he's saying matches what I'm telling you."

"If you're doing such things, there are bound to be other people working with you."

"They just told me to work with this officer. I haven't been at it very long."

In fact, I'd been working with them for quite a while, but no one knew. Believe me, they try their best to break you. Once you're done with the interrogation, it's time for round two: beatings, torture, and even death. Believe me, I was strong when I entered prison, and I was strong when I left. I'm still strong to this day. I never cried or showed weakness in front of the enemy. The torture was very intense. I'll tell you about something that happened to me one night. I'd been without food for two days. I told a female guard that I needed a drink of water. She said there wasn't any. I said, "I'm thirsty. I need to drink." The interrogator came and told the guard, "She wants to drink."

Now these were Lahad's people. The Israelis hire their lackeys but keep watch from afar. They pay attention to what's going on; they don't depend on the interrogators alone. They supervise. They're listening. They disrespect their own agents and collaborators, and they respect those who stand their ground. This even was the case with me. I'll tell you the rest of the story now.

They had an empty *halawa* container that had traces of leftover tomato sauce in it. The female guard put some water in it for me to drink. I threw it back in her face, asking, "Why would you give this to me? How could you put water in this used dirty container and expect me to drink it?" I threw it right in her face. The interrogator came in and yelled at her. He asked her, "Why are you giving her water in that?" The guard replied, "She wanted a drink." I said, "The hell with the way you treat people here. And you want us, the resistance, to submit to you?! I won't drink anymore. I don't want to drink."

Then the interrogator went back into his office and brought me a glass of water. I said, "I don't want to drink." I didn't drink for two days after that. I said to the guard, "Uncuff me and just let me get my hands on you. Then you'll see who will win." They're such cowards.

Anyway, one day she said, "She won't confess. You need to pin her against the wall with her arms over her head." I told her, "I've said all I have to say." My tactic was to delay the interrogation as long as I could, so I could give my siblings and their friends more time to escape. If I could help them get away, I would because if they got caught, it would be disastrous. She ordered me to stand against the wall and put my arms over my head. Some officers came in and pulled out a bed. They said, "We're going to have a long night together unless you confess." They meant to imply that they would rape me.

"I don't have anything to add. I said all I have to say."

The officers became very rude and yelled at me. Ask Kifah [Afifi]: she was there with me! That day, Kifah and the other girls in that prison heard about this and liked me immediately, before even having met me. They liked me because they'd heard so much about how I acted during interrogations and my boldness—that's a trait we all shared!

The interrogation ended; they closed the case file, and I was moved to the cell block, where I met the rest of the girls. Some had medical conditions, some were under extreme emotional duress. Some girls hadn't done anything at all, really, and were being held for no reason. Trust me on that. They hadn't done anything, either outside prison or inside. Believe me, the women who actively participated in the resistance and were arrested entered and left prison with unfaltering strength. But the other women, those who hadn't done anything . . . they felt that their entire lives had fallen to pieces as soon as they entered prison. So many women's lives were destroyed. They hadn't had any role in the resistance, which meant that they didn't have any belief to sustain them while inside. They were discounted both inside and outside of prison and even in their roles as wives and mothers. Everything was doomed to fail. I've kept up with many of them; I'd know.

Khiam Prison

In prison, they used to bring us olives with breakfast. We would save the pits and whittle them. There was this girl from the Harb family who made a needle out of a piece of wire. I wish I still had it. But I lost it. We used to pull threads out of our wool sweaters and make rosaries with them. We hid them in our clothes, and we'd take them with us even to the shower because as soon as we went to the bathroom, our cells would be raided and searched. The guards searched the cells. We had many confrontations with these guards, several confrontations, but if you stayed strong, they didn't dare mess with you. The female guards were from Marjaayoun, our areas, from the villages of al-Kherbe and Qlaiaa, and it was as if they were already thinking about what would happen after all of this ended. But I was fierce. I was really strong. They were the enemy, and that meant that I wouldn't engage in a give-and-take with any of them. There were lines I would not cross.

Sometimes they'd be so lenient with me that some of my fellow prisoners would say, "If we didn't know how strong she is, we'd think she were a collaborator!" They knew that the guards treated me well because they were afraid of me. I asked those female guards once, "Why are you so lenient with me? If I so much as see you outside, outside this prison, you can be sure that I'll put a bullet straight through your head."

"Would you really do that?" one of them responded.

"I would, I swear to God. I don't compromise when it comes to the blood of a martyr or someone's dignity. Don't you forget that two of my brothers were martyred, and your people still have not returned their bodies. You think if you treat me a little better than the others that you're absolving yourself for when this is over? Do you really think that when I see you in our area in the South, I'll have mercy on you? In your dreams. If I could have my way with you right now, right here in this prison, I'd bury you right where you're standing."

We had this window facing the al-Dardara Valley, and one time I was talking through it with the women in another cell. A guard opened the window and said, "Get the hell down from the window."

"You bitch, who do you think you're talking to, telling *me* to get the hell down from the window? If you call yourself a guard, open the door right now and come in here," I told her.

She ran away back to her office, and I started banging on my cell door. She filed a report on me, claiming I'd cursed at her, so they put me in solitary confinement for three days. I mocked the warden and said to him, "Three days? OK, three days then."

My cellmates and I talked things over at night, and we decided to stage a protest. They would smuggle food to the bathroom for me, and we'd all say I was on a hunger strike. We really cooperated with each other, there was a lot of love; we loved each other. For example, if my comrade needed something, I'd leave it in the toilet tank lid for her. There was one toilet that was out of order, so its tank was empty. There was mutual affection and camaraderie. We'd do anything for each other. Like if someone's family was far away, and she needed a change of clothes or some other thing, we'd leave it for her in the toilet tank. When her turn came to shower, she'd take them from the tank. They had no idea what we did. They had no idea, as long as nobody informed. We used to help each other, and we loved each other. Those were the good times. Even now, whenever we see each other, we remember those days fondly. I could talk forever about the suffering we endured in prison. There is so much to say. Once a prisoner starts talking, she'll never stop. There will always be more to say. Every minute, every second, is so full of suffering; even the space between the minutes is filled with suffering.

The hardest days were holidays. You miss your family and long for them so much. You don't know how long you're going to be in prison; there is no sentence; they just lock you in and leave you there. Some women I asked said they had been there for two, three, four years. And all the while you have no news about any of your relatives. You long for your family, but there's a wall between you and them, and you don't know anything about what's going on with them. It's the worst when there's a holiday or some anniversary. . . . All of this scars you. But you have to be brave and try not to be affected by it. Some women used to cry—each person has a different breaking point. Some women were able to withstand it; others weren't. But we were all strong. We used to sing, entertain each other, joke around. We had to pass the time somehow.

We invented our own games. We used to peel oranges, dry out the peels and use a bar of soap to draw a checkers board on a piece of black cloth. We played on that.

One morning they brought us rotten fava beans; there were worms inside. When they opened the door and said, "Sanaa, come take your breakfast." I said, "What is this? What is it? Worms and cockroaches!" The other women heard me. I said, "What are we, animals?! The state is providing at least one or two dollars of food per prisoner per day. Our food comes from the Lebanese state. And you bring us rotten food? Is Israel the one feeding us? Had it been Israel feeding us, they would've closed down the prison and left."

Anyway, the guard said, "We'll bring in the nurse to examine the food."

I told her, "Go get him then! What the hell, this food is inedible. You think I'm making this up?!"

I closed the door and hopped up to the window. I warned my cellmates, "Ladies, the fava beans are completely rotten. When they bring the food, don't take it. If anyone does, they'll have me to answer to. When the guards are out of sight, you'll have hell to pay! We won't take their food. I don't care how upset you are. We won't eat."

The next day they brought us bulgur cooked in tomato sauce. We could smell that the semolina was rotten. Some women ate, and they told me to come eat with them. I said, "No, thank you, I don't want any." I don't even know what food they brought us that night. Something clicked inside me, and I just refused to eat. They used to give us an apple or orange with lunch, and two days into my refusal to eat, they'd given us an orange. I was hungry, and I ate it. At eleven o'clock, I asked my cellmates, "Is there any bread, girls?" They said they'd only eaten plain bread that day. I knocked on the door three times. It was a code we'd agreed to use. Someone responded, and I asked her if they had any bread. She said yes. I threw her my scarf, and she put some bread in it and fastened the scarf around it. I pulled it back to me. There were also some dry orange peels. I swear, I ate those, too; I put them in the bread and ate them together like a sandwich. They said, "What are you doing?!" I said I couldn't take it any longer. I felt dizzy. I was very skinny. They said, "You're crazy!" I told them I'd eat anything . . . a monkey, even the sewage outside. When you're in prison, you'd even eat poison. They asked me, "How come you didn't eat the fava beans?" I said, "They were rotten! There were cockroaches in there. I swear there were cockroaches on them."

I told the guards, "If you're going to give us this food, I'm going to complain and make a big fuss!" They didn't change anything back then. But that story about the orange peels, it really means a lot to me. Sometimes I think about how I dared eat that food. We really suffered a lot, but those were really great times, too, I swear.

We never really argued with each other, but we did have some differences of opinion. Like if one of us was more partial to Hizbullah or the AMAL movement. There was a lot of love for each other; our suffering was one. If someone got upset, it would only last five minutes, then everyone would make up. There really wasn't any hostility or hatred. None at all. I spent two years and two months in a cell with Nawal Baidoun. After three months of interrogation, I was sent to the cell she was in, where I used to see her pacing up and down. She was under extreme psychological pressure, in really bad shape, and she was skinny, skinny, skinny. I asked the other girls, "Why is she like this?" and they'd say, "Let her be."

"But why is she like that?"

She wouldn't talk to anyone; she didn't really engage with them. But I started talking to her, asking her about what was going on in the outside world. I felt like she was really smart, but the others didn't understand her. Because she was under intense psychological pressure and emotionally fragile, the other women kind of recoiled from her. She's a schoolteacher from Bint Jbeil; she's very respectable. She was brought to prison, and that was that.

Resistance and Militancy, Political and Personal Reflections

I'm tough. It's all the suffering. . . . First of all, two of my brothers were martyred. It was hard on us as a family. We used to see how devastated my mother was, crying out for her two martyred sons. We'd go demand that their bodies be returned to us, and they'd tell us, "They're not here. Leave." This all creates a lot of hatred and hostility and makes you want to take revenge on the enemy. They only returned my brothers' bodies to us in 2000, the year of the liberation of the South. They had been kept in the Marjaayoun barracks—there were around twenty-three young men that the enemy had buried there in the area. By nature, I'm quite courageous, and I have been since I was much younger. When I was being held in Khiam prison, my courage only increased. All that suffering makes you stronger.

But I've always been courageous. Had I not been, I wouldn't have marched into the office of one of Lahad's South Lebanon Army officers and told him I wanted a man's uniform. I didn't even know him, and he had no clue who I was, either. I said to him, "I want you to bring me some uniforms from storage. I need two that have the Israeli star on them."

The guys had sent me to his office, and he ended up helping me. But he was wearing Lahad's army uniform, after all, so he could very well have reported on me. He handed me the uniform, and I took it and left. This officer was from my village, from Blat. After I took the uniform, I hid it in the lining of my suitcase and crossed through the Kfar Tebnit checkpoint on my way to Saida. I had taken a risk and told the taxi driver who went to Saida what I was doing. He refused to take me and told me he didn't want any trouble. He seemed to be a patriotic man since he didn't report me; I think he was afraid. I reassured him that I wasn't going to cause him any problems. I've always been courageous, but I became more so in Khiam. My bravery multiplied tenfold. I became stronger, and I'm still standing tall today despite all the suffering I've endured. What do you think? Am I strong or not?

You say I am the model of strength? I'll tell you something, I'm not afraid. I'm bold and frank. I don't lie. If you hurt me, I don't vent to a third party about it; I confront you to your face. You know? Like, for example, when the ladies told me that Sayyid Hassan Nasrallah had honored a girl who'd been a collaborator in prison. I didn't hold back. I didn't care. I didn't care about his turban or his title. "Why would you put us in such a situation? Why would you honor her, specifically? There are so many Communist women infinitely more honorable than her. At least they were arrested and released with their integrity intact."

Even if these women didn't belong to any party, the fact that they were arrested and suffered at the hands of the enemy should be enough. Even though I was active, my party never really followed me closely. But now I feel like they wanted me to join their ranks because they saw how tough and brave I was. Even though there are many women in the party, there aren't many like this.

Even if you gave me a million dollars, I would never betray a fellow activist or give up a resistance fighter. I wouldn't even say a word about them. I was interrogated numerous times in prison, and I never said one word about the people who had helped me. I never gave them up, and I wouldn't have sold them out, no matter what. I knew a lot about them, and I used to see them in action. Still, I never said a word. I had gone into that field willingly, and despite the beatings I endured, I knew I wouldn't talk. I still suffer to this day from pain in my feet, rheumatism, and backaches. I suffer from so many different pains. I really suffer. They tortured me. They used whips and electric shocks and water. You name it. I suffered so much, it's a wonder I'm still in my right mind and have the ability to talk to people and understand them. Alhamdulillah, it's a blessing.

They used many methods of torture—electric shocks, whips, they'd make you kneel, and then they'd stomp all over your feet . . . but the psychological torture was even worse than the physical pain. Sometimes you'd be withheld food for a long time. . . . They always used to threaten you while name-dropping your family members—"I'm going to bring your mother and father and sister, and I'm going to do this and this and that"—pure psychological torture. But that didn't break me, I swear to God. It didn't work on me. I'd taunt him back, "Go ahead, bring them in. Do what you have to do!" He'd say, "We're going to bring your sister in," and I'd tell him, "Bring whoever you want! This is all the information I have. I have nothing else to say!"

They would threaten, but there was no sexual assault. No, no, no. Let them try! It was just empty threats. They'd threaten that they were going to do this and that to me, but I knew they wouldn't actually do those things. I knew they wouldn't sexually assault anyone because they didn't want to risk getting anyone pregnant and then have children to deal with. They just wanted information. The rest was just lies. There was this interrogator I could tell was Druze from his name: Yahya Abu Qamar, from the village of Mari. I had been beaten up really badly, and he'd witnessed the beatings. He asked me, "What's wrong?" I said, "Nothing."

"Are you in pain?"

"No." I said to him, "I don't feel pain when I get hit. Even if you were to beat me with a whip"—and then he interrupted me and said, "I didn't hit you."

I continued, "You think if you beat me with a whip and make me kneel on the ground, you're hurting me?! Think again! I never once cried out in pain, and I never once cried any tears. Not one tear! Or haven't you noticed?"

"That's what I wanted to ask you about."

"It didn't hurt. You might as well have been hitting the wall. I swear to God."

"Let me ask you something. With how much they beat you with that whip, how come you didn't once cry out in pain? Others, men, would scream and beg for the beatings to stop!"

I told him it hadn't hurt and that actually for me it felt like nothing more than a passing breeze. I swear to God, he then told me, "I don't want to interrogate you." I swear on my mother's grave, he unlocked my handcuffs and took the bag off my face and said, "I want to talk to you. For heaven's sake, just tell me what your deal is!" And I wondered what *his* deal was—he's an interrogator!

Then he said, "Do you want some water?"

"No, thank you. If I want to drink, I'll drink in my cell. I won't take one drop from any of you. Not one drop. I could be dying of thirst, and I wouldn't take any water from you."

"Coffee?"

"No, thank you. And you'd better not think that you can buy me off with a cup of water or coffee."

"God, no. It's just that yesterday my own skin hurt from watching them beat you so roughly. And you didn't even flinch."

"Why do you think that is? It's because I don't give a damn. Do whatever you want, wallah."

The interrogator was telling me that just watching me get beaten up and whipped the day before had been painful for him and that in the next room there were young men screaming for their own torture to stop. If only you could've seen the blood and whips on the floor. I don't blame those men for screaming out in pain. You should've seen the size of those whips.

After he undid my handcuffs and lifted the bag covering my face, the interrogator said he wanted to ask me something. "With all the torture that rained down on you yesterday, I kept waiting for you to just ask them to stop."

What he doesn't know is that when you're arrested, you go to prison to die, not to collaborate with the enemy. You don't go to prison just to be weak and to stoop to their level. Right? People were humiliated, and for what? I'd die with my dignity, or I wouldn't have joined the resistance in the first place. Do you see what I mean? Why would you join and struggle with the resistance and then change sides and work with the enemy once arrested?

Resistance Work and the Communist Party

We used to work—I started this kind of work automatically; I was motivated to join the resistance without anyone having to ask me to. I did the work without any training. I love resistance work. No one had to tell me about it or ask me to join the struggle; I was the one who presented myself. I knew I'd either die or be arrested. It was out of a personal sense of duty that I wanted to offer something to my land, my country, my people. Unfortunately, though some people respect, love, and appreciate you for this, many others have renounced me because of it.

A lot of potential suitors refused to marry me. You know how it goes. They think maybe there's something wrong with you, or maybe you've been assaulted. I'd tell them, "You're likely to end up with someone you met at a bar! Here's someone who's been released from prison—and you're all so lost in your prejudice against her you can't understand that she's never been touched!" Unfortunately, that's how things go. But believe me, the drive to offer help and join the resistance really came from me. If only they had let us continue down that path, we would've accomplished so much more. You know . . .

I found out that someone had presented my name to the Communist Party back then and told them that I shouldn't be left behind since my situation was very challenging. You know what I mean? It was sad, you know, it was a sad situation with what had happened within my family, but I'm proud of the drive that I had personally. So many people joined the party and received payments from it but never did anything worthwhile. The party asked me to do very little—the initiative came from me. My family and I gave a lot and suffered a lot, too. My brother was arrested, and I grew up watching them hatching their plans and building their bombs. I witnessed them getting ready to go plant those bombs, how they'd leave at night and set them up somewhere. This really made me love them. I was so young back then, and I saw how much my mother suffered, with two of my brothers martyred. All of this is what set me up. I just grew to love this work; I felt like I needed to do something to avenge my brothers. I'm sure you know what I mean.

I worked for and admired the party because it operates honestly and transparently. I helped them in ways they weren't necessarily aware of. That ended up being better than joining their ranks officially. You know? It was when I was released from prison that they brought me in. And now they consider me to be one of them, but circumstance stood in the way of me continuing my work. Whenever there's a protest or celebration, I join them; I know people there now, and the party really considers me to be one of them. In party terms, I belong to them because I worked for them. I was arrested in their name. But the party doesn't give you your strength. If you don't have it already, the party can't give it to you. It must come from within. That's why Abu Wahid liked me so much—because I have that strength.

I'm proud of myself. Some people say that my strength is masculine, but I refuse to subscribe to this kind of thinking. I'm in control of my own space, and no one dares come violate that. Why be otherwise? Why be meek and let people boss me around? Why stoop to that level? If you aren't strong, you won't succeed. Right? But I'm fair. I don't like it when people try to deceive or hurt me. I treat people fairly so long as they do the same. That's how I function.

Within the party, though, I did sometimes experience discrimination as a woman and find that men had more privileges. There were a few young men, they'd been arrested, who really wanted to be the center of attention after their release. They were always thinking about themselves and themselves alone. But all of us had done similar work! The mere fact of getting arrested and being held by the enemy means that you will be tortured, even if you're not affiliated with any specific party. Those working with them and against them, whoever really, everyone will go through the same process. But the whole point is whether you keep going or give up. If you stand your ground and maintain your position against the enemy all throughout your time in prison, any party should welcome you into its fold once you are released. Your experience has proven that you believe in a cause and were arrested, but you have maintained your dignity since your arrest resulted from confronting the enemy. Even after release, you held on to your honor. Other people . . . I was in the party myself, and I witnessed how some people would show off. I'd be in meetings with them, and after I saw that behavior, I left the party. Now I've joined them again. I'm hoping something will come out of the Communist Party after all. We hope to get some things done. They assured me that they have my name on file at the leadership office in Beirut, so I've officially joined their ranks.

Release

I was arrested in 1989 and released in 1991, so I was inside for three years. When you get out, the state should welcome you, respect you, honor you at least. Unfortunately, we experienced none of that. After we were released, we started meeting in Beirut; this was before Rafic Hariri was martyred in 2005. The state should acknowledge women prisoners. We were just a few women and were demanding that the state create a monthly stipend for us, at least five hundred thousand Lebanese pounds [around US$300]. Some of the women had no family, and some had never gone to school.

The idea was that, for example, in case someone got married and her husband turned out not to be a good person, she'd be able to rely on this monthly stipend from the state. But then they started focusing on the minutiae. Some women formed a committee, but each person was only looking out for herself and her own affairs. I was excluded, and a lot of other women were excluded, too. I was one of those people who were left behind.

I always used to participate whenever I heard about a protest. I'd be the first one there; I'd arrive at two in the afternoon and return home after eleven at night. I was always in the streets, all over, but so many others didn't join me. The people getting paid were those who never participated. It's those who were left out that did. Unfortunately. Had I not been tough, had a strong personality, and landed myself a job—and, remember, my employer was a good person, he was sympathetic to my activism as he also had a family member who'd been martyred and thus appreciated my role in the struggle—had all of this not been the case, I would've ended up just like everybody else, without a job. You need connections to get a job. No matter how educated you are, you need connections; otherwise, you won't find work.

They'd ask, "What party are you affiliated with?"

"The Communist Party."

"Let them get you a job."
You know what I mean?

Problematic Partisanship

The same is true of health care. After I was released from prison, I went to the Council for South Lebanon, controlled by Nabih Berri, to ask for financial support for the dental problems caused by the beatings I'd suffered on my face. When we were released from prison, our finances were tight. Riad Abdallah kept trying to get me to collaborate with him. He was part of the Israeli Mossad, from Khiam. This happened around 1991. I told him I wouldn't work with him. He threatened to take me back to Khiam prison, and I said, "I was there for three years. I'm willing to go back for another thirty, no problem. But I won't work for you. Whatever! I miss my friends anyway. I'll go back there willingly. But I'll never work for you." They kept after me, so I left and moved to Saida in 1991. Back then, moving from your village to the city, it took some time to settle in and for people to get used to you. I stayed with my brother until I finally found work in 1996. I got myself a job.

More women had started moving here to Saida from the village, and by chance they moved to the same area I live in now. We are all from the same area, and we happened to have moved very close to each other. But we didn't even know one another! It was pure coincidence that we started spotting each other in the shops. They told me that the Council for South Lebanon was providing medical services. I said, "I've just started working, and I went to see a dentist. I'm going to fix my teeth. The whole thing will cost $600. I'll break it down into $100 payments to the dentist every month. I don't need the Council of the South."

But then one of them, a devout veiled woman, said, "I fixed my teeth with their help. You should go! Yours are worse than mine were; you should've gone way before I did! Go see them, take your medical chart and present it to them."

"You think so?" I asked her, and she said she'd even go with me.

Long story short, we got my medical chart, which said it would cost me around $1,200 to fix my teeth. I told my doctor to change the total to

$600 because there was no way the council would agree to cover the whole cost. I'd pay the other half out of my own pocket. He agreed, and off we went. When we got there, the receptionist at the council looked at me and asked, "What party are you affiliated with?"

"The Communist Party."

"Let them pay your medical expenses," she said.

"This is how you're categorizing people now?" I asked her, and she said yes. I said, "No problem."

"You're always welcome here, please come again!" she told me. She had no idea what I was about to do.

I humiliated the Council of the South in *As-Safir* newspaper because of how they'd treated me. I swear it was brutal. I wish I had the issue so I could show it to you. Doha Chams herself came all the way here to interview me. The title of the interview was "The Brave Woman Sanaa Ali Ahmad." I couldn't get my hands on any copy of that issue after 1997 or 1998.

I headed back to the Council of the South after that. They were really angry, and they made that pretty clear to me. They even kicked me out. Then they phoned me. It was that same lady, the receptionist, on the phone.

"Yes?" I asked.

"Are you Sanaa Ali Ahmad?" she asked.

"Yes I am."

"You've said some pretty bad things about the Council of the South in *As-Safir* newspaper. You need to publish an apology in that paper and say you were wrong," she said.

I told her, "Keep dreaming. You think I'd ever take back what I say? Weren't you the one who told me to go seek help from my own party?"

"I don't remember."

"If you don't remember, I'll remind you. It was 9:30–10:00 in the morning, and you were sitting there all wrapped up in your hijab. You asked me what party I was affiliated with, and I said the Communist Party. To which you replied, 'Get your help from the Communist Party then.' I said thank you, but you thought I was coming here to beg and go on my way. Are you happy with the result now? I said what I said, and you and your Council of the South can do what you want, I won't take anything back. I said what I said."

She stayed on the line for almost an hour and a half. She said I had until the next day to publicly apologize. I told her, "Keep dreaming! The Zionists were here and couldn't control me any more than you're trying to. You think a bitch like you can shut me up?"

She said they were going to contact Doha and tell her to retract the article.

"Do whatever you want. I won't withdraw a thing. And if Doha retracts the interview, I'll complain publicly." I called Doha myself and told her what had happened, and I was very pleased to hear her say, "Let them dream on. I couldn't believe I'd finally gotten my hands on a story like yours—it's not going anywhere."

Doha is great! She's a really nice and likeable person. She came all the way to my house, and we hit it off instantly. She told me I was very brave. University students from the Lebanese American University came along for the interview, and they recorded it on a CD that they still have. They said they'd give me a copy.

I've told Doha several times that I want a copy of the issue the interview was published in. It's important for me to have it. She lent it to a Lebanese American University student to help her with her research, but she hasn't returned it to Doha yet. It's my fault for having given it to her in the first place back in 1997!

After Prison

I left prison as strong as when I got there. I landed myself a job, and I stayed strong. I married, and that didn't work out, but I'm still strong. I got married in 2006 and divorced in 2017. I was the one who asked for the divorce. I didn't want to be married anymore because when you have a certain history, when you've been part of the resistance struggle, and someone comes along and tries to treat you as less than, as inferior, you really don't have to accept it. Even the enemy wasn't able to discount me or control me! *You knew what my commitments were when we married, and you told me it was fine.* But he forbade me from participating in any celebrations, and he'd stop me from meeting with my comrades, male and female. *Why would you want to marginalize me like this? What gives you the right?* I found myself in a situation I didn't want to be in anymore. Whenever you say the word *prisoners*, he loses it! Stop! Why did he agree to marry me then?! I agreed to this because he'd seemed to embrace all of me; I thought he was going to help me make up for all my suffering. *But you turned out to be even worse than them. That's why I left you.*

We met in Saida, and he seemed like a decent, respectable guy. But later it turned out that he was one person in public and someone else entirely in private. My deepest desire had been to find someone who had also been in prison. Even if he was unable to care for himself anymore, I wouldn't have minded; I would have stayed with him and looked after him for the rest of our lives. No matter what, we wouldn't get upset with each other. We would understand each other's suffering and stick with each other through it all. I don't know. But there's no way I'd go back now. I won't leave one prison for another. God forbid. I'm comfortable now, with my work and my home; I don't have to answer to anyone. I'm doing well. My parents have passed, and my sisters are all married.

No one ever pressured me to stay married or get remarried. They stood by me and understood that I was suffering with him. They said, "As long as you're strong and doing what you know is right, it's nobody's business." That's life. You're set so long as you can think straight. Just look at me: I did the right thing, and I'm okay; I'm living alone and working and have never needed help from anyone.

Acknowledgments

Appendix

Reading Guide

Bibliography

Index

Acknowledgments

What the War Left Behind is the culmination of years of work in a large project, "Women's War Stories: Building an Archive of Women and the Lebanese Civil War," that we coauthors and translators have worked on from 2016 to the present. The project has been deeply collaborative from its inception, and thus acknowledgments hardly cover the extent of the ways that numerous people need to be both thanked and honored. The people listed here are only some of the many who worked on and discussed the project with us. People contributed to the book in diverse ways. We apologize for any omissions.

First and foremost, we thank all of the women who participated in the "Women's War Stories" project. They, of course, include not only the eight women whose stories are featured here but also all the other women we interviewed and talked to as part of the larger project and those who facilitated our meeting other women.

Next, we thank the artist Tagreed Darghouth, who generously has allowed us to use art from her collection "The Tree Within." This is the second time that her beautiful artwork has graced the cover of a book we put together, and we are grateful for this.

The "Women's War Stories" project was funded largely by an Insight Grant from the Social Sciences and Humanities Research Council of Canada (SSHRC). We would like to acknowledge our departments at McGill University for support during the tenure of the project—the Institute of Islamic Studies and the Department of History and Classical Studies.

We would also like to acknowledge the work of the editors, including copy editors, at Syracuse University Press and mention here the press's commitment to publishing academic work on Lebanon. We profoundly thank the anonymous reviewers of the manuscript for their thorough readings, helpful corrections, and thought-provoking comments on the manuscript.

At McGill University, many undergraduate and graduate researchers participated in different ways in the larger project and elements of this book. We would like to acknowledge here the work of Hanine El Diri, Ralph Haddad, Nayla Joy Zayn, Reem Abdulmajid, Heather Porter-Abu Deiab, and Layal Sami. We would also like to single out Sarah Abdel-Shamy's contributions as a graduate researcher who dedicated a great deal of effort to the project.

Another graduate researcher and translator, Caline Nasrallah, deserves her own section of thanks. Caline participated in and was dedicated to this project from the beginning, working on some of the most difficult and time-consuming parts of it without fail. During the COVID pandemic, Caline and Michelle worked with hours of interview material, translating and at times retranscribing them. This project and this book owe a great deal to Caline's dedication and translational skills.

We also thank the following people who contributed in many different ways to making this project a success. We extend our profound gratitude to Fatme Charafeddine from the American University of Beirut library as well as Tawfiq Mansuri (Abou-Wahid), Muhammad Hashisho, Afif al-Sayyid, Bachir Osmat, Rima Saab, Raed H. Charafeddine, Ahmad Shahhal, Samah Idriss, Jamal Wakim, Sami Ofeish, Tony Haykal, Abdel Razzaq Takriti, Abdul Haleem Fadlallah, Liliane Hamzé, Wehbe Hamzeh, Khalid Halabi, Hassane El-Achkar, Najat Mahmoud El-Achkar, Hayat Mahmoud Chaker, Wajih Abi Saab, Nada Saab, Janan Jurdi, Ghazi Abi Saab, Aziz Choudry, Katy Kalemkerian, and Layla Younes.

Michelle would also like to extend a big thanks to Yasmine Nachabe Taan as well as to the larger Nachabe, Fakih, Taan, Merhej family for help, hosting, and support in Lebanon over the many years of this project (and more). Yasmine's contributions—personal and professional—have helped to shape this book and this project. Thank you, Yasmine, for always being ready to talk about work!

Finally, we both extend a special, singular thanks to the person without whom this book would not be what it is today, Rula Jurdi Abisaab. Thank you, Rula, for everything you have done for this book and this project. This book is for you.

Sample Consent Forms
in Arabic and English

Participant Informed Consent Form in Arabic

(استمارة موافقة مسبقة لمشارك (مشاركون

رقم الاسم:

أنتِ مدعوة للمشاركة في مشروع البحث التالي:

قصص عن نساء في الحرب: بناء أرشيف للنساء والحرب الأهلية اللبنانية

ا-الباحثون:

ميشيل هارتمان: أستاذة، معهد الدراسات الإسلامية،

michelle.hartman@mcgill.ca

مالك أبي صعب، أستاذ، قسم التاريخ/ معهد الدراسات الإسلامية،

malek.abisaab@mcgill.ca

جامعة مكغيل، مونتريال، مقاطعة كيبك، كندا هاتف: ****514-398 1 00

برعاية: مجلس بحوث العلوم الاجتماعية والإنسانية في كندا (SSHRC)

ب-هدف البحث:

جمع قصص من نساء عايشن الحرب الأهلية في لبنان حول تجاربهن الخاصة . أي أن المقصود هو تجميع ما أمكن من قصص لفهم ما واجهته النساء ودراسة العوامل المؤثرة عليهن خلال هذه الفترة. وبالتالي فإن هذه المعلومات والقصص ستُستخدم لدراسة وتحليل حياة المرأة ودورها في المجتمع خلال الحرب. كذلك ستصبح هذه القصص والمعلومات متوفرة لجمهور الباحثين وذلك من أجل تعميم المعرفة والفائدة العلمية ولاطلاع العالم على تجارب ومعاناة المرأة في لبنان وما واجهنه من تحديات ومسؤليات وادوار قمن بها خلال الحرب.

ج-طريقة إجراء المقابلات:

سنطلب من السيدات والآنسات اللواتي وافقن على المشاركة في هذا المشروع أن يروين لنا قصصهن المميزة التي خبرنها خلال الحرب. وسنقوم نحن بدورنا بتسجيل هذه القصص على مسجلات رقمية

بالطبع بعد موافقتك الخطية. إن المعلومات التي أعطيتها لنا ممن اختيارك ستطرح للمناقشة والدراسة من قبل افراد او مجموعات اكادمية تهتم بدراسة المرأة في الشرق الأوسط. قد تستغرق هذه المقابلة-الحوار ساعة أو أكثر وسيقوم بإجرائها أحدنا أو كلانا. أما مكان إجراء المقابلة فسيتم بالتشاور بين الطرفين بما يتلائم مع ظروف كل منا.

د-ملاحظة:

بأمكانك أن تطلبين إيقاف المقابلة او حتى إلغاؤها ساعة تشائين. كذلك نود إعلامك أننا لن نسمح لأحد الاطلاع على مضمون المقابلة وما جاء فيها غير أعضاء فريق العمل. ولا يمكن لأحد خارج هذا الفريق الأطلاع بدون موافقة كل أعضاء فريق البحث.

ه-المخاطر والمضايقات:

نعلم أن قصص الحرب ممكن أن تكون مزعِجة وأن أيام الحرب كانت صعبة. لذلك، قد تشعرين باعتلالات نفسية أو عاطفية. إذا واجهت هذا في أي وقت، من حقكِ إيقاف المقابلة فوراً. ممكنك أن تطلبين إيقاف المقابلة لبرهة، أو أخذ استراحة، أو طلب إكمال المقابلة في وقتٍ لاحق. إن هذا لن يؤثر على علاقتك مع الباحثين، أو مشروع البحث أو الجامعة أو أي طرف أخر. تجدر الاشارة الى أن إجراء مقابلة بين شخص وشخص تكون عادةً أكثر مريحة من المقابلة بين شخص ومجموعة فيرجى منك أخذ العلم أنك تستطيعين إيقاف المقابلة عند شعورك بعدم الراحة.

و-المشاركة:

يجب التأكيد على النقاط التالية:

أولاً: المشاركة الاختيارية، يجب التأكيد بدايةً أن مشاركتك في هذا البحث هي، وبشكل كلي، تطوعية إختيارية. إن هذا يعني أنه بإمكانك رفض الاجابة على أي سؤال وحتى العزوف عن متابعة المقابلة في أي وقت.

ثانياً: الانسحاب من مشروع البحث، ممكنك أخذ قرار الانسحاب من هذا المشروع في أي وقتٍ ولأي سبب. إن قرارك بالانسحاب أو عدم الاجابة على أسئلة معينة، لن يؤثر على علاقتك مع الباحثين او جامعة مكغيل أو أي مجموعة أخرى مرتبطة بالمشروع.

ثالثاً: الخصوصية، يرجى أخذ العلم أنه بإمكانك عدم الافصاح عن اسمك. بالمقابل ممكنك إستخدام اسم آخر او إستخدام رمز معين. كذلك ممكنكِ أن تطلبين منا إختيار أسم لكِ. اذا كنتِ تفضلين الخيار الأخير فسنعمل على نقل المعلومات التي صرّحتِ بها بطريقة تجعل معرفة مصدرها مستحيلاً. من جهتنا سنقوم فقط بنسب المعلومات التي ستصرحين بها لكِ عندما توافقين انتِ تحديداً على ذلك. وسنطلب من كل المشاركين في هذا المشروع إبقاء جميع المعلومات والمحادثات سرية. بالاضافة ، لن تعرض أمام أي شخص أو مجموعة من الأشخاص، أو منظمة، غير الباحثين، كل التسجيلات الصوتية أو المرئية لمحادثاتك والنصوص المكتوبة. ستبقى هويتك الحقيقية مرتبطة باسمك المستعار فقط ضمن ملف يحفظ على حاسوب(كومبيوتر) مع كلمة مرور، يوضع في مكتبٍ مقفل وستكون البيانات مُتاحة للباحثين فقط.

ز- ملاحظة أخيرة:

اذا كان لديكِ أي سؤالٍ في أي وقت من الأوقات يتعلق بمشروع البحث هذا او بالاجراءات المتعلقة به يمكنك مراجعةأحد الباحثين أو كلاهما: مالك أبي صعب أو ميشيل هارتمان على -3986077 (514) أوعلى البريد الالكتروني الموجود أعلاه.

بالاضافة نرجو أخذ العلم أنه إذا لديك أي أسئلة أو شكاوى تتعلق بالأصول الأخلاقية وتخص مشاركتك في المشروع ولا ترغبين إستشارة أي شخص من فريق البحث، يمكنك التواصل مع مديرة مكتب اخلاقيات البحوث في جامعة ماغيل على الرقم التالي: 514.398.6831 أو على البريد الالكتروني lynda.mcneil@mcgill.ca

نحن مستعدون أيضاً لتزويدك بمعلومات للاتصال بمراجع طبية وعلمية محلية تساعدكِ على التفكير والتحدث عن الحرب أو مشاكل حياتية واجهتِها آن ذاك. أخيراً، يرجى أخذ العلم أنه بإمكانك الحصول على نسخة عن هذا المستند للأحتفاظ به.

تمّ مراجعة هذا المشروع والموافقة عليه من قِبل مجلس أخلاقيات البحوث، جامعة ماغيل (0416-457# Research Ethics Board) (file)

قرار الموافقة:

أود أن يتم التعرف على هويتي من خلال ذكر اسمي في البحث

(أود استخدام اسمٍ آخر (اسم مستعار

أوافق على تسجيلِ المحادثة صوتيا

(أوافق على تسجيل المحادثة مرئياً(فيديو

قام الباحثان/الباحث بشرح المعلومات في هذا المستند وقمت بقراءته وفهمه. إن توقيعي في الأسفل يعني موافقتي على المشاركة في الدراسة. إن الموافقة على المشاركة في هذه الدراسة لا تجردني من حقوقي، كما أنها لا تعفي الباحثين من مسؤولياتهما.

توقيع المشاركة _____ تاريخ _____

توقيع الباحث _____ تاريخ _____

Participant Informed Consent Form in English

You are invited to participate in the following research project:

Title of Research: Women's War Stories: Building an Archive of Women and the Lebanese Civil War

Researchers: Michelle Hartman, Professor, Institute of Islamic Studies michelle.hartman@mcgill.ca

Malek Abisaab, Professor, Dept. of History / Institute of Islamic Studies, malek.abisaab@mcgill.ca

    Faculty of Arts, McGill University, Montreal QC, Canada,

    Tel: 00 1 514-398-****

Sponsor: Social Science and Humanities Research Council of Canada (SSHRC)

Information

Purpose of the research: To collect stories of women who lived in Lebanon during the Lebanese Civil War from your own point of view. We wish to collect as many stories as possible and understand what women experienced and what they analyzed as the most important things that affected them during this period. We hope then to use these stories to think more deeply about women's lives and their roles in society during the war. We hope to make these stories available to a wider public and share the stories of women—especially when their stories are less likely to be told and less likely to be heard—with a broader public.

What is involved: Participants in this research study will be asked to share their stories about living in Lebanon during the Civil War. This part of the project consists of group discussions, and you have been asked to participate because you already did an individual interview with us. This conversation (1–2 hours) will be held with one or both of the researchers and one or more other women in a convenient mutually agreed upon location. If you choose to participate in this conversation, it will be audio recorded only if all of the members of the group consent to this. If you do not consent to this, you may withdraw from participating at any time.

    **You have the right to stop participating in the conversation or ask to stop the taping at any time. This is true of all of the members of the group. Any audio recording will not be shown to anyone outside of the research project team or people in the group without the permission of everyone in the group. All members of a group must give their explicit consent for any sharing of material.

Risks and discomforts: We know that stories of the war can be uncomfortable and that this was a very difficult time. You may therefore feel psychological and/or emotional discomfort. If this happens at any time, you have the right to stop participating immediately. You can also ask to pause, take a break, and leave the conversation. No such break or stop in conversation will affect your relationship with the researchers, the project, the university, or any other group. You should be aware that speaking in a group setting is different than individual conversations and feel comfortable participating or not.

Participation

Voluntary participation: Your participation is entirely voluntary and you can choose to decline to answer any question or even to withdraw at any point from the project.

Withdrawal from the study: You can stop participating in the study at any time, for any reason, if you so decide. Your decision to stop participating or to refuse to answer particular questions will not affect your relationship with the researchers, McGill University, or any other group associated with this project.

Confidentiality: Your Decision

You may choose to be identified by name in the study or for your identifying information to be kept confidential. Should you choose to tell stories in the group and to the researchers but wish your identity to remain confidential, you may choose another name to use to participate and represent you in the study (or ask us to choose this name). If you do this, we will report all information in a way to make direct association with you impossible. Anything you say will only be attributed to you with your permission. We will ask all members of the group to keep all information shared and all conversations that happen confidential as well. All other information you supply will be held in confidence, meaning no other person, people, or organization other than the researchers and others in the group will have access to the audio-taped conversations and their transcripts. Your true identity will be linked to your pseudonym only in a document and on a computer protected with a password and kept in a locked office. Only the researchers will have access to your data.

Do You Have Any Questions about the Research?

If you have questions at any time about the study or the procedures, you may contact either or both of the researchers, Malek Abisaab or Michelle Hartman at (514) 398-6077 or by email (addresses supplied above). This project has been reviewed and approved by the McGill University Research Ethics Board (REB-I) (file # ****).

If you have any ethical concerns or complaints about your participation in this study and want to speak with someone not on the research team, please contact the McGill University Ethics Manager at 00 1 514.398.6831 or by email at: lynda.mcneil@mcgill.ca.

You will receive a copy of this form to keep for your records.

We are prepared to provide you with contacts for local resources to support you in thinking or talking about the war or issues related to your life during the war.

Consent

I wish to be identified in the research by name. ____ YES ____ NO
I wish to use another name (pseudonym). ____ YES ____ NO
I agree to be audiotaped. ____ YES ____ NO

The information in this document has been explained to me by the researcher/s, and I have read it myself and understood it. My signature below indicates that I agree to participate in this study. I understand that agreeing to participate in this study does not waive any of my rights or release the researchers from their responsibilities.

Participant's name (Print) _____

Participant's signature _____ Date _____

Researcher's signature _____ Date _____

Reading Guide

In this guide, we outline and describe the groups/organizations, political parties, prisons, events, newspapers, people, and places central to this book to help readers understand the material it covers.

We offer very brief descriptions in the listings in each category to give a sense of how they are used in the stories of the women presented. These lists are not at all comprehensive but rather are meant to guide the reader through the stories and histories presented here, and we encourage a deeper reading and investigation into all of them from more sources.

For ease of use, each entry in each section is indexed to the chapter(s) where it is used, and the entries are arranged from chapter 2 to chapter 9.

Groups/Organizations

Committee of the Families of the Kidnapped and Disappeared　　　(Chap. 2)

This committee was founded by Wadad Halwani and other affected people to advocate for their loved ones and other people who went missing during the war. It remains active today.

Literature and Culture　　　(Chap. 3)

One of the foremost social and cultural institutions in Saida, established in 1955 to spread cultural awareness through all parts of society, especially among disadvantaged communities.

United Nations Development Program (UNDP)　　　(Chap. 3)

Founded in the 1950s by the General Assembly of the United Nations and operating in Lebanon since 1960, continuing operations through the period of the war until today (https://www.undp.org/lebanon/undp-lebanon-and-un).

League for Democratic Feminist Action   (Chap. 5)

Left-wing political organization founded during the Civil War as part of the Popular Front for the Liberation of Palestine, discussed in chapter 5 in relation to other women's organizations at the time.

Lebanese Women's Council   (Chap. 5)

An umbrella organization for the Lebanese women's movement founded in 1952. Referred to here in relation to the Lebanese women's movement in general and to the prominent feminist activist Linda Matar in particular.

MMKN   (Chap. 6)

Association founded after the war in 2010, its abbreviation evoking the Arabic word *mumkin*, meaning "it's possible," the group's slogan. Devoted to education and empowerment (https://www.mmkn.org/).

Aamiliyeh

An educational program affiliated with the Charitable Islamic 'Amili Society, a Shi'i Muslim association. The latter was established in 1923 to develop a sense of identity and culture in productive individuals in order to contribute to building a viable society. It opened schools nationwide.

Renaissance Women's Gathering   (Chap. 7)

Discussed extensively by Elissar Zein as a group founded in conjunction with the principles of the Syrian Social Nationalist Party and secular nationalist principles for women's empowerment.

Women of the Mountain Association   (Chap. 7)

A collective that came together after the war in 1994, with Elissar Zein as one of its founding members, to promote action and activities in the region of Mount Lebanon.

Committee for Resistance Support   (Chap. 7)

Founded by women in Islamic resistance and others, knitting for fighters in the resistance across party lines.

Islamic Action Committees   (Chap. 8)

Founded in the late 1960s before the Civil War as an outgrowth of the Association of Shaykh Muhammad Mahdi Shamseddine, named for the one-time leader of the Islamic Shi'a Council. These committees gathered to study and work on so-cial issues through Islam and Islamic principles and sought to bring in community members with a more secular orientation in their political affiliations and work.

Martyrs' Foundation and al-Rasoul al-Aazam Center
for Industry and Commerce   (Chap. 8)

Hajjeh Zahra speaks about these two groups together as being established to provide support to families of martyrs and wounded people in the resistance strug-gle. She talks about the latter center setting up field hospitals and providing direct help to the resistance and the former in relation to directly meeting with families.

Political Parties

Communist Action Organization (CAO)   (Chaps. 2, 4, 8)

Two leftist political groups merged and formed the CAO in 1969: the Orga-nization of Lebanese Socialists, an offshoot of the Movement of Arab National-ists, and the Organization of Socialist Lebanon, a faction of the Arab Socialist Ba'ath Party. The CAO was officially founded in 1971 purportedly as an alterna-tive communist organization to the reformist pro-Soviet Lebanese Communist Party. With the outbreak of the Lebanese Civil War in 1975, the CAO built an elaborate alliance with the Communist Party, and they fought together against the Lebanese right-wing militias. The two parties were core components of the Lebanese National Movement and strong advocates of the coalition with the PLO. In 1982, jointly with the Lebanese Communist Party, the Arab Socialist Action Party, and other nationalist parties, it started the Lebanese National Re-sistance Front (Jammoul) against the Israeli occupation of Lebanon.

Lebanese Forces   (Chaps. 2, 3, 4, 7)

Originally an umbrella organization of right-wing, mainly Christian mili-tias founded during the Civil War, including the Phalangists and National Lib-eral Party, and later becoming a party in its own right after the war. Like the Phalangists, the Lebanese Forces are discussed as the opposing right-wing forces against which people were engaged in literal and figurative battles.

Phalangist Party   (Chaps. 2, 4, 7, 8)

A right-wing militia and political party initially founded in 1936 as a Ma-ronite Christian paramilitary youth organization, inspired by fascist principles.

At times on their own and at others together with the Lebanese Forces, the Phalangists are discussed as the right-wing, opposing side in battle—literally and figuratively.

People's Democratic Party   (Chaps. 3, 8, 9)

An offshoot of the Arab Socialist Action Party, founded in 1969 as a Marxist-Leninist party that advocates nonclassical reformist methods to change the political regime in Lebanon. During the Civil War, it fought against the right-wing militias and joined the Lebanese National Resistance Front (Jammoul).

Lebanese Communist Party   (Chaps. 3, 8, 9)

Founded in 1924 and affiliated with the Syrian Communist Party until 1964. During the French rule of Lebanon, it called for abolishing the privileges of foreign companies and canceling the debt the French imposed on the Syrian and Lebanese people. In post-French Lebanon, the party played a significant role in founding Lebanese syndicates in various economic sectors and in defending women's rights. It was decisive in the confrontations between capital and labor that culminated in the promulgation of the Labor Law. After 1968, the party shifted its focus toward the national struggle against imperialism and Zionism, and during the Civil War it played a leading role in defending Palestinians, building the Lebanese National Movement, and supporting a political change of the Lebanese sectarian regime. In 1982, jointly with the Communist Action Organization, the Arab Socialist Action Party, and other nationalist and leftist parties, it started the Lebanese National Resistance Front (Jammoul) against the Israeli occupation of Lebanon.

"Islamic Resistance"   (Chaps. 3, 7, 8, 9)

This general term is used to refer to political parties and other formations that operate using Islamic principles as their guidance in resistance to occupation. In Lebanon, such groups include AMAL and Hizbullah but also less organized, less formal political formations built on largely but not exclusively Shiʿi bases.

AMAL Movement   (Chaps. 3, 5, 8, 9)

The acronym AMAL stands for Afwaj al-Muqawamah al-Lubnaniyyah (literally: Lebanese Resistance Regiments), but the movement was originally called the Harakat al-Mahrumin (Movement of the Dispossessed). It was founded in 1974 and gained prominence during the war, especially in representing Shi'i Muslims from South Lebanon. In chapters 3, 5, and 9, AMAL is referred to in conjunction with Hizbullah and as a contrast to other parties. Chapter 8, however, delves into some of inner dynamics of the movement and places it in its context in detail.

Hizbullah   (Chaps. 3, 8, 9)

Hizbullah was founded as a Shi'i Islamist party in Lebanon after the Israeli invasion of 1982, its name literally translated meaning "Party of God." Originally a resistance organization, today it is a political party as well. The party is mentioned in passing in three chapters, both to highlight the time when it was not a major player on the political scene and to situate it in relation to other resistance parties over time. The way it is spoken about here shows the importance that the party plays today.

Progressive Socialist Party   (Chap. 3)

Founded in 1949 with a base in the Druze community of Mount Lebanon. During the Civil War, it was a part of the Lebanese National Movement in support of Arabism and the Palestinians. In chapter 3, it is referred to as one of the parties more open to women's participation and activism than some other parties both earlier and today.

Jumblatti Socialists   (Chap. 6)

Referring to members of the Progressive Socialist Party, naming the party's founder and leader, Kamal Jumblatt, and ironically alluding to the fact that after the war it moved away from socialism and to how its new leader, Walid Jumblatt, had become affiliated with Rafic Hariri, who had decidedly nonsocialist financial and economic plans for post–Civil War Lebanon.

Popular Front for the Liberation of Palestine (PFLP)   (Chaps. 4, 5, 7)

Also referred to as just "the Popular Front," a Marxist-Leninist political party founded in 1967 as part of the overall PLO and holding a more revolutionary line than the more moderate Fatah. In chapters 4, 5, and 7, the group is discussed in some detail because the women interviewed were members and talk about its inner workings.

**Organization of Socialist Lebanon and Organization
of Lebanese Socialists** (Chaps. 4, 5)
   See **Communist Action Organization**.

Dhofar Liberation Front (Chap. 4)
   An Arab nationalist coalition with the declared objective of expelling the British and Al Bu Said Sultanic Rule in Oman. After it adopted Marxism-Leninism in 1968, its name was changed to the Popular Front for the Liberation of the Occupied Arab Gulf. In chapter 4, it is referred to in conjunction with the Popular Front for the Liberation of Palestine as two groups whose active members were targeted by the Egyptian government, making it difficult to travel.

Fatah (Chaps. 4, 5, 7, 8)
   Still the largest faction of the PLO, as it was during the Lebanese Civil War. At times, these names, Fatah and PLO, are used interchangeably. Led by Yasser Arafat during the Lebanese Civil War, Fatah officially was forced into exile from Beirut to Tunis with the Israeli invasion, though some fighters and commanders remained. Both Fatah specifically and the PLO more generally are referred to in several chapters, particularly in connection to work for Palestinian liberation.

Ba'ath Party (Chaps. 4, 8)
   Originally founded in Syria in 1946 by Michel Aflaq and Salah al-Din Bitar, teachers who grew up in the Maidan neighborhood of Damascus and studied in France. Its ideology is premised on the belief that the larger Arab nation, or *umma*, needed to be resurrected and united. It denounced class struggle and instead advocated Arab socialism, which called for unity among Arab people to end injustice. In 1963, it became the ruling party in Syria and ruled in Iraq from 1968 until 2003.

Arab Nationalist Movement (Chap. 4)
   Scholars have recently been translating the name of this movement with the more accurate "Movement of Arab Nationalists." The defeat of the Arab armies in the 1948 war with Israel motivated political activists and intellectuals to explore alternative ways to resist the devastating effect of the Nakba. They founded the Arab Redemption Brigade in 1949, whose name was changed later to the Arab Nationalist Movement; they rejected political compromises with Western imperialists and believed that only revolutionary violence would help them achieve their goals. The movement focused on raising the consciousness of the Arab people to

lead to unity and development. President Gamal Abdel Nasser of Egypt joined the movement and shifted its ideological orientation toward Arab socialism.

Arab Socialist Action Party   (Chap. 5)

Founded in 1969 out of the Popular Front for the Liberation of Palestine and developing a platform to be an alternative to the reformist Communist Parties in the Arab world, which advocated regionalism. Its goal was to establish an Arab Communist Party reflecting a belief in Arab unity. It adopted Marxism-Leninism but attempted to maintain its distance from the Soviet Union. It separated from the PFLP in 1981. Together with the Lebanese Communist Party and Communist Action Organization, it formed the armed resistance front, the Lebanese National Resistance Front (Jammoul), against the Israeli occupation in 1982.

Fatah al-Intifada   (Chap. 5)

Although sharing the word *fatah* in its name, this faction split off from Fatah in 1983 during the Civil War, allying itself with Syria, which backed it against the leadership of Yasser Arafat. In chapter 5, we see that this party pays for the funeral expenses of an active member of the Palestinian resistance, an allusion to Arafat's alliance with Syria.

Syrian Social Nationalist Party (SSNP)   (Chap. 6)

A secular party founded in 1932 in Lebanon to advocate for the reunification of Greater Syria and the establishment of a unitary state across it. During the war, it was allied with the leftist Lebanese National Movement and fought against the right wing. The party is important in chapter 6 because of joint projects it engaged in with the secular left resistance.

National Liberal Party / al-Ahrar   (Chap. 8)

Founded in 1958, this nonsectarian party was associated with Christian nationalism and right-wing politics. Over time, it was allied with the Phalange Party. Its associated militia was called the Tigers. Referred to in chapter 8 together with the Phalange Party not only as being the opposite of Islamist activists and militants but also as being so far removed as to be in an entirely different world.

Lebanese National Resistance Front (LNRF)   (Chap. 9)

Also known as "Jammoul," this underground alliance of resistance parties founded in 1982 was active throughout the 1980s as a follow-up to the Lebanese

National Movement. In chapter 9, the LNRF is discussed in relation to resistance in the South against the Israelis and the South Lebanese Army (the Israelis' proxy militia) and is referred to in different ways, including as "Lahad's guys" (see Antoine Lahad).

Prisons

Ansar   (Chap. 3)

An Israeli prison camp hastily built near the town of Nabatieh to detain large numbers of people active in the resistance in South Lebanon in 1982. The site of a notorious prison massacre and mass arrests, Ansar is referred to in chapter 3 as where the men rounded up in Saida during the invasion were removed to and held.

Khiam   (Chaps. 3, 9)

This prison for men and women was built on the site of former army barracks in South Lebanon and starting in 1975 was run by the South Lebanese Army and overseen by the Israelis. In chapter 9, we read some details of Sanaa A.'s incarceration there. In chapter 3, it is referred to along with Ansar as the place where men in Saida were removed to and detained after being rounded up on the beach. Prison memoirs by women who were held in Khiam include *Resistance: My Life for Lebanon* (Bechara 2003) and *Memoirs of a Militant* (Baidoun 2021).

Ramleh   (Chap. 8)

Referring to two separate prisons, one for women and one for men, inside occupied Palestine near the town of the same name. A number of Lebanese political prisoners were taken and held there during the Lebanese Civil War, as Hajjeh Zahra describes in the story of her imprisonment in chapter 8. Also known as "Ayalon prison."

Events

1967 War   (Chaps. 4, 5)

This war is also referred to as the June War or Six-Day War of 1967, noting its brevity. Fought between the Israeli Defense Forces and an alliance of Egypt, Syria, and Jordan, the former completed its victory in a short time, destroying infrastructure and occupying more territory than Israel had previously held, including the West Bank, the Golan Heights, and the Sinai Peninsula. As chapters

4 and 5 discuss, this war has come to symbolize the defeat of Arab nationalism and politicized some young people.

Black September Massacres (1969–70)   (Chap. 4)

Mentioned in relation to one of the young fighters in a training camp who lived through them. In this period of armed clashes between the Jordanian Armed Forces and the PLO, thousands of Palestinians were killed, and many of Palestine's fighters left for Lebanon to participate in the Civil War, as did the young man described in chapter 4.

Strike at the Ghazieh Branch of the Régie de tabac (1970)   (Chap. 4)

Preceding the Civil War, this major strike at the most important branch of the government tobacco monopoly's factory in South Lebanon is discussed as part of the political formation and awakening of Arab L. because she was sent there to speak to women workers as part of her party's labor organizing.

Assassination of Maarouf Saad (1975)   (Chaps. 3, 4)

The assassination of this important political figure in the crucial southern city of Saida is understood to be one of the catalysts that set off the Lebanese Civil War. In chapters 3 and 4, it is mentioned as crucial in the political awakening and formation of women in the lead-up to the war.

Saida Port Strike (1975)   (Chaps. 3, 4)

This strike by fisherpeople in Saida was a crucial moment in escalating the outbreak of the Civil War in this important city, the capital of South Lebanon.

Outbreak of the Lebanese Civil War (April 13, 1975)   (Chaps. 2, 8)

The "official date" associated with the outbreak of the Civil War is April 13, 1975, a point when clashes between many rival groups and sides were escalating, including the fisherpeople's strike and the assassination of the Nasserite leader Maarouf Saad. An attack by the Phalangist militia on a bus carrying mainly Palestinians in the Ain al-Remmaneh neighborhood is often cited as the event that marks the start of the war.

Camp David Accords (1978)   (Chap. 4)

An agreement brokered by the United States and signed by President Anwar Sadat of Egypt and Prime Minister Menachem Begin of Israel, leading to a recognition of Israel and normalization of relations with it by Egypt. It is discussed in relation to people being imprisoned for opposition to the accords.

Israeli Invasion of Saida and Beirut (1982)   (All Chapters)

Preceded by the Israeli invasion of 1978, the invasion of these two cities in 1982 had a major impact on the war and Lebanon, not only Beirut and Saida, but the entire country, as can be seen by how they are mentioned in every chapter. We also focus on this invasion in chapter 1.

Aoun War (1989)   (Chaps. 5, 8)

In 1989, Michel Aoun, the commander in chief of the Lebanese army, began his so-called War of Liberation against Syrian troops occupying Lebanon at the time. A year after he started the war, the country was subject to a de facto partition between East and West Beirut, and Aoun was the leader of major parts of the former.

Amnesty Law (1991)   (Chap. 2)

Part of the deals struck during the meetings held in Saudi Arabia that led to the official end of the Civil War in 1990, later referred to as the Ta'if Accords (1989). The law gave people who participated in the war a general amnesty and freedom from prosecution. This amnesty meant that many of the militia leaders and other war participants who committed war crimes have remained active in Lebanese public life and politics to this day.

Qana Massacre (1996)   (Chap. 7)

Israeli air strike killing more than one hundred Lebanese civilians and wounding more than a hundred along with United Nations peacekeepers stationed in and near the small southern Lebanese village of Qana on April 18, 1996.

Assassination of Rafic Hariri (2005)   (Chaps. 2, 9)

The wealthy billionaire businessman Rafic Hariri, with deep ties to Saudi Arabia, was assassinated by a car bomb in 2005, leading to massive instability in the country. Prior to his death, he was the architect of massive and controversial rebuilding projects. One of them involved the demolition of buildings, appropriation of land, and construction of new luxury complexes in the heart of Beirut's downtown, rendering it unrecognizable and inaccessible to most of the Lebanese population.

July War (2006)   (Chap. 7)

A short war waged on Lebanon by Israeli forces, mainly targeting the South and the southern suburbs of Beirut, massively destroying infrastructure, and leaving more than 1,300 people dead. In chapter 7, it is referred to as a follow-up site of organizing and activism drawing on knowledge and experiences learned during the Civil War.

Newspapers

Al-Hurriyya   (Chap. 4)

Initially the mouthpiece of the Arab Nationalist Movement, founded in Beirut in 1960. In 1969, it became a joint organ of the Communist Action Organization in Lebanon and was later affiliated with the Democratic Front for the Liberation of Palestine.

Al-Hadaf   (Chap. 5)

Founded in 1969 as a weekly political and cultural magazine to be an official outlet of the Marxist-Leninist, pan-Arab Palestinian liberation party the Popular Front for the Liberation of Palestine and ultimately becoming the major leftist platform for Arab radicals.

Al-Thawri   (Chap. 5)

Founded in 1971 in Beirut as a weekly political magazine and eventually the official organ of the Arab Socialist Action Party, a Marxist-Leninist party.

Al-Watan   (Chap. 4)

Official paper of the Lebanese National Movement, a coalition of nationalist and communist Lebanese parties that formed an alliance with the PLO.

Al-Anwar   (Chap. 5)

A long-running daily newspaper (1959–2018) with an Arab nationalist, Nasserist bent, viewed over time as politically centrist, though employing left-leaning writers.

Al-Shiraa   (Chap. 5)

Founded in 1948 as a weekly news magazine, carrying a pro-Nasser message and financially supported by President Muammar Qaddafi of Libya.

As-Safir   (Chap. 9)

Left-leaning, pan-Arab newspaper that ran from 1974 to 2016, initially financially supported by President Muammar Qaddafi of Libya and in support of the PLO and the Lebanese National Movement.

People (Nonfamily Members)

Salim al-Hoss   (Chap. 2)

Served as prime minister of Lebanon from 1998 to 2000 and identified as an extraordinary prime minister given his efforts to fight corruption, embrace transparency, and develop a national nonsectarian policy for the Lebanese government.

Camille Chamoun   (Chaps. 2, 5, 8)

Served as president of Lebanon from 1952 to 1958, with a major revolt in 1958 bringing an end to his presidency. Among the founders of the National Liberal Party (al-Ahrar) and he remained an important right-wing Christian political figure throughout the Civil War until his death in 1987.

Rashid Broum and Family   (Chap. 3)

Rashid, Suad, Ghassan, and Samia Broum passed away on June 8, 1982, because of the Israeli raid on Saida, capital of South Lebanon. Rashid and Suad were members of the leadership of the People's Democratic Party, a communist party of Lebanon. They are discussed in chapter 3 as close friends of Rima Z., who speaks about their impact on her political development. See Farah 2015.

Adel Osseiran   (Chap. 4)

A prominent right-wing Shi'i politician affiliated with another major notable Shi'i, Kamil al-As'ad, who intermittently served as the Speaker of the House between 1964 and 1984. Osseiran became a deputy in the Lebanese Parliament for the first time in 1943. Both Osseiran and As'ad belonged to important landowning families and consistently supported the pro-Western policies of President Camille Chamoun.

Ghalib al-Turk   (Chap. 4)

The governor of South Lebanon during the administration of President Fouad Chihab. He was identified by many southerners as the best leader in South Lebanon because of his efforts to develop the local infrastructure and his unwavering support for cultural activities in the province. He awarded Arab L. the "Prize of the South" for the paper she wrote on Palestine as a high school student.

Mariam Makki   (Chap. 4)

A comrade of Arab L. who helped her to mobilize the Ghazieh branch of tobacco workers against the tobacco monopoly, the Régie co-intéressée libanaise des tabacs et tombac.

Umm Mahmoud   (Chap. 4)

A woman tobacco worker who worked with Arab L. in organizing other female workers at the Ghazieh branch of the Régie.

Nouhad al-Damr   (Chap. 4)

A leftist woman worker who, like Umm Mahmoud, helped Arab L. in agitating with the Régie workers in the strike at the Ghazieh branch of the Régie in 1970.

Wardeh   (Chap. 4)

A comrade of Arab Loutfi who assisted her in mobilizing the Régie workers at the Ghazieh branch to confront the administration in 1970.

Kamal Jumblatt   (Chaps. 4, 7)

Leader of the Progressive Socialist Party, which during the Civil War was part of the broad alliance of leftist parties called the Lebanese National Movement, formed in support of the PLO. He was assassinated in 1977. He is discussed here in his capacity as the leader of the National Movement and as the major chief of the Druze community who argued with Yasser Arafat. His son Walid is also mentioned in chapter 7 as the head of Druze militants who were responsible for killing innocent people during the Mountain War (1982–89).

Yasser Arafat   (Chaps. 4, 8)

The chairman of the PLO and leader of Fatah, nicknamed and known as "Abu Ammar." At the time of the outbreak of the Lebanese Civil War, the PLO was an underground guerilla organization recognized as fighting on behalf of the Palestinian people. Arafat's role as a leader changed significantly over time, and it is notable here how he is referred to as an activist and revolutionary rather than as a statesman and diplomat, which he served as later in his life. Arafat ended his revolutionary role with the signing of the Oslo Agreement with Israel in 1993.

Abdel-Halim Hafez   (Chaps. 4, 5)

Iconic Egyptian singer whose famous song "Ahwak" was listened to by fighters during the Civil War. The song expresses longing for the beloved. In chapter 5, he is mentioned as a nationalist who stirred feelings in people through music.

Bizri Family   (Chap. 4)

A prominent Sunni Muslim family based in Saida, South Lebanon. Members of this elite family have occupied major religious, political, and administrative positions in society and the state bureaucracy since the Ottoman Empire.

May Sayegh   (Chap. 4)

Mentioned in chapter 1 for her autobiography about the siege of Tal al-Zaatar, Sayegh is a Palestinian poet and was a prominent political activist with the PLO during the war. She is mentioned in chapter 4 in relation to a documentary film about women in the PLO. We interviewed her as part of our project, though her story is not featured in this book.

Fatima Ghandour   (Chap. 4)

A professor of philosophy at the Lebanese University and a friend of Arab L. Both witnessed a detonation of a bomb against an Israeli military vehicle in Saida, South Lebanon.

George Habash   (Chaps. 4, 5)

Leader of the Popular Front for the Liberation of Palestine, also known and referred to by his nickname "al-Hakim," or "the Doctor," because he graduated from medical school before devoting his life to the Palestinian struggle as an activist and militant. Habash died in 2008.

Nawal Baidoun   (Chap. 9)

Mentioned in chapter 1 for her book *Memoirs of a Militant* (2021), Baidoun is an Islamist activist who was incarcerated in Khiam prison with Sanaa A. (chapter 9) and Souha Bechara, who wrote the memoir *Resistance: My Life for Lebanon* (2003).

Saeb Salam   (Chap. 5)

A major Sunni Muslim political leader who was known during his time as minister of the interior in 1946 for his firm policies in dealing with the strike of the Régie workers, when scores of protesters were killed or wounded. In the early

1970s, he became the prime minister and was seen as a primary supporter and advocate of Saudi Arabia. During the Civil War, he opposed the Lebanese National Movement, especially its attempts to build—in the absences of the state—alternative democratic administrative bodies to protect and safeguard people's everyday lives. At the time of the Israeli invasion and blockade of Beirut in 1982, in his role as the head of the Islamic Caucus he exerted tremendous pressure on the PLO to withdraw from Beirut.

Rashid Karami   (Chap. 5)

Born in 1921 to an Arab nationalist family in Tripoli, North Lebanon, Karami was elected to the Lebanese Parliament in 1951. He became the prime minister in 1955, a position he held several times until his assassination in 1987. He is viewed often as an honest, transparent, and serious prime minister. He opposed the policies of right-wing parties, especially those of Camille Chamoun, and supported the PLO, Syria, and Arab nationalist parties in Lebanon. He played a major role in efforts to end the Civil War and was a leading figure of the National Salvation Front, which was founded to quash the treaty between Lebanon and Israel of May 17, 1983.

Naim Moghabghab   (Chap. 5)

A cofounder of the right-wing National Liberal Party/al-Ahrar, headed by the pro-Western Lebanese president Camille Chamoun. Moghabghab was elected to the Parliament twice, in 1951 and 1957. He decisively opposed the anti-Chamoun revolution of 1958, which ultimately led to his assassination in 1959.

Sami al-Solh   (Chap. 5)

Born in Ottoman Palestine in 1887 to the notable al-Solh family. In his early years, he joined a secret society that advocated Arabism against the Ottoman elite, who imposed Turkism. After studying law in France, he was appointed a judge by the French government holding the mandate over Lebanon. He supported the policies of President Camille Chamoun, which antagonized Muslims and Arab nationalists in Lebanon. He served as prime minister of Lebanon five times in his long political career.

Gamal Abdel Nasser   (Chap. 5)

An important Arab leader who, with other Egyptian army officers, staged a coup d'état against the Egyptian monarchy in 1952. In 1956, Nasser nationalized the Suez Canal and used its revenue to build the Aswan Dam. This act aggravated Britain and France, which were in control of the canal. With Israel, France and Britain started the tripartite attack against Egypt but failed to change Nasser's decision. He emerged victorious and became a popular Arab leader because he stood against colonial aggression and defended Arab dignity. Nasser called on Arabs to unite as one nation, the ideology of Arab nationalism that is still associated with his name. While in power, he introduced land reforms in Egypt that helped landless peasants. He also initiated the short-lived United Arab Republic, combining Egypt and Syria (1958–61). He adamantly supported the PLO, and his popularity remained strong among the Arab masses even after his sudden death in 1970.

Abu Maher al-Yamani   (Chap. 5)

A cofounder of the Arab Nationalist Movement and the Popular Front for the Liberation of Palestine. He was also a leading figure of the Palestinian labor movement. Popular Front leader George Habash nicknamed him "Damir al-Thawrah," or the "Conscience of the Revolution."

Salah Salah   (Chap. 5)

A Palestinian militant who joined the Arab Nationalist Movement and the Popular Front for the Liberation of Palestine at their genesis. He is known as an advocate of the "One-State Solution" for Palestinians and Israelis in which both peoples would live as equals within one democratic state.

Leila Khaled   (Chap. 5)

Iconic symbol of Palestinian revolutionary womanhood, active in resistance in Lebanon during the war as a member of the Popular Front for the Liberation of Palestine. Most notoriously involved in the hijacking of airplanes in the late 1960s, she remained and remains to this day active in the struggle for the liberation of Palestine. She has written her memoirs (Khaled 1975) and is the subject of a biography (Irving 2012).

Abu Abed   (Chap. 5)

The man in charge of the Popular Front for the Liberation of Palestine office in downtown Beirut who met Batul H. before she left for the training camp in Amman.

Linda Matar   (Chap. 5)

A leading feminist activist who founded the Lebanese Women's Rights Committee in 1947, an organization affiliated with the Lebanese Communist Party. Matar played a pioneering role in defending oppressed women and seeking justice for and equality between women and men.

Hussein Maroush   (Chap. 5)

A Popular Front party official who supervised the activities of Batul H. and other women comrades.

Bilal   (Chap. 5)

A sexist Popular Front party official who tried to hamper the role of Batul H. and other female members.

Antoun Saadeh   (Chap. 6)

Founder of the Syrian Social National Party, a secular party with an ideology premised on the geographical and cultural unity of Greater Syria (to be formed from modern-day Lebanon, Syria, Jordan, Palestine, Iraq, Kuwait, and Cyprus). Saadeh was executed by the Lebanese government in 1949 for his radical ideas.

Intissar   (Chap. 6)

One of the women who was a leader in Kamal Jumblatt's local socialist women's association and is referred to first name only in chapter 6. Used as an example of different styles of women's organizing in more and less organized, more and less funded political formations.

Mounir Shafiq (Abu Fadi)   (Chap. 7)

A prominent Palestinian thinker and writer who started his political life as a Communist but turned to Islamism in 1981. He joined Fatah in 1968, where, with a group of leftist members, he founded the Student Battalion, which played a significant role in resisting the Israeli invasion of Lebanon in 1982. Both the Student Battalion and its partner organization, the National Committees, joined the ranks of the National Lebanese Resistance Front (Jammoul) and engaged in the armed resistance against the Israeli occupation, especially in Mount Lebanon.

Suad Ml'aeb   (Chap. 7)

A Druze female fighter who with her sister and other women formed a group, which Umm Ziad Adnan led. They were commissioned to ambush the invading Syrian army in 1976.

Dalal Mughrabi   (Chap. 7)

A Palestinian woman and member of the Student Battalion. With other comrades, she penetrated the Israeli defense system in 1978 and attacked targets within Israel to avenge Israel's assassination of three Palestinian leaders. She is often upheld as an exemplary Palestinian female fighter.

Amin al-Andari (Abu Wajih)   (Chap. 7)

A militant known for his bravery, dedication, and self-sacrifice and noted in particular for his dangerous trips to smuggle food, medicine, and weapons into the Palestinian refugee camp Tal al-Zaatar when it was under siege.

Abu Mahmoud (Hilal Rislan)   (Chap. 7)

A Syrian Druze man who served as the governor of Aleppo and ambassador to China. He left Syria for Lebanon in 1970 to support the Palestinian resistance. There he founded the National Committees, the partner association of the Student Battalion. He had Maoist leanings and, together with Mounir Shafiq, was considered one of the ideologues of the Student Battalion.

Halim Zahr   (Chap. 7)

A local notable who was a relative of Umm Ziad from the locally prominent Muslim Druze Zahr family living in Abadiyeh, Mount Lebanon. He helped her find a new home so she could get some distance from the difficulties with her mother-in-law.

Amin Zahr   (Chap. 7)

Known as the doctor of the poor people because of his commitment to helping the less fortunate. Umm Ziad mentions his house when she is recounting the Israeli bombing of her town.

Sayyid Hassan Nasrallah   (Chaps. 8, 9)

Born to a poor Shi'i family in South Lebanon, this charismatic leader was one of the founders of Hizbullah. In 1978, Nasrallah went to Najaf to study in the seminary there. In Najaf, he was exposed to the Islamist al-Da'wa Party. He returned to Lebanon in 1978 and continued his religious education in Baalbek in eastern Lebanon. During his stay in Baalbek, he taught Shi'i youth about the meaning and aims of jihad. With the Israeli invasion of Lebanon in 1982, Nasrallah set out to form the "Party of God" with other leading Shi'i clerics. At the time, he was only twenty-two years old. At the age of thirty-two, Nasrallah was elected secretary-general of Hizbullah.

Rajeh Gharz al-Din   (Chap. 7)
  A member of the Arab Socialist Action Party from Ras el-Matn, Mount Lebanon. He studied in Egypt and after graduation received guerilla training in Palestinian military camps in Jordan. He was martyred in the occupied West Bank in 1969 and is considered to be one of the first Druze martyrs in Palestine after the War of 1967.

Enaam Hamza   (Chap. 7)
  A female radical warrior from Aabey, Mount Lebanon, who joined the Lebanese National Resistance Front (Jammoul) and engaged in guerilla warfare against the Israeli occupying forces in the Shab'a Hills in the West Beqaa. She was martyred in 1990 and is acknowledged as one of the first female Druze martyrs.

Hajj Bilal   (Chap. 7)
  Hajj Bilal Daghir was the Hizbullah official in charge of Mount Lebanon, or the eighth sector. Umm Ziad mentions that she met with him to give him sweaters knitted by the Committee for Resistance Support for the Hizbullah fighters.

Fouad al-Najjar   (Chap. 7)
  A Druze man from Abadiyeh, Mount Lebanon. Mentioned by Umm Ziad because his house was hit by an Israeli air raid and his son-in-law injured.

Imam Khomeini (Ayatollah Ruhollah Khomeini)   (Chap. 8)
  Imam who led the Islamic Revolution in Iran (1978–79). His theory of *wilayat al-faqih* (literally: "deputyship of the jurist") held that a qualified jurist could become the full and legitimate deputy of the Hidden Imam, a revolutionary model that inspired Hizbullah as well as many other Shi'i revolutionary groups around the globe.

Musa al-Sadr   (Chap. 8)

A Shi'i religious scholar born in Iran who studied law at the University of Tehran. In 1959, Sadr came to Lebanon as the representative of a major Shi'i Iraqi cleric. He created the Supreme Islamic Shi'a Council in Beirut in 1969 to administer personal-status laws for the community and to mediate between the Shi'i community and the Lebanese state. He founded the Movement of the Dispossessed in 1974, which is better known by its Arabic acronym AMAL. This movement denounced the political marginality and economic deterioration of the Lebanese Shi'i community and brought attention to the plight of the South under intense Israeli attack. Sayyid Musa Sadr disappeared in Libya in 1978.

Ahmad al-Assaad   (Chap. 8)

A provincial leader and landed rural chief who dominated Shi'i politics and divided farming tax revenues on peasant landholdings with other Shi'i landed aristocracy. He won many parliamentary elections and was appointed a minister in several governments.

Sayyid Mustafa   (Chap. 8)

The eldest son of Ayatollah Ruhollah Khomeini, who helped his father in the revolutionary activities against the shah of Iran. He was killed during his arrest in Najaf, Iraq, in 1977.

Shaykh Muhammad Mahdi Shamseddine   (Chap. 8)

A Shi'i cleric who became the vice president of the Supreme Islamic Shi'a Council after the disappearance of Imam Musa Sadr in 1978. He advocated civil resistance against the Israeli occupation of Lebanon and Palestine.

Shaykh Ragheb Harb   (Chap. 8)

A Shi'i prayer leader from Jibsheet, South Lebanon, who was one of the early Islamist activists in the South who strove to raise awareness about the occupation and Zionist ideology. He saw the plight of Palestinians and southern Lebanese as one and the same—the result of Zionist colonialism and US hegemony. He was martyred in 1984.

Antoine Lahad   (Chaps. 8, 9)

General who became the leader of South Lebanon Army in 1984 after the death of the Israeli collaborator Saad Haddad. The South Lebanon Army was an

Israeli surrogate army trained and financed by Israel, created after the invasion of South Lebanon in 1978. In 1988, Souha Bechara, an activist for the Lebanese National Resistance Front (Jammoul), attempted to assassinate Lahad. He survived and fled to Israel after the Israeli withdrawal in 2000. He died in 2015.

Aql Hashem (Chap. 8)

An army officer in the South Lebanon Army from Debel, South Lebanon, who collaborated with the Israeli occupying army. He was feared and detested by the people under occupation and was killed by the Islamic resistance in 1999.

Husayn Abdel-Nabi (Chap. 8)

Known as "al-Jalbout" (the Weasel), one of the most senior officials in the security apparatus run by the Israelis and Saad Haddad. He was notorious for spreading havoc and terror throughout South Lebanon as well as for unparalleled criminality. He was executed by the Islamic resistance in 1994.

Saad Haddad (Chap. 8)

A defector from the Lebanese army, Major Saad Haddad collaborated with the Israeli army and established the South Lebanon Army in 1978 as a proxy army. He used it as a local force to fight the PLO and its allies—the Islamist, leftist, and nationalist parties. He died in 1984 and was succeeded by Antoine Lahad.

Abu l-Fadl al-Abbas (Chap. 8)

Half-brother of Imam Husayn (d. 662), the son of Imam ʿAli b. Abi Talib (d. 661), whom Shiʿi Muslims believe was the legitimate successor of Prophet Muhammad (d. 632). Hajjeh Zahra used his name as a fake name to conceal the actual name of the leader of the cell of the Islamic resistance with whom she was working in Beirut.

Shaykh Subhi al-Tufayli (Chap. 8)

Born in 1948, one of the founders of Hizbullah and its first secretary-general (1989–91). In his early political career, he criticized Musa Sadr and the Supreme Islamic Shiʿa Council for their reconciliatory position toward the Lebanese government and the Christian Right. He later broke away from Hizbullah and criticized its political tactics. He rejected the Taʾif Accords (1989), which ended the Civil War in Lebanon, and accused Hizbullah of losing sight of its original commitment to change the state system. He opposed the alliance of Hizbullah and the Syrian government because he believed that Syria was attempting to gain US approval. In 1997, al-Tufayli led what was called the "Revolt of the Hungry" against the Lebanese government, which Hizbullah did not support. He also rejected *wilayat al-faqih*, a core component of Hizbullah's ideology.

Nabih Berri   (Chaps. 8, 9)

One of the most influential politicians in Lebanon and the leader of the AMAL movement since 1980. As leader, he significantly contributed to the diminishing importance of the traditional Shi'i leadership. Berri led the war on the Palestinian camps in Beirut in 1985 and a harsh war with Hizbullah in the late 1980s. AMAL under Berri is considered a formidable ally of Syria, and after the Ta'if Accords Berri sought to increase the number of Shi'is in official positions and roles to match their demographic size in the country and to capitalize on their role in the liberation of South Lebanon. Berri has held the position of Speaker of the Lebanese Parliament since 1992.

Kifah Afifi   (Chap. 9)

A revolutionary Palestinian woman from the Shatila refugee camp who survived the massacre there in 1982. Three of her brothers were martyred in battles with the Israelis and their Lebanese allies. She was captured by the Israelis in South Lebanon after a failed guerrilla operation in 1988. She was later transferred to the Khiam detention camp, where she was subjected to torture. She was released in 1994. Kifah's name was used to scare Sanaa A. during her own interrogations in prison.

Riad Abdallah   (Chap. 9)

Born in the town of Khiam, an agent for the Israeli army who served in the South Lebanon Army, specifically as a torturer in the Khiam prison. During the Israeli invasion of South Lebanon in 1978, he was appointed head of the security service in the town. He was notorious for arresting, imprisoning, and torturing scores of innocent people. He fled to the United Arab Emirates after the liberation of South Lebanon. He tried to recruit Sanaa A. to be a collaborator after her release.

Doha Chams   (Chap. 9)

A Beirut-based journalist, writer, and blogger. Mentioned by Sanaa A. because Chams interviewed her and helped her publish the report about the bias and discrimination in the Council of the South.

Places (All Chapters)

Neighborhoods and Areas in Beirut

Ain al-Remmaneh

Located south of Beirut and on the east side of the Damascus–Beirut highway, across from Chiah, Ain al-Remmaneh was totally populated by Christians. It is now known as the place where the spark of the Civil War was ignited. On April 13, 1975, members of the Phalangist Party murdered civilian passengers on a Palestinian bus passing through the neighborhood.

Azarieh

The Lazarist office building located in downtown Beirut, designed in 1953 by the French engineer Andre Leconte (1894–1990) and becoming a major commercial center in Beirut.

Bir al-Abed

A slum in Dahyeh populated by Shi'i Muslims and the birthplace of Hizbullah. In Bir al-Abed, the CIA made a failed assassination attempt against an important Shi'i *'alim*, Sayyid Muhammad Husayn Fadlallah (1935–2010) in 1985, killing eighty innocent people as a result.

Chiah (Maroun Misk Street)

A suburban slum located to the south of Beirut, on the west side of the Beirut–Damascus highway, and on the demarcation line with Ain al-Remmaneh. Populated before the Civil War by middle- and working-class Christians and Muslims who constituted the workers of the adjacent industrial areas, Chiah became a major stronghold for the Lebanese National Movement and the PLO during the war. It experienced a long history of fighting with Ain al-Remmaneh, which was controlled by right-wing militiamen. Maroun Misk Street in Chiah was heavily populated by Shi'i Muslims and constantly bombarded during the Civil War.

Corniche el-Mazraa

A major street that cuts through the Mazraa neighborhood in West Beirut, an area that includes al-Basta, Khandaq al-Ghameeq, Ras al-Nabaa, Tariq al-Jadida, Qasqas, and the Sports City Stadium. Inhabited mostly by Sunni

Muslims, during the Civil War it was considered an area loyal to the Lebanese National Movement and the PLO.

Dahieh

The name "Dahieh" refers to the southern suburbs of Beirut, populated mostly by Shi'i Muslims. In the early 1950s, a large wave of migrants moved from the rural regions to the cities, especially Beirut, because of the deteriorating conditions of peasant life caused by unchecked population growth, land shortages, irresponsible government policies, and attacks by Israel, especially in South Lebanon and the western Beqaa Valley. Migrants from South Lebanon, mostly Shi'i Muslims, found a refuge in these southern suburbs of Beirut, while those from East Lebanon, Muslims and Christians, targeted the eastern suburb of Beirut. These suburbs created what became known as the Poverty Belt (Hizam al-Bu's), which encircled Beirut from east to the west.

East Beirut and West Beirut

During the Civil War, Beirut was divided into two major parts: East Beirut, which was inhabited by diverse Christian denominations (Maronite Catholic, Greek Orthodox, Melkite Catholic, Armenian Orthodox, Armenian Catholic, and Protestant) and was politically dominated by a right-wing coalition, the Lebanese Front, which included the Lebanese Forces, a paramilitary organization. West Beirut was populated by various Muslim sects, Sunni (the majority), Shi'i, and Druze, and by a minority of Christians. Also in contrast to East Beirut, West Beirut was the hub of several leftist groups: Arab nationalists, Syrian nationalists, and Communists. West Beirut was hospitable to the Palestinian refugees and embraced their militant organization, the PLO. The Green Line separated the two parts of Beirut. The neighborhoods in East Beirut prominent during the Civil War most often mentioned in this book are Achrafieh, Ain al-Remmenah, al-Saifi, Gemmayzeh, Nabaa, Karantina, Burj Hammoud, Hazmieh, Sin al-Fil, Badaro, Dikouane. In West Beirut, they include al-Hamra, Mazraa, Chiah, Ras al-Nabaa, al-Fakhani, al-Kola, Msaytbeh, Basta, Vardan, Raouché, Zarif, el-Kantari, Burj Abu-Haidar, Aisha Bakkar, Ras Beirut, Ain Mreisseh, Qoraytem, Wadi Abu-Jamil, and Manara.

Hayy Madi

A Shi'i Muslim neighborhood integrated into the southern Dahieh. It became the hub for shoe factories that attracted many skilled laborers who were displaced from East Beirut and had become unemployed because of the Civil War.

Horsh Beirut

One of Beirut's only green areas, Horsh Beirut is also called the Pine Park. Located in West Beirut, it borders the airport road and is surrounded by Qasqas, Mazraa, Sabra, Ghobeiry, Chiah, Forn el-Shebbak, Tariq al-Jadida, and Badaro. The total area of the Horsh is three hundred thousand square miles, and during the Israeli invasion of 1982 many Palestinian refugees fled the camps to the Horsh, which then was targeted by Israeli air raids.

Mar Mitr

A neighborhood in Achrafieh, a Christian area in East Beirut. An important Greek Orthodox church, Saint Dimitrios, is located in Achrafieh, thus the name of the community.

Mathaf

This area surrounds the National Museum of Beirut, after which it is named. Located on the Green Line, it was known as a crossing point between West and East Beirut during the Civil War.

Msaytbeh

A religiously mixed, crowded neighborhood in West Beirut.

Nabaa

Geographically located near the East Beirut neighborhoods Burj Hammoud and Karantina. Populated by poor families who migrated from the Lebanese peripheries, mostly Shi'is, who provided manual labor for industries based in East Beirut. It hosted Armenian Christians and Palestinian craftspeople as well as Syrian, Egyptian, Pakistani, and Bengali workers. During the Civil War, Nabaa, Karantina, and the Palestinian refugee camp Tal al-Zaatar became known as "Muthallath al-Sumud" (the Steadfast Triangle) and symbolized the thwarting of attempts at ethnic cleansing by fascist Lebanese militias. The fascist forces considered these poor neighborhoods "alien," given the social, political, and religious backgrounds of the people living in them. On the eve of the Civil War, a significant number of the Shi'i residents of Nabaa supported the Lebanese Communist Party and the Arab Socialist Ba'ath Party.

Ras al-Nabaa

A poor Muslim neighborhood in West Beirut, geographically close to the Beirut–Damascus highway that divided East and West Beirut, known as the Green Line. The neighborhood is also close to downtown Beirut and the war zone. Before the Civil War, people from different religious denominations lived in Ras al-Nabaa. During the war, Sunni Muslims formed the majority.

Tahwita (Tahwitat Forn el-Chebbak)

Part of a suburban town Forn el-Chebbak, which is a Christian constituency, and administratively belonging to the province of Ba'bda in Mount Lebanon. Tahwita's walls were built to protect the banks of the Beirut River, which passes through Forn el-Chebbak. During the Civil War, Tahwita was a military training field for one of the major paramilitary groups in that area.

Zarif

A locality in West Beirut close to Verdun Street, al-Sanayeh Park, and Kontari. Populated by middle- and upper-class Muslims, a majority of whom are Sunnis and a minority Shi'is and Druzes. There were a few Christian Lebanese and Armenian families before the Civil War, most of whom left the neighborhood during the war.

Zoqaq al-Blat

A quarter in West Beirut located between Mazraa, Zarif, and Riyad al-Solh Square, downtown. It is a lower-class residential neighborhood that attracted displaced families from South Lebanon and Syrian Kurdish immigrants because of its proximity to downtown Beirut, where job opportunities were abundant.

Other Places in Lebanon

Akkar

A province in North Lebanon, with a mixed Christian and Muslim population. The economy of the area heavily relied on agriculture; thus, many Akkari people experienced a trajectory similar to that of families in other peripheral territories. Many found jobs in the Lebanese army or in the police forces, but the majority immigrated to urban centers and joined industrial or commercial undertakings or worked in agriculture.

Beqaa Valley

A Lebanese province to the east of Beirut that constitutes more than 41 percent of Lebanon and 52 percent of the total agricultural area in Lebanon. It has a mixed Muslim and Christian population of various religious denominations, with a majority of Shi'is. On the eve of the Civil War, more than 65 percent of the people of Beqaa lived in villages and therefore relied completely on agriculture; the rest lived in towns such as Zahle, Baalbek, Hermel, Rashayya, and Hasbayya. From the mid-1950s to 1969, as in other peripheral areas in Lebanon, it witnessed a decline in agricultural revenues, government-initiated agricultural reforms, land shortages, overpopulation, poor irrigation plans, high prices for fertilizers and insecticides, and lack of subsidies from the government, all of which attracted rural urban migrants to Beirut. From 1969 onward, political instability and Israeli violence contributed to a new wave of migration from the Beqaa to Beirut.

Chouf

The southern province of Mount Lebanon, located to the southeast of Beirut. It has a mixed Christian, Maronite Catholic, Greek Orthodox, and Muslim population, the latter mostly Druze, Sunni, and some Shi'i. The political life in the Chouf has been controlled to a large extent by the Druze Jumblatt family. Its leader, Kamal Jumblatt, and later his son Walid were supporters of the late Egyptian president Gamal Abdel Nasser. During Nasser's administration, a war broke out between the pro-Israeli Lebanese Forces and a coalition of Syrian, Palestinian, and Lebanese nationalist parties led by Walid Jumblatt's Socialist Progressive Party. The outcome of the War of the Mountain (1982–89) was disastrous to the Lebanese Forces. This in turn weakened the Lebanese government of Amin Gemayel, which was pressured to cancel the short-lived May 17 Peace Treaty with Israel. The human cost of the Mountain War was profound as hundred of thousands of civilians lost their homes, and thousands on both sides were killed or wounded.

Marjaayoun

An important Christian-majority town in South Lebanon, it was a center for the pro-Israeli South Lebanon Army and the capital of the so-called Free Lebanon State (Buffer Zone), protected by the Israeli army. It is also the birthplace of the founder of the South Lebanon Army, Saad Haddad.

Nabatieh

A major Shi'i city in South Lebanon occupied by Israel in 1982 and liberated in 1985. On Muharram 10, 1983, the Israeli occupying army fired at a Shi'i crowd of thousands commemorating the death of Imam Husayn, the grandson of Prophet Muhammad, in Nabatieh, killing two men and wounding scores of others. The angry crowed attacked the Israeli armed vehicles and set fire to them. The incident sparked the First Intifada and consolidated the armed resistance against the Israeli army.

"The North"

The northern province of modern-day Lebanon has a mixed Muslim and Christian population of various religious denominations. Most areas of northern Lebanon, especially Akkar and Tripoli, faced total negligence from the Lebanese state, which contributed to rural disintegration, economic deterioration, political instability, and, consequently, waves of migration to urban centers. These developments also encouraged antistate struggles and leftist leanings among the population. In the post–Civil War era and with the decline of communism, Sunni Islamism was the alternative.

"The South"

The southern province of modern-day Lebanon, historically known as "Jabal Amil," is predominantly Shi'i but has a significant Maronite Catholic population and a smaller Sunni one. Saida (Sidon), Sour (Tyre), Nabatieh, and Bint Jbeil are the major cities of the South. The state's economic plans neglected the South as well as other peripheral areas while focusing on Beirut and Mount Lebanon. In addition to Israeli raids, the South suffered from major socioeconomic problems and political instability, which resulted in large migrations of people toward urban centers, especially the southern suburbs of Beirut. Before the Israeli invasion in 1982, most of the poor Shi'is joined various leftist parties and Palestinian organizations to challenge the Lebanese state in order to improve their socioeconomic and political conditions and to defend their families against Israeli aggression.

West Beqaa

The western part of the Beqaa is a fertile agricultural area with a mixed Muslim and Christian population. From 1948, it became a combat zone for Israel, the PLO, and Lebanese leftist guerilla groups. It was occupied by Israel from 1982 to 2000.

Southern Villages, Towns, and Cities

Abbasiyya

A Shi'i coastal farming town in the Sour District, South Lebanon. It was occupied by Israel in 1967. The Israeli army killed 110 people there in a massacre in 1977 and martyred 90 villagers during the invasion of South Lebanon in 1978. It was liberated in 2000.

Blat

A small town in the Marjaayoun District, South Lebanon, that has a mixed Christian and Muslim population, with a Shi'i majority, most of whom rely on agriculture for a living. It was liberated from Israeli occupation in 2000. The birthplace of Sanaa A., whose story is told in chapter 9.

Bra'chit

A town in the Bint Jbeil District, South Lebanon, that has a mixed Christian and Shi'i population, with a Shi'i majority. One-third of the residents of Bra'chit rely on farming, especially tobacco and wheat; the remaining people work in commerce, small business, and the state bureaucracy. Bra'chit borders the infamous Israeli "Buffer Zone" and thus was invariably subject to Israeli incursions, the abduction of ordinary people, and house bombings, which caused death and injuries. The national and Islamic resistances retaliated against Israeli aggression and launched many attacks to defend the village. Peace was finally restored to Bra'chit with the withdrawal of Israel in 2000.

Chakra

A Shi'i town in the Bint Jbeil District, South Lebanon, and a prominent place for traditional Shi'i learned families. Geographically, it overlooks the Saluki Valley (Wadi al-Hujeir), which was a battlefield between the Islamic resistance and the Israeli army in 2006.

Ghazieh

A large Shi'i town in the Zahrani District, South Lebanon. Emigrants from other southern villages were driven to Ghazieh during Israeli incursions because of its proximity to Saida, the capital city of South Lebanon, and the job opportunities on offer from industry there, especially the Régie tobacco monopoly. The AMAL movement is the dominant political power in Ghazieh.

Jwaya

A Shiʻi village in the Sour District, South Lebanon, from which a significant number of people immigrated to the United States or to African and Latin American countries. Those who remained found work in farming olives and cereals such as wheat and barley. The Israeli occupying army transformed the Social Club of Jwaya into a prison, where it detained and tortured nationalist and Islamic militants. Jwaya was liberated in 1985.

Kfar Tebnit

A Shiʻi village in the Nabatieh District, South Lebanon. People work in farming olive, tobacco, and pine trees, which the Israeli army routinely scorched during the occupation to punish the villagers for their antioccupation activities. Under the Israeli occupation, two-thirds of the people of Kfar Tebnit were forced out, fifty-six houses were bulldozed, and scores of people were martyred or wounded.

Al-Kherbe

A small Christian village in the Marjaayoun District, South Lebanon, whose name was changed by the Lebanese government to "Burj al-Muluk" in 1967. Farming olives is a major means of subsistence. Liberated from the Israeli occupation in 2000.

Qlaiaa

A Christian village in the Marjaayoun District, South Lebanon, that overlooks the Litani River and includes the fertile Marj al-Khiam Plain. Farming, independent professional work, and commerce are the main jobs of most people in Qlaiaa. Scores of young men and women from the village joined the South Lebanon Army and fled to Israel when the latter withdrew in 2000.

Saida (Sidon)

The capital city of South Lebanon. After the liberation of Lebanon from the Israeli army in 2000, Saida unofficially became known as the "Capital of the Resistance." A coastal city forty kilometers from Beirut, it has a mixed Christian and Muslim population, with a majority of Sunni Muslims. During the Civil War, the Saida port became the only outlet to the world for sea transport or people who lived in the areas under the control of the Lebanese National Movement and the PLO. In addition, Saida is the location of the largest Palestinian refugee camp in Lebanon, Ain al-Hilweh, as well as of the smaller camp Mieh Mieh.

Sharqia

A Shi'i town in the Nabatieh District, South Lebanon. Before and during the Civil War, the major political parties in Sharqia were the Lebanese Communist Party, the Arab Socialist Ba'ath Party (Iraqi branch), and the Democratic Socialist Party led by the Shi'i magnate Kamil al-As'ad. After the Israeli invasion in 1982, Hizbullah became the major political force in Sharqia.

Sharq Saida

Located to the east of Saida, this group of Christian villages has Jezzine as its administrative capital. In 1985, fighting broke out between the pro-Israeli Lebanese Forces and the South Lebanon Army, on one side, and the nationalist parties in Saida, on the other side, after the withdrawal of the Israeli army from the area, which led to the displacement of Christian villagers and the destruction of their properties.

Sojod

A Shi'i village in the Jezzine District, South Lebanon, ninety-three kilometers from Beirut. Tobacco and wheat are the major crops produced by the farmers of Sojod. Bordering the Israeli "Buffer Zone," Sojod was consistently under bombardment, which eventually caused the complete destruction of residential properties and farms, forcing the displacement of most of its people. The Israeli army destroyed the Sojod mosque and set fire to the *hussainiya* there in 1989.

Sour (Tyre)

A coastal city in South Lebanon eighty kilometers from Beirut that has a mixed Christian and Muslim population, with a Shi'i majority. Sour is home to three Palestinian refugee camps, el-Buss, Burj el-Shemali, and Rashidieh. The city of Sour and the Palestinian camps there suffered greatly during the two Israeli invasions of 1978 and 1982 and during the War of the Camps between AMAL and the Palestinians (1985–88).

Tebnine

A town in the Bint Jbeil District, South Lebanon, that a mixed Christian and Muslim population, with a Shi'i majority. People in Tebnine rely on agriculture to make a living. In the Israeli war on Lebanon in 1993, Tebnine was heavily bombarded, which devastated its properties. Tebnine is the birthplace of the Speaker of the Lebanese Parliament, Nabih Berri.

Eastern Villages and Towns (Beqaa)

Baalbek

The major city of the East Beqaa, eighty-five kilometers from Beirut, which has a mixed Christian and Muslim population, with a Shi'i majority. The city is famous for its antiquities and ancient ruins from the Phoenician, Greek, Roman, Byzantine, and Islamic periods. It also has a religious significance for the Shi'is as the location of the tomb of Khawla bint al-Husayn, the daughter of Imam Husayn. Baalbek was the incubating environment of Hizbullah.

Rashayya

A town in the West Beqaa (East Lebanon) about eighty-five kilometers from Beirut that has a mixed Christian and Muslim (Druze and Sunni) population, with a Druze majority. Rashayya appears prominently in the Lebanese national narrative of its independence. Politically, the Druze parties, associated with the Jumblatt and Yazbak families, dominate political life. People work in farming and professional jobs. The town was hit hard during the two Israeli invasions in 1978 and 1982, and many Christian residents deserted their homes.

Riyaq

A town in the Zahle District of the Beqaa Valley that has a mixed Christian and Muslim population, with a Christian majority. Two major transportation facilities were built in Riyaq: a railway center founded during the Ottoman rule and an airport constructed during the French Mandate. The airport was attacked by Israel in the war of 2006. The majority of the villagers rely on farming, commerce, and services for their livelihoods.

Saadnayel

A Sunni town in the Zahle District of the Beqaa Valley. Farming is the major economic activity of people there. Saadnayel constituted a strong popular base for the Lebanese leftist parties and the Palestinian resistance.

Villages and Towns in Mount Lebanon

Aabey

A town in the Aley District, Mount Lebanon, that has a mixed Christian and Druze population, with a Druze majority. Farming, professional jobs, and employment in the private and public sectors are the people's major production activities. During the Mountain War (1982–89), Aabey became a battlefield between the Lebanese Forces and the Lebanese army of Amin Gemayel (1982–88) on the one side and the Lebanese nationalist parties led by the Progressive Socialist Party on the other. The Druze of Aabey and the surrounding villages fled the area when they heard the news of the massacre at an adjacent town, Kfar Matta.

Aaraya

A Christian town in the Baabda District, Mount Lebanon, located in the war zone near Chouit and bordering Kahali. People rely on farming and employment in small industrial firms for their livelihoods. The Free Patriotic Movement, led by General Michel Aoun, is the dominant party in Aaraya.

Al-Abadiyeh

A town in the Baabda District, Mount Lebanon, that has a mixed Christian and Druze population, with a Druze majority. Farming, professional jobs, and employment in the private and public sectors are the sources of livelihood. Diverse political parties exist in the town, all affiliated with the Lebanese National Movement; however, the dominant one is the Progressive Socialist Party, led by Walid Jumblatt. As in other nearby towns and villages, most Christian families fled during the Civil War.

Ain Ainoub

A town in the Aley District, Mount Lebanon, that has a mixed Christian and Druze population, with a Druze majority. Farming, small professional jobs, and employment in private and public sectors are the sources of livelihood. Diverse political parties affiliated with the Lebanese National Movement exist in Ain Ainoub; however, the dominant one is the Progressive Socialist Party, led by Walid Jumblatt. It was a major battlefield during the Civil War, and, consequently, most Christian families fled their homes there.

Aley

A city in the Aley District, Mount Lebanon, that has a mixed Christian and Druze population, with a Druze majority. It is a commercial center and summer resort, and the southern part of it has industry. Aley also has public-administration buildings and private hospitals. Diverse political parties affiliated with the Lebanese National Movement exist in Aley; however, the dominant one is the

Progressive Socialist Party, led by Walid Jumblatt. It was a major battlefield during the Civil War, with fighting against the Lebanese army led by Amin Gemayel and the Lebanese Forces.

Aytat

A Druze village in the Aley District, Mount Lebanon. Most people work in farming, professional jobs, and employment in the private and public sectors. Diverse political parties affiliated with the Lebanese National Movement exist in Aytat; however, the dominant one is the Progressive Socialist Party, led by Walid Jumblatt. It was a major battlefield during the Civil War; many homes were destroyed, and many young people were killed.

Baakline

The largest Druze city in the Chouf District, Mount Lebanon, with a Christian minority. The dominant political party in Baakline is the Progressive Socialist Party, led by Walid Jumblatt. During the Mountain War (1982–89), many Druze families fled their villages, located in battle zones, and sought refuge in Baakline.

Baalchmay

A town in the Baabda District, Mount Lebanon, that is a summer resort situated midway between the cities of Aley and Bhamdoun and has a mixed Christian and Druze population, with a Druze majority. People rely on farming, leasing properties (i.e., renting to summer vacationers), and running convenience stores along the Beirut–Damascus highway, which passes through the town. Two political parties are dominant in the town—the Progressive Socialist Party, led by Walid Jumblatt, and the Lebanese Democratic Party, led by Talal Arsalan. During the Civil War, Christians fled the town, leaving their properties.

Baysour

A major Druze town in the Aley District, Mount Lebanon. People support themselves through farming, professional jobs, service, and employment in the private and public sectors. Diverse political parties affiliated with the Lebanese National Movement exist in Baysour; however, the dominant one is the Progressive Socialist Party, led by Walid Jumblatt. The people of Baysour rose up against the invading Israeli army in December 1983, when the latter tried to arrest a nationalist militant. The impact of the Civil War on Baysour was severe, and the human cost was enormous—more than one hundred people were martyred, and thus Baysour's symbolic name became "Mother's Martyrs."

Bchamoun

A town in the Aley District, Mount Lebanon, with a mixed population of Christians and majority Druze. The town sheltered several political leaders who defied the French mandatory authorities in 1943, demanded complete independence, and established the Government of Bchamoun. Diverse political parties affiliated with the Lebanese National Movement exist in Bchamoun; however, the dominant one is the Progressive Socialist Party, led by Walid Jumblatt. During the Mountain War (1982–89), Christians left the town.

Beit Meri

A town and a summer resort in the Matn District, Mount Lebanon, that has a mixed Christian and Druze population, with a Christian majority. People rely on farming, tourism, and renting properties to summer vacationers to make a living. During the Civil War, the town was under the control of right-wing militiamen and was a major military base for their troops, especially those engaged in the Battle of Tal al-Zaatar and Aley–Kahali.

Bhamdoun

A mainly Christian summer resort town in the Aley District, Mount Lebanon, and a major service center on the Beirut–Damascus highway. During the Civil War, 40 percent of its buildings were destroyed, and most civilians fled the fighting. Bhamdoun experienced intense fighting during the Israeli invasion of 1982. Lebanese nationalist forces, supported by Syria and the Palestinian resistance, attacked the town in September 1983 on their way to regain control of the areas in Mount Lebanon that were liberated from the Israeli occupation.

Charoun

A Druze town in the Aley District, Mount Lebanon, very close to Bhamdoun. Farming, professional jobs, employment in the service private and public sectors are the sources of livelihood. The Progressive Socialist Party and the Syrian Social Nationalist Party are the dominant political groups. The Israeli army occupied Charoun and the surrounding towns in 1982, but the towns were liberated a year later.

Chouit

A town in the Baabda District, Mount Lebanon, between al-Abadiyeh and Aaraya, the latter of which was constantly at loggerheads with Chouit during the Civil War. It has a mixed Christian and Druze population, with a Druze majority. Farming, professional jobs, employment in the private sector, and the few local industries are the sources of livelihood for most people. The Socialist Progressive Party led by Walid Jumblatt is the dominant political group in Chouit. Christians fled their homes in Chouit during the Civil War.

Dahr al-Wahsh

A small Christian town in the Aley District, Mount Lebanon, located on the Beirut–Damacus highway between the cities of Aley and Kahali. Dahr al-Wahsh was a battleground during the Civil War, especially during the confrontation between the Syrian army—commissioned by the Arab League to end the Civil War according to the Ta'if Accords—and insubordinate divisions of the Lebanese army led by General Michel Aoun in 1990. Many observers described the confrontation as a massacre as hundreds of Syrian and pro-Aoun Lebanese soldiers were killed.

Damour

A major coastal town on the Beirut–Sour highway in the Chouf District, Mount Lebanon, with a majority-Christian population. People rely on farming fruit trees and garden vegetables and the services provided by tourism, such as at beaches, to make a living. During the Civil War, Lebanese right-wing militiamen turned the town into a military stronghold, with roadblocks at which people from other sects, Palestinians, and Lebanese Nationalist Movement (LNM) militants were kidnapped. Damour was attacked by the PLO-LNM in early 1976, with a devastating impact on its people, who fled to East Beirut. It became a sanctuary for Palestinian refugees who survived the massacre at Tal al-Zaatar in August 1976. With the Israeli invasion of 1982, Palestinians withdrew from Beirut, and the displaced residents of Damour returned to the town.

Dhour al-Abadiyeh

This hilly part of al-Abadiyeh bordering the Beirut–Damascus highway is a summer resort. The population is mostly Druze, with a diverse community of vacationers. Farming and leasing properties are the major sources of people's income in the area. The dominant political party is the Progressive Socialist Party, led by Walid Jumblatt. The area was severely damaged during the Civil War, especially during the Israeli invasion in 1982.

Al-Hilaliyah

A Druze town in the Baabda District, Mount Lebanon, situated between al-Abadiyeh and Roueisset el-Ballout. Farming, professional jobs, and employment in the private sector are how people support themselves. Walid Jumblatt's Socialist Progressive Party is the dominant political group in al-Hilaliyah. The town was located relatively far away from the battle zone during the Civil War.

Kfar Silwan

A town in the Baabda District, Mount Lebanon, that has a mixed Christian and Druze population. Farming fruit trees is its major economic asset. The dominant political group is the Progressive Socialist Party, led by Walid Jumblatt. During the second phase of the Civil War (1982–90), the Christian residents of Kfar Silwan fled their homes.

Mari

A village in the Hasbaiya District, South Lebanon, that has a mixed Christian and Druze population. The Progressive Socialist Party, the Lebanese Democratic Party, and the Syrian Social Nationalist Party are the dominant political groups. Farming, raising livestock, making crafts, and employment in public institutions are the major economic activities of most people.

Monte Verde

A small hilly Christian locality, part of a town called Ayn Saadeh, in the Matn District of Mount Lebanon. It is a summer resort that became residential given its proximity to Beirut. During the Civil War, the area was controlled by right-wing militiamen who fought against the Palestinian camp Tal al-Zaatar.

Ras el-Matn

A mountain town in the Baabda District, Mount Lebanon, that is a summer resort and has a mixed Christian and majority Druze population, with a Druze majority. People rely on farming, leasing properties (i.e., renting to summer vacationers), employment in professional occupations, and working in the service industry to make a living. The Progressive Socialist Party is the dominant political group. Christians largely fled the town during the Civil War. Ras el-Matn became a central base for the transportation and communication lines of the Lebanese National Resistance Front (Jammoul) during the Israeli occupation of Beirut and Mount Lebanon.

Roueisset el-Ballout

A Druze town in the Baabda District, Mount Lebanon, situated between al-Hilaliyah and Ras el-Matn. Farming, professional jobs, and employment in the private sector form the livelihood of most people. The Socialist Progressive Party and the Syrian Social Nationalist Party are the dominant political groups. The town was geographically distant from the battle zones of the Civil War. Like most places of that area, however, it was occupied by the Israeli army in 1982. A Palestinian guerilla group kidnapped eight Israeli soldiers stationed in Roueisset el-Ballout during the invasion of 1982. They were later released in exchange for 4,600 Palestinian and Syrian prisoners held by Israel.

Souq el-Gharb

A mostly Greek Orthodox, Christian town in the Aley District, Mount Lebanon, and a summer resort. With the Israeli invasion of 1982, the town became a battlefield between the invading army and the PLO–Lebanese National Movement fighters. When the PLO troops withdrew from Lebanon, the war resumed in Souq al-Gharb between the Lebanese Forces, supported by the Lebanese army during the administration of Amin Gemayel (1982–88), and a consortium of nationalist parties led by the Progressive Socialist Party of Walid Jumblatt. During these confrontations, the Lebanese Forces occupied the Palestinian Orphanage and transformed it into a center for torturing their opponents.

Bibliography

Interviews

Adnan, Umm Ziad. Abadiyeh, Lebanon, July 2019.
Ali Ahmed, Sanaa. Haret Saida, Lebanon, June 2018.
Halwani, Wadad. Beirut, July 2016.
Hashim, Batul Ali [pseudonym]. Beirut, July 2017.
Loutfi, Arab. Montreal, Mar. 2017.
Sh'ayb, Hajjeh Zahra Abdel Latif. Beirut, Aug. 2019.
Zaazaa, Rima. Saida, Lebanon, June 2016.
Zein, Elissar. Bchamoun, Lebanon, July 2016.

Works Cited

Abdul Hadi, Faiha. 2015a. *Adwar al-mara'a al-filistiniyya: Mundhu muntasaf al-sitinat hatta 'am 1982* [Palestinian women's roles: From the middle of the 1960s to 1982]. Al-Birah: Markaz al-Mar'a al-Filistiniya lil-Abhath wal-Tawfiq.
———. 2015b. *The Role of Palestinian Women from the Mid-1960s to 1982*. Al-Birah: Palestinian Women's Research Center.
Abisaab, Malek, and Rula Abisaab. 2017. *The Shi'ites of Lebanon: Modernism, Communism, and Hizbullah's Islamists*. Syracuse, NY: Syracuse Univ. Press.
Accad, Evelyne. 1990. *Sexuality and War: Literary Masks of the Middle East*. New York: New York Univ. Press.
Amireh, Amal. 2000. "Framing Nawal El Saadawi: Arab Feminism in a Transnational World." *Signs: Journal of Women in Culture and Society* 26, no. 1: 215–49.
Baidoun, Nawal Qasim. 2020. *Mudhakkirat al-munadila fi mu'taqal al-Khiyam*. Edited with an introduction by Malek Abisaab and Michelle Hartman. Beirut: Dar Ab'ad.

———. 2021. *Memoirs of a Militant: My Years in the Khiam Women's Prison.* Translated by Michelle Hartman and Caline Nasrallah. Northampton, MA: Interlink.

Bechara, Souha. 2002. *Muqawama.* Translated by Antoine Abu Zeid. Beirut: Dar al-Saqi.

———. 2003. *Resistance: My Life for Lebanon.* Translated by Gabe Levine. Brooklyn, NY: Soft Skull.

Bechara, Souha, and Cosette Ibrahim. 2011. *Ahlumu bi-zinzanah min karaz* [I dream of a prison made of cherries]. Beirut: Dar al-Saqi.

———. 2014. *La fenêtre: Camp du Khiam.* Translated by Rawdha Cammoun-Claveria. Tunis: Editions Elyzad.

Béchara, Souha, with Gilles Paris. 2000. *Résistante.* Paris: J. C. Lattès.

Bizri, Dalal. 2017. *Dafatir al-harb al-ahliyya al-lubnaniyya 1975–1990* [Journals of the Lebanese Civil War 1975–1990]. Beirut: Arab Center for Research and Policy Studies.

Chahine, Antoinette. 2007a. *Crime d'innocence.* Beirut: Dar an-Nahar, 2007.

———. 2007b. *Jurm al-bara'ah.* Translated by Marie al-Touq. Beirut: Dar an-Nahar.

cooke, miriam. 1996. *War's Other Voices: Women Writers on the Lebanese Civil War.* Syracuse, NY: Syracuse Univ. Press.

Dublin, Thomas. 1998. *When the Mines Closed: Stories of Struggles in Hard Times.* Ithaca, NY: Cornell Univ. Press.

Duplan, Nathalie, and Valérie Raulin. 2005. *Le cèdre et la croix: Jocelyne Khoueiry, une femme de combats.* Paris: Presses de la renaissance.

Eggert, Jennifer Philippa. 2022. *Women and the Lebanese Civil War: Female Fighters in Lebanese and Palestinian Militias.* New York: Palgrave Macmillan.

Farah, Natalie. 2015. "Film Revives a Life Lost in Lebanon's Civil War." *Gulf News,* July 29. At https://gulfnews.com/entertainment/arts-culture/film-revives-a -life-lost-in-lebanons-civil-war-1.1558100.

Georgis, Dina. 2013. *The Better Story: Queer Affects from the Middle East.* Binghamton: State Univ. of New York Press.

Ghoussoub, Mai. 1998. *Leaving Beirut: Women and the Wars Within.* London: Saqi, 1998.

Gluck, Sherna Berger, and Daphne Patai, eds. 1991. *Women's Words: The Feminist Practice of Oral History.* New York: Routledge.

Hammad, Eva Stahl (Samira). 2000. *An International Who Didn't Leave the Tal.* N.p.: n.p.

Hartman, Michelle. 2020. "Zahra's Uncle? Or Where Are Men in Women's War Stories?" *Journal of Arabic Literature* 51, nos. 1–2: 83–107.

Hartman, Michelle, and Malek Abisaab, eds. 2022. *Women's War Stories: The Lebanese Civil War, Women's Labor, and the Creative Arts.* Syracuse, NY: Syracuse Univ. Press.

Al-Hilou, Jihan. 2009. *Al-Mara'a al-filistiniyya: Muqawama wal taghayyruat al-ijtima'iyya: Shahadat hayya lil-mara'a al-filistiniyya fi lubnan 1965–1970* [Palestinian women: Living testimonies by Palestinian women in Lebanon 1965–1970]. Al-Bireh: Markaz al-Mara'a al-Filistiniyya lil-Abhath wal-Tawfiq.

———. 2022. *Making Palestine's History: Women's Testimonies.* Nottingham, UK: Spokesman, 2022.

Iacovetta, Franca, Katrina Srigley, and Stacey Zembryzcki. 2018. Introduction to *Beyond Women's Words: Feminisms and the Practices of Oral History in the Twenty-First Century*, edited by Katrina Srigley, Stacey Zembryzcki, and Franca Iacovetta, 1–23. New York: Routledge.

Irth Lubnan mina al-'unf al-siyasi [Lebanon's legacy of political violence]. 2013. Beirut: Al-Markaz al-Dawli lil 'Adala al-Intiqaliyya.

Irving, Sarah. 2012. *Leila Khaled: Icon of Palestinian Liberation.* London: Pluto.

Kahf, Mohja. 2014. "Packaging Huda: Sha'rawi's Memoirs in the United States Reception Environment." In *Going Global: The Transnational Reception of Third World Women Writers*, edited by Amal Amireh and Lisa Suhair Majaj, 148–72. New York: Routledge.

Khaled, Laila, with George Hajjar. 1975. *My People Shall Live: Autobiography of a Revolutionary.* Toronto: NC Press.

Khweiri, Jocelyn. 1999. "From Gun Powder to Incense." In *Women and War in Lebanon*, edited by Lamia Shehadeh, 209–28. Gainesville: Univ. Press of Florida.

Maasri, Zeina. 2008. *Off the Wall: Political Posters of the Lebanese Civil War.* London: I. B. Tauris.

Makdisi, Jean Said. 2007. *Beirut Fragments: A War Memoir.* New York: Persea.

Maksoud, Hala. 1996. "The Case of Lebanon: Women and the Civil War in Lebanon." In *Arab Women: Between Defiance and Restraint*, edited by Suha Sabbagh, 89–94. New York: Olive Branch.

Mikdadi Tabbara, Lina. 1979. *Survival in Beirut: A Diary of Civil War.* London: Onyx.

Mundus, Hani. 1974. *Al-'Amal wa al-'ummal fi al-mukhayyam al-falastini: Bahth midani 'ann mukhayyam Tal al-Za'tar* [Work and workers in Palestinian refugee camps: Field work in the Tal al-Zaatar Camp]. Beirut: Palestine Liberation Organization Research Center, 1974.

————. 1977. *Tariq Tal al-Za'tar* [The road to Tal al-Zaatar]. Beirut: Markaz al-Abhath al-Filastiniyya.

Nabulsi, Karma, and Abdel Razzaq Takriti, eds. 2016. The Palestinian Revolution. Website, Oxford Univ., 2016. At learnpalestine.politics.ox.ac.uk.

Nasr, Salim. 2013. *Susyulujya al-harb fi Lubnan: Atraf al-sira' al-ijtima'i wa al-iqtisadi, 1970–1990* [A sociology of the Lebanese War: Sites of social and economic struggle]. Beirut: Dar al-Nahar.

Nofel, Mamdouh. 2006. *Maghdusha: Qisat al-harb 'ala al-mukhayamat fi Lubnan* [Maghdusha: The story of the War of the Camps in Lebanon]. Ramallah: Muwatin, Palestinian Institute for the Study of Democracy.

Nuwayhed al-Hout, Bayan. 2004. *Sabra and Shatila, September 1982*. London: Pluto.

Patai, Daphne. 2018. "When Is Enough Enough?" In *Beyond Women's Words: Feminisms and the Practices of Oral History in the Twenty-First Century*, edited by Katrina Srigley, Stacey Zembryzcki, and Franca Iacovetta, 48–55. New York: Routledge.

Petran, Tabitha. 1987. *The Struggle over Lebanon*. New York: Monthly Review Press.

Saab, Jocelyne, dir. 1988. *La tueuse*. Canal+.

Safa, Muhammad. 2021. *Mawsu'at mu'taqal al-Khiyam: Al-Qissah al-kamilah* [Encyclopedia of Khiam prison: The whole story]. Beirut: Dar al-Farabi.

Sayegh, May. 1988. *Al-Hisar* [The siege]. Beirut: Al-Mu'assasah al-Arabiyyah lil-Dirasat wal Nashr.

Schulze, Kristen, Martin Stokes, and Colin Campbell. 1998. "Communal Violence, Civil War and Foreign Occupation: Women in Lebanon." In *Women, Ethnicity and Nationalism: The Politics of Transition*, edited by Rick Wilford and Robert Miller, 130–46. New York: Routledge.

Shehadeh, Lamia Rustum, ed. 1999. *Women and War in Lebanon*. Gainesville: Univ. Press of Florida.

Sneifer, Regina. 1995. *Guerres maronites, 1975–1990*. Paris: Harmattan.

————. 2006. *J'ai déposé les armes: Une femme dans la guerre du Liban*. Ivry-sur-Seine, France: Atelier.

————. 2008. *Alqaytu al-silah: Imra'ah fi khidamm al-harb al-lubnaniyah* [I put down my arms: A woman in the Lebanese War]. Translated by Rula Dhubyan. Beirut: Dar al-Farabi.

Srigley, Katrina, Stacey Zembryzcki, and Franca Iacovetta, eds. 2018. *Beyond Women's Words: Feminisms and the Practices of Oral History in the Twenty-First Century.* New York: Routledge.

Traboulsi, Fawwaz. 2007. *A History of Modern Lebanon.* London: Pluto.

Yawmiyyat al-harb al-lubnaniyya [Chronicle of the Lebanese War]. 1977. Beirut: Munazamat al-Tahrir al-Filastiniyya.

Index

MALEK ABISAAB is associate professor at McGill University, where he teaches in the Department of History and Classical Studies and the Institute of Islamic Studies. His books with Syracuse University Press include *Militant Women of a Fragile Nation* (2010), *The Shiʻites of Lebanon: Modernism, Communism, and Hizbullah's Islamists*, coauthored with Rula Jurdi Abisaab (2014), and *Women's War Stories: The Lebanese Civil War, Women's Labor, and the Creative Arts*, coedited with Michelle Hartman (2022).

MICHELLE HARTMAN is professor in the Institute of Islamic Studies at McGill University. With Syracuse University Press, she has published two books, *Breaking Broken English: Black–Arab Literary Solidarities and the Politics of Language* (2019) and *Native Tongue Stranger Talk: The Arabic and French Literary Landscapes of Lebanon* (2014) and has coedited with Malek Abisaab the collection *Women's War Stories: The Lebanese Civil War, Women's Labor, and the Creative Arts* (2022).